Building Skills in
MATHEMATICS

Authors

Loye Y. "Mickey" Hollis
Houston, Texas

Jack M. Ott
Columbia, South Carolina

Dorothy S. Strong
Chicago, Illinois

Merrill

Contents

Editorial and Production Staff

Series Editor: Garnet A. Lewis; *Book Editors:* Patricia K. Nye,
Angela Stovall; *Production Editor:* Janice E. Wagner;
Series Designer: Kevin Buckland; *Illustrator:* Glenn Wasserman;
Artist: Jeffrey A. Clark

ISBN 0-675-03815-4

Find the sum or difference.

1. 7 + 9   **2.** 12 − 4   **3.** 8 + 5   **4.** 13 − 8

5. 6 + 4   **6.** 11 − 6   **7.** 7 + 8   **8.** 17 − 9

Complete.

9. 8 + _____ = 8   **10.** 3 + 7 = 7 + _____   **11.** _____ + 6 = 6 + 5

Find the missing addends.

12. 4 + ☐ = 9   **13.** ☐ + 6 = 13   **14.** 8 + ☐ = 17

Write the fact family for each group of numbers.

15. 5, 11, 6   **16.** 9, 4, 5   **17.** 7, 15, 8

Add or subtract.

1.	398	2.	607	3.	4,734	4.	4,106	5.	5,036
	− 85		+ 292		− 1,631		+ 1,752		3,721
									+ 1,011

6.	7,758	7.	263	8.	8,037	9.	3,542	10.	9,684
	− 216		+ 522		− 1,021		+ 5,443		− 7,502

Solve.

11. A library has 8,259 books. There are 137 poetry books. How many books on other subjects are in this library?

12. Juan saved $43 one month, $22 the next month, and $31 the third month. How much did Juan save in the three months?

Addition Facts, Addition Properties

Use addition to combine groups of objects.

$$5 + 4 = 9$$
addend   addend   sum

$$\begin{array}{r} 5 \\ +4 \\ \hline 9 \end{array}$$
addend
addend
sum

If you change the order of addends, the sum is the same.

$$8 + 6 = 14 \qquad 6 + 8 = 14$$

When you add 0 and a number, the sum is that number.

$$8 + 0 = 8 \qquad 0 + 4 = 4$$

EXERCISES Add.

1. $6 + 2$

2. $7 + 5$

3. $2 + 8$

4. $3 + 6$

5. $3 + 0$

6. $9 + 6$

7. $0 + 6$

8. $5 + 5$

9. $\begin{array}{r} 8 \\ +3 \\ \hline \end{array}$

10. $\begin{array}{r} 2 \\ +7 \\ \hline \end{array}$

11. $\begin{array}{r} 8 \\ +0 \\ \hline \end{array}$

12. $\begin{array}{r} 9 \\ +9 \\ \hline \end{array}$

13. $\begin{array}{r} 8 \\ +2 \\ \hline \end{array}$

14. $\begin{array}{r} 0 \\ +5 \\ \hline \end{array}$

15. $\begin{array}{r} 4 \\ +9 \\ \hline \end{array}$

16. $\begin{array}{r} 8 \\ +7 \\ \hline \end{array}$

17. $\begin{array}{r} 2 \\ +5 \\ \hline \end{array}$

18. $\begin{array}{r} 7 \\ +0 \\ \hline \end{array}$

Complete.

19. $7 + 6 = $ _____ $+ 7$

20. _____ $+ 8 = 8 + 4$

21. $6 + $ _____ $= 6$

Solve.

22. Chad's cat had 3 kittens. Lisa's cat also had 3 kittens. Find the total number of kittens.

23. In Mrs. Brown's class, 8 boys and 4 girls have dogs. How many children have dogs?

Three or More Addends

When adding three or more addends, grouping
different ways does not change the sum.

$$\underbrace{2 + 3}_{5} + 1 \atop 5 + 1 = 6 \qquad \text{or} \qquad 2 + \underbrace{3 + 1}_{4} \atop 2 + 4 = 6$$

When you group, look for sums of ten. Tens are easy to add.

$$\underbrace{8 + 2}_{10} + 6 = 16 \qquad\qquad 9 + \underbrace{5 + 5}_{10} = 19$$

EXERCISES Add.

1. $2 + 6 + 4$

2. $5 + 1 + 6$

3. $2 + 4 + 3$

4. $8 + 0 + 5$

5. $6 + 4 + 9$

6. $8 + 2 + 6$

7. $6 + 5 + 4 + 3$

8. $4 + 2 + 4 + 3$

9. $1 + 5 + 3 + 5$

10.
$$\begin{array}{r} 4 \\ 3 \\ 1 \\ +4 \\ \hline \end{array}$$

11.
$$\begin{array}{r} 2 \\ 5 \\ 5 \\ +6 \\ \hline \end{array}$$

12.
$$\begin{array}{r} 6 \\ 3 \\ 1 \\ +1 \\ \hline \end{array}$$

13.
$$\begin{array}{r} 8 \\ 4 \\ 0 \\ +2 \\ \hline \end{array}$$

14.
$$\begin{array}{r} 2 \\ 6 \\ 5 \\ +3 \\ \hline \end{array}$$

Solve.

15. Farmer Brown has 3 sheep, 8 cows,
and 5 pigs. How many animals does
he have?

16. Miss Black found 3 red gloves, 4 blue
gloves, and 6 black gloves. How many
gloves did she find?

17. The truck stopped at 5 homes on
Monday, 3 homes on Tuesday, and 7
homes on Wednesday. At how many
homes did the truck stop?

18. There are 3 girls jumping rope, 2 boys
playing catch, 4 children swinging,
and 8 boys playing ball. How many
children are playing?

Missing Addends

Use addition facts to find **missing addends**.

Paul wrote 5 thank-you notes in the morning. Before he went home, he gave the teacher a total of 13 notes. How many notes did he write in the afternoon?

$$5 + \boxed{} = 13 \qquad 5 + \boxed{8} = 13$$

Paul wrote 8 thank-you notes in the afternoon.

EXERCISES *Find the missing addend.*

1. $1 + \boxed{} = 9$ **2.** $\boxed{} + 4 = 12$ **3.** $6 + \boxed{} = 12$ **4.** $\boxed{} + 5 = 14$

5. $4 + \boxed{} = 11$ **6.** $8 + \boxed{} = 13$ **7.** $\boxed{} + 6 = 14$ **8.** $8 + \boxed{} = 8$

9. $\boxed{} + 7 = 12$ **10.** $\boxed{} + 5 = 9$ **11.** $8 + \boxed{} = 16$ **12.** $2 + \boxed{} = 6$

13. $9 + \boxed{} = 13$ **14.** $8 + \boxed{} = 17$ **15.** $\boxed{} + 2 = 11$ **16.** $\boxed{} + 3 = 7$

17.
$$\begin{array}{r} 4 \\ + \boxed{} \\ \hline 7 \end{array}$$

18.
$$\begin{array}{r} \boxed{} \\ + \ 8 \\ \hline 13 \end{array}$$

19.
$$\begin{array}{r} 7 \\ + \boxed{} \\ \hline 8 \end{array}$$

20.
$$\begin{array}{r} \boxed{} \\ + \ 7 \\ \hline 12 \end{array}$$

21.
$$\begin{array}{r} 4 \\ + \boxed{} \\ \hline 10 \end{array}$$

22.
$$\begin{array}{r} \boxed{} \\ + \ 5 \\ \hline 10 \end{array}$$

23.
$$\begin{array}{r} 7 \\ + \boxed{} \\ \hline 15 \end{array}$$

24.
$$\begin{array}{r} \boxed{} \\ + \ 0 \\ \hline 6 \end{array}$$

25.
$$\begin{array}{r} 8 \\ + \boxed{} \\ \hline 17 \end{array}$$

26.
$$\begin{array}{r} \boxed{} \\ + \ 7 \\ \hline 14 \end{array}$$

Solve.

27. Bill saw 7 blue birds. Then he saw some robins. He saw 12 birds in all. How many robins did he see?

28. Joan and Brad bought 15 balloons. Brad bought 6 balloons. How many did Joan buy?

Subtraction Facts

You can **subtract** to find how many are left.

John and Bettie had 17 grapes.
They ate 9 grapes. How
many grapes are left?

$$17 - 9 = 8$$ There are **8** grapes left.

You can subtract to **compare** two numbers.

Chris had 8 books. Kyle had 5 books.

How many more books
did Chris have?

$$\begin{array}{r} 8 \\ -5 \\ \hline 3 \end{array}$$

Chris had **3** more books.

How many fewer books
did Kyle have?

$$\begin{array}{r} 8 \\ -5 \\ \hline 3 \end{array}$$

Kyle had **3** fewer books.

EXERCISES **Subtract.**

1. $6 - 4$ **2.** $12 - 5$ **3.** $9 - 4$ **4.** $18 - 9$

5. $10 - 6$ **6.** $15 - 7$ **7.** $6 - 0$ **8.** $13 - 5$

9. $\begin{array}{r} 17 \\ -\ 8 \\ \hline \end{array}$ **10.** $\begin{array}{r} 10 \\ -\ 3 \\ \hline \end{array}$ **11.** $\begin{array}{r} 4 \\ -0 \\ \hline \end{array}$ **12.** $\begin{array}{r} 16 \\ -\ 8 \\ \hline \end{array}$ **13.** $\begin{array}{r} 12 \\ -\ 4 \\ \hline \end{array}$

14. $\begin{array}{r} 11 \\ -\ 4 \\ \hline \end{array}$ **15.** $\begin{array}{r} 16 \\ -\ 7 \\ \hline \end{array}$ **16.** $\begin{array}{r} 8 \\ -8 \\ \hline \end{array}$ **17.** $\begin{array}{r} 12 \\ -\ 9 \\ \hline \end{array}$ **18.** $\begin{array}{r} 14 \\ -\ 6 \\ \hline \end{array}$

Solve.

19. There are 6 rabbits. Two of them are white. The rest are black. How many are black?

20. Mr. Wilson had 15 signs to paint. He painted 8. How many more does he need to paint?

Related Facts

Addition and subtraction are related.

$$7 + 8 = 15 \qquad 15 - 8 = 7$$

Subtraction can undo addition.

$$16 - 9 = 7 \qquad 7 + 9 = 16$$

Addition can undo subtraction.

EXERCISES *Write a related fact.*

1. $3 + 6 = 9$

2. $6 - 1 = 5$

3. $12 - 7 = 5$

4. $8 + 4 = 12$

5. $17 - 8 = 9$

6. $5 + 8 = 13$

7. $7 + 7 = 14$

8. $4 + 6 = 10$

9.
$$\begin{array}{r} 2 \\ +4 \\ \hline 6 \end{array}$$

10.
$$\begin{array}{r} 15 \\ -\ 8 \\ \hline 7 \end{array}$$

11.
$$\begin{array}{r} 12 \\ -\ 6 \\ \hline 6 \end{array}$$

12.
$$\begin{array}{r} 8 \\ +8 \\ \hline 16 \end{array}$$

Write the fact family for each group of numbers.

2, 3, 5	$2 + 3 = 5, \quad 3 + 2 = 5, \quad 5 - 3 = 2, \quad 5 - 2 = 3$

13. 7, 8, 15

14. 5, 9, 4

15. 12, 4, 8

16. 7, 6, 13

_____

_____

_____

_____

Solve.

17. Mrs. Barnes made 6 pies. She wants to make a total of 10 pies. How many more does she need to make?

18. Marsha gave 8 pictures to Sue. Marsha had 4 pictures left. How many pictures did Marsha have before?

Patterns in Computation: Checking Sums and Differences

You can use basic facts to add or subtract greater numbers. Then, use a related fact to check your work. Study the pattern below.

	Check			Check			Check
3	8		88	55		5,555	8,888
+ 5	− 5 ✔		− 55	+ 33 ✔		+ 3,333	− 3,333 ✔
8	3		33	88		8,888	5,555

Use basic facts and related facts to add, subtract, and check other large sums and differences.

```
                                            Check
  4      8      7      4  ⟶   4,874        2,603
 − 2    − 6    − 0    − 3  ⟶  − 2,603       + 2,271
  2      2      7      1  ⟶   2,271        4,874
```

Add or subtract. Use a related fact to check your answers.

	1. 7	2. 77	3. 222	4. 9,999	5. 9,999
	+ 2	+ 22	+ 777	− 7,777	− 2,222

	6. 23	7. 753	8. 85	9. 259	10. 398
	+ 52	+ 136	− 32	− 148	− 126

	11. 130	12. 274	13. 2,461	14. 583	15. 5,375
	+ 253	+ 722	+ 326	− 61	− 251

	16. 7,281	17. 5,038	18. 9,684	19. 4,837	20. 5,687
	+ 1,517	+ 3,721	− 7,502	− 2,027	− 4,536

7

Maintenance

Add.

1. 4 + 6   **2.** 8 + 5   **3.** 6 + 0   **4.** 7 + 6

5. 8 + 8   **6.** 0 + 4   **7.** 9 + 7   **8.** 3 + 9

9. 4 + 2 + 5   **10.** 1 + 3 + 8 + 2   **11.** 7 + 3 + 4 + 4

Find the missing addend.

12. 5 + ☐ = 13   **13.** ☐ + 7 = 14   **14.** 4 + ☐ = 10   **15.** ☐ + 8 = 17

Subtract.

16. 5 − 3   **17.** 7 − 6   **18.** 12 − 4   **19.** 3 − 0

20. 17 − 8   **21.** 10 − 5   **22.** 18 − 9   **23.** 6 − 6

24. 9   **25.** 16   **26.** 4   **27.** 13   **28.** 15
     −5   − 7   −1   − 6   − 9

Solve.

29. There are 8 houses on the left side of the street. There are 6 houses on the right side. How many houses are on the street?

30. Mrs. Evans bought 12 donuts. Her children ate 7 of them. How many are left?

31. The home team has 5 runs. The other team has 13 runs. How many runs are needed to tie the score?

32. Billy has 6¢. He needs 12¢ to buy an eraser. How much more money does he need?

Addition with No Renaming

The football team gained 263 yards passing. They also gained 122 yards rushing. How many yards did they gain?

First add the ones.	*Next add the tens.*	*Then add the hundreds.*	*Change the order to check your answer.*
263 +122 5	263 +122 85	263 +122 385	122 +263 385 ✔

They gained 385 yards.

EXERCISES Add.

1. 34 +12	**2.** 56 +21	**3.** 81 + 8	**4.** 123 +123	**5.** 251 +126
6. 308 +130	**7.** 444 +104	**8.** 2,176 + 213	**9.** 3,870 +1,128	**10.** 2,275 +1,314

Add. Check your answers.

11. 46 +22	**12.** 804 +152	**13.** 4,321 +1,455

Solve.

14. The team scored 52 points on Friday. They scored 43 points on Saturday. What was the total of points scored?

15. A bus traveled 162 miles the first day. It traveled 212 miles the second day. How far did the bus travel?

Subtraction with No Renaming

One day, 124 students packed their lunch. The rest of the students bought lunch. There were 346 students at school. How many students bought lunch?

First subtract the ones.	*Next subtract the tens.*	*Then subtract the hundreds.*	*Check by adding.*
$\begin{array}{r} 346 \\ -124 \\ \hline 2 \end{array}$	$\begin{array}{r} 346 \\ -124 \\ \hline 22 \end{array}$	$\begin{array}{r} 346 \\ -124 \\ \hline 222 \end{array}$	$\begin{array}{r} 124 \\ +222 \\ \hline 346 \end{array}$ ✔

222 students bought lunch.

EXERCISES *Subtract.*

1. $\begin{array}{r} 57 \\ -23 \\ \hline \end{array}$
2. $\begin{array}{r} 63 \\ -41 \\ \hline \end{array}$
3. $\begin{array}{r} 49 \\ -26 \\ \hline \end{array}$
4. $\begin{array}{r} 31 \\ -20 \\ \hline \end{array}$
5. $\begin{array}{r} 267 \\ -\ 45 \\ \hline \end{array}$

6. $\begin{array}{r} 482 \\ -\ 61 \\ \hline \end{array}$
7. $\begin{array}{r} 769 \\ -237 \\ \hline \end{array}$
8. $\begin{array}{r} 454 \\ -121 \\ \hline \end{array}$
9. $\begin{array}{r} 2{,}357 \\ -\ 154 \\ \hline \end{array}$
10. $\begin{array}{r} 3{,}688 \\ -1{,}164 \\ \hline \end{array}$

Subtract. Check your answers.

11. $\begin{array}{r} 45 \\ -24 \\ \hline \end{array}$
12. $\begin{array}{r} 84 \\ -63 \\ \hline \end{array}$
13. $\begin{array}{r} 368 \\ -\ 57 \\ \hline \end{array}$

14. $\begin{array}{r} 819 \\ -409 \\ \hline \end{array}$
15. $\begin{array}{r} 5{,}426 \\ -3{,}114 \\ \hline \end{array}$
16. $\begin{array}{r} 8{,}753 \\ -8{,}243 \\ \hline \end{array}$

Solve.

17. A store had 48 books to sell. During the week 36 books were sold. How many books are left to sell?

18. Kevin wants to buy a book for 96¢. He has saved 83¢. How much more money does he need?

Copyright © 1988 by Merrill Publishing Co., Columbus, Ohio 43216

Problem Solving

Use these problem-solving steps.

Read the problem. ➤ **Decide** what to do. ➤ **Solve** the problem. ➤ **Examine** the solution.

The children ate 15 hamburgers and 6 hot dogs at the zoo picnic. How many more hamburgers did they eat than hot dogs?

$$15 - 6 = 9$$

The children ate 9 more hamburgers than hot dogs.

EXERCISES *Decide what to do. Write ADD or SUBTRACT.*

1. There are ☐ boys and ☐ girls at the picnic. How many children are at the picnic?

2. There are ☐ hot dogs left. There were 10 hot dogs. How many hot dogs were eaten?

Solve.

3. There are 15 children at the zoo. Marti has prepared 6 cups of juice. How many more cups of juice are needed?

4. There are 9 raisin cookies and 8 chocolate cookies. How many cookies are there in all?

5. Jake is to bring apples for everyone. He has 9 red apples and 7 yellow apples. How many apples does he have in all?

6. Roberta has 7 cents in her bank. Her mother gave her 8 cents. How much money does Roberta have now?

11

Problem Solving

Read each story. Then put a number in the blank so the story makes sense.

1. Carl had 15 marbles. He lost ____ marbles in a game. He has 9 marbles left.

2. On Monday, the bookstore had 236 children's books to sell. On Tuesday, ____ more books were delivered. Now the store has 357 children's books to sell.

3. Mr. Wade had ____ tickets to sell. He sold 53 tickets today. Tomorrow, he wants to sell the other 46 tickets.

4. Sally attended our school 163 days last year. This year she attended only 124 days before she moved. Sally attended our school a total of ____ days.

5. Kristy had ____ posters to hand out. She handed out 33 posters before lunch. After lunch she handed out the other 53 posters.

6. Kellie traveled 130 miles to get to her grandmother's house. She traveled ____ miles to get home. She traveled 293 miles in all.

7. Jerry took ____ pictures at the park. He also took 10 pictures at the zoo. He used all 24 pictures on the roll of film.

8. Mr. Smith is a car dealer. He ordered 546 new cars to sell. He has sold 425 of the new cars. Now he has ____ new cars left to sell.

Chapter 1 Test

Add or subtract.

1. 6 + 2   **2.** 8 + 7   **3.** 9 + 9   **4.** 6 + 8

5. 13 − 4   **6.** 9 − 4   **7.** 17 − 9   **8.** 16 − 8

9. 3 + 7 + 5   **10.** 6 + 2 + 4   **11.** 1 + 8 + 9

12. 5 + (4 + 3)   **13.** (4 + 8) − 5   **14.** 8 + (9 − 6)

15. 52
       +26

16. 37
       +11

17. 268
       +130

18. 421
       +156

19. 3,285
       +1,401

20. 64
       −31

21. 97
       −45

22. 343
       −122

23. 555
       −232

24. 5,526
       −2,503

Write the fact family for each group of numbers.

25. 2, 6, 4   **26.** 11, 5, 6   **27.** 8, 15, 7   **28.** 6, 9, 15

_____   _____   _____   _____

_____   _____   _____   _____

_____   _____   _____   _____

_____   _____   _____   _____

Solve.

29. Bettie decided to bake 36 cookies. She has baked 14 cookies. How many more does she need to bake?

30. On Saturday, 1,326 people watched a ball game. On Sunday, 1,142 people watched a game. How many people watched the two games?

Write in words.

1. 407　　　　　**2.** 1,900　　　　　**3.** 45,006　　　　　**4.** 123,070

Complete.

5. 70 = _____ tens　　　**6.** 2,700 = _____ hundreds　　**7.** 4,560 = _____ tens

Replace each ◯ with <, >, or = to make a true sentence.

8. 49 ◯ 40　　　　　**9.** 6,278 ◯ 6,287　　　　**10.** 241,010 ◯ 241,100

Round to the nearest hundred.

11. 348　　　**12.** 561　　　**13.** 176　　　**14.** 3,095　　　**15.** 4,690

Write in standard form.

1. 75 million, 1 thousand　　**2.** 2 million, 36 thousand, 4　　**3.** 9 million, 80

Replace each ◯ with <, >, or = to make a true sentence.

4. 748,043 ◯ 748,034　　　　　　**5.** 62,007,132 ◯ 62,007,130

Solve. Use the bar graph.

6. How many points did Gary score?

7. How many more points did Ron score than Bill?

Points Scored

Name

Bill
Ron
Gary

0 2 4 6 8 10 12 14
Points

Solve. Use only the facts you need.

8. There are 673 children at Franklin School. The school prepared 775 newsletters this month. 53 of them were damaged. How many newsletters were left?

Numbers to 999

You can write any numeral with these ten **digits**.

The number named by each digit depends on its
place-value position.

The numeral 324 means 3 hundreds, 2 tens, and 4 ones.

You can write this numeral in the following ways:

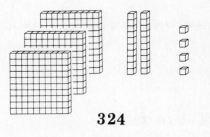

Standard Form	324
Words	three hundred twenty-four
Expanded Form	300 + 20 + 4

324

EXERCISES *Write in standard form.*

1. 8 tens   **2.** 7 hundreds   **3.** 5 ones   **4.** 60 + 3

5. 200 + 90   **6.** 800 + 40 + 1   **7.** 900 + 4   **8.** nineteen

9. seventy-two   **10.** eight hundred thirteen   **11.** five hundred forty-two

Write in words.

12. 17   **13.** 44   **14.** 87

15. 198   **16.** 579   **17.** 919

Write in expanded form.

18. 33   **19.** 12   **20.** 88

21. 461   **22.** 729   **23.** 999

24. 209   **25.** 518   **26.** 730

Numbers to 999,999

Study each place-value position in the chart.

The chart shows the numeral **761,528**.
A *comma* separates the thousands
place from the hundreds place.

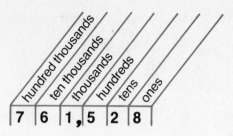

This numeral can be written in the following ways:

Standard Form	761,528
Words	seven hundred sixty-one thousand, five hundred twenty-eight
Expanded Form	700,000 + 60,000 + 1,000 + 500 + 20 + 8

EXERCISES **Write the number named by each 5.**

1. 9,527   **2.** 15,409   **3.** 548,222   **4.** 257,003

Write in standard form.

5. two thousand, five hundred six   **6.** fifteen thousand, eighty-nine

7. 8,000 + 700 + 40 + 9   **8.** 300,000 + 5,000 + 60 + 8

9. nine hundred thirty-three thousand, one hundred seven

Write in words.

10. 7,609   **11.** 17,540   **12.** 94,062

13. 321,002   **14.** 983,404

Write in expanded form.

15. 5,314   **16.** 28,140   **17.** 59,021

18. 79,981   **19.** 384,208   **20.** 999,909

More about Numbers

There are many different ways to name **1,000**.

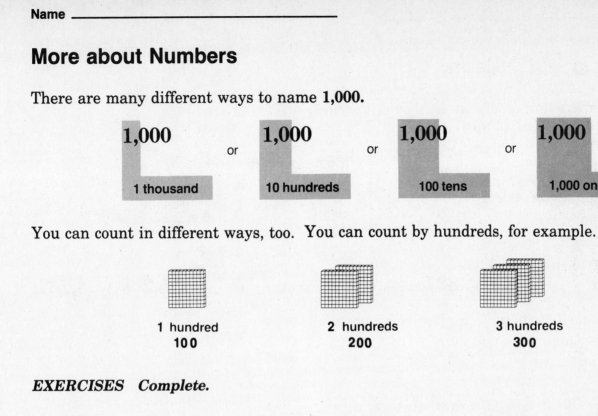

1,000	or	**1,000**	or	**1,000**	or	**1,000**
1 thousand		10 hundreds		100 tens		1,000 ones

You can count in different ways, too. You can count by hundreds, for example.

1 hundred	2 hundreds	3 hundreds
100	**200**	**300**

EXERCISES *Complete.*

1. 20 = ____ tens

2. 50 = ____ tens

3. 90 = ____ tens

4. 230 = ____ tens

5. 560 = ____ tens

6. 200 = ____ hundreds

7. 800 = ____ hundreds

8. 3,400 = ____ hundreds

9. 6,830 = ____ tens

10. 4,700 = ____ hundreds

11. 2,880 = ____ tens

12. 9,100 = ____ hundreds

Complete each number pattern.

13. 560, 570, 580, _____, _____, _____, 620

14. 3,200, 3,300, 3,400, _____, _____, 3,700

15. 6,740, 6,750, 6,760, _____, _____, 6,790, _____, _____, 6,820

Solve.

16. Cindy walks her dog for 30 minutes each day. After 10 days, how many minutes does she walk her dog? (Hint: 30 tens)

17. Paul saves 10¢ each week from his allowance. He does this for 10 weeks. How much money does Paul save? (Hint: 10 tens)

Comparing and Ordering

You can compare and order numbers by comparing
the digits in each place-value position.

Compare 819 and 821.

Compare 5,268 and 5,257.

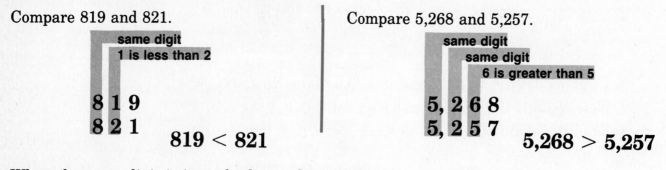

When the same digit is in each place-value position,
the numerals name the same number.

EXERCISES   *Write using the symbols <, >, or =.*

1. 28 is less than 29   2. 463 is greater than 462   3. 747 is equal to 747

4. 3,664 is greater than 3,649   5. 8,233 is less than 8,238

Fill in the circle with <, >, or = to make a true sentence.

6. 34 ◯ 43   7. 96 ◯ 93   8. 129 ◯ 131   9. 304 ◯ 304

10. 867 ◯ 856   11. 701 ◯ 711   12. 1,212 ◯ 1,012   13. 5,874 ◯ 5,864

Circle the lesser number in each pair of numbers.

14. 53, 52   15. 44, 54   16. 743, 558   17. 612, 618

18. 996, 994   19. 3,218, 2,812   20. 4,080, 4,090   21. 8,311, 8,301

Order the numbers from least to greatest.

22. 576, 467, 671   23. 4,338, 2,610, 1,426

Rounding Numbers

The number line below can be used to round 384 to the nearest hundred.

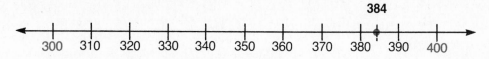

384

300 310 320 330 340 350 360 370 380 390 400

Since 384 is closer to 400 than 300, it rounds to 400.

To round without using a number line:

- **Look at the digit to the *right* of the place being rounded.**
- **Round up if the digit to the right is 5, 6, 7, 8, or 9.**
- **Round down if the digit to the right is 0, 1, 2, 3, or 4.**

To the nearest hundred, 1,538 rounds to 1,500.
To the nearest thousand, 17,622 rounds to 18,000.

EXERCISES *Locate each number on the number line.*
Round to the nearest hundred.

800 810 820 830 840 850 860 870 880 890 900

1. 888	**2.** 813	**3.** 850	**4.** 842	**5.** 893
6. 851	**7.** 804	**8.** 849	**9.** 877	**10.** 835

Choose the correct answer for rounding to the nearest thousand.

11. 3,298   3,000   4,000   **12.** 6,519   6,000   7,000

13. 19,405   19,000   20,000   **14.** 78,712   78,000   79,000

Round to the underlined place-value position.

15. 2,0<u>3</u>3	**16.** 4,<u>6</u>70	**17.** 9<u>5</u>5	**18.** 8,2<u>6</u>4	**19.** 18,<u>8</u>26
20. 2<u>6</u>,903	**21.** 5<u>1</u>,210	**22.** 48,<u>8</u>06	**23.** 79,3<u>3</u>6	**24.** 9<u>0</u>,826
25. 32,8<u>5</u>8	**26.** 19,<u>2</u>46	**27.** 2<u>9</u>,125	**28.** 42,<u>3</u>80	**29.** 99,<u>8</u>99

Maintenance

Add.

1. $6 + 4$ **2.** $9 + 0$ **3.** $8 + 5$ **4.** $7 + 4$ **5.** $3 + 9$

6.
$$\begin{array}{r} 23 \\ +56 \\ \hline \end{array}$$
7.
$$\begin{array}{r} 67 \\ +22 \\ \hline \end{array}$$
8.
$$\begin{array}{r} 727 \\ +162 \\ \hline \end{array}$$
9.
$$\begin{array}{r} 4 \\ 4 \\ +3 \\ \hline \end{array}$$
10.
$$\begin{array}{r} 5 \\ 1 \\ +7 \\ \hline \end{array}$$

Subtract.

11. $9 - 4$ **12.** $11 - 3$ **13.** $8 - 0$ **14.** $14 - 7$ **15.** $16 - 9$

16.
$$\begin{array}{r} 58 \\ -43 \\ \hline \end{array}$$
17.
$$\begin{array}{r} 67 \\ -21 \\ \hline \end{array}$$
18.
$$\begin{array}{r} 88 \\ -37 \\ \hline \end{array}$$
19.
$$\begin{array}{r} 46 \\ -14 \\ \hline \end{array}$$
20.
$$\begin{array}{r} 97 \\ -62 \\ \hline \end{array}$$

Write the number named by each 6.

21. 168   **22.** 693   **23.** 4,076   **24.** 16,823   **25.** 864,105

Write in standard form.

26. six hundred twenty-nine   **27.** eight thousand, one hundred two

28. fifty-three thousand, thirteen   **29.** four hundred thousand, eleven

Fill in the circle with $<$, $>$, or $=$ to make a true sentence.

30. $87 \bigcirc 78$ **31.** $417 \bigcirc 407$ **32.** $671 \bigcirc 671$ **33.** $4,265 \bigcirc 4,255$

Round to the underlined place-value position.

34. 3<u>4</u>2   **35.** <u>6</u>91   **36.** <u>8</u>,463   **37.** 5,<u>2</u>88   **38.** 9,1<u>1</u>8

39. 1<u>3</u>,262   **40.** 2<u>4</u>,509   **41.** 63,1<u>4</u>4   **42.** 8<u>3</u>,456   **43.** 77,<u>7</u>77

Millions

Millions			Thousands			Ones		
hundreds	tens	ones	hundreds	tens	ones	hundreds	tens	ones
	4	3,	0	0	0,	8	0	0

Study each place-value position in the chart at the left.
Each group of three digits is called a **period**. The periods are separated by commas.

The chart shows the numeral **43,000,800.**

- The digit 4 names **4 ten millions** or **40 million.**
- The digit 3 names **3 one millions** or **3 million.**
- The digit 8 names **8 hundred ones** or **800.**

EXERCISES *Place commas between the place-value periods.*
Then read each numeral.

1. 37214   2. 248309   3. 8832117   4. 98026707   5. 630126789

Write the number named by each 2.

6. 4,631,258   7. 6,529,380   8. 12,844,113   9. 523,004,413

10. 43,268,000   11. 194,026,513   12. 89,002,895   13. 772,638,475

Write in standard form.

14. 3 million, 47 thousand, 200   15. 53 million, 208 thousand, 23

16. thirty-three million, five hundred ten thousand, seventeen

Write in words.

17. 5,040,600   18. 63,070,004

Fill in each circle with <, >, or = to make a true sentence.

19. 54,300,146 ◯ 54,700,247   20. 607,890,003 ◯ 607,890,003

Problem Solving

Use the plan below to solve a problem.

Read the problem. ▶ **Decide** what to do. ▶ **Solve** the problem. ▶ **Examine** the solution.

EXERCISES *Solve. Use the chart.*

Favorite Desserts	Number of Times Listed
ice cream	14
cake	8
pie	10
cookies	6
jello	12
fruit	6

1. How many times was jello listed?

2. How many times were cookies listed?

3. What is the total number of times jello and cookies were listed?

4. How many more times was ice cream listed than cookies?

5. What two desserts were listed the most?

6. What two desserts were listed the least?

Complete this graph. Use the chart above.

7.

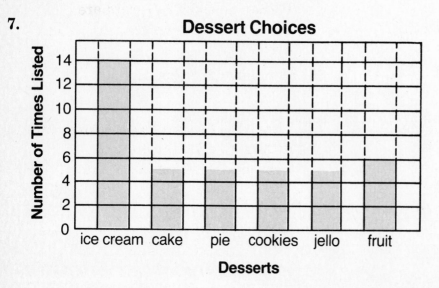

22

Problem Solving

Sometimes a problem has too many facts.

Use the plan below to solve problems.

Read the problem. ▶ **Decide** what to do. ▶ **Solve** the problem. ▶ **Examine** the solution.

Solve. Use only the facts you need.

1. The trailer truck holds 3,900 watermelons. Jack has 2,850 melons. He sells 1,768 melons. How many melons does he have left?

2. It was 95° at the zoo on Saturday. The zoo sold 229 balloons on Saturday. On Sunday 287 balloons were sold. How many balloons were sold all together?

3. Aleta owns over 150 records. She buys a record for $6.98. She also buys a songbook for $3.75. How much money does she spend?

4. Tickets to the ball park cost $2.50. The ball park has 525 seats. Only 286 seats are filled. How many seats are empty?

5. Morse School sends 43 children to the Amusement Park. The children buy 226 tickets for rides and 187 tickets for the fun house. How many tickets do the children buy?

6. There are 15 girls and 12 boys in Mrs. Clark's third grade. Tickets for the fun house cost 65¢ each. How many children are in Mrs. Clark's third grade?

Chapter 2 Test

Write the number named by each 4.

1. 1,435   **2.** 28,047   **3.** 54,268   **4.** 1,047,252

Write in standard form.

5. nineteen thousand, two hundred   **6.** three million, five hundred forty-six

Write in words.

7. 8,728   **8.** 9,030,070

Write in expanded form.

9. 5,607   **10.** 12,870   **11.** 434,050   **12.** 303,671

Complete.

13. 60 = _____ tens   **14.** 870 = _____ tens   **15.** 4,200 = _____ hundreds

Fill in the circle with <, >, or = to make a true sentence.

16. 289 ◯ 287   **17.** 1,473 ◯ 1,482   **18.** 653,004 ◯ 653,004

Round to the underlined place-value position.

19. 8<u>9</u>4   **20.** 1,<u>3</u>61   **21.** 18,<u>5</u>17   **22.** 268,<u>3</u>20   **23.** 17<u>2</u>,998

Solve. Use the bar graph.

24. How many people said they liked chocolate ice cream the best?

25. How many more people said they liked vanilla than strawberry?

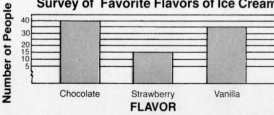

Survey of Favorite Flavors of Ice Cream

Add.

1. 74
    + 8

2. 65
    + 28

3. 419
    + 93

4. 542
    + 278

5. 935
    + 156

6. 8,546
    + 2,726

7. 67,503
    + 17,343

8.   46
     287
    + 59

9. 487
    206
    + 174

10. 4,558
    1,169
    + 7,742

Round to the nearest hundred. Estimate.

11. 286
    + 139

12. 762
    + 541

13. 548
    + 813

14. 382
    + 657

Subtract.

1. 42
    − 9

2. 84
    − 35

3. 536
    − 77

4. 743
    − 168

5. 620
    − 195

6. 2,635
    − 1,719

7. 3,014
    − 1,634

8. 88,205
    − 19,156

9. 742,050
    − 153,629

10. 523,460
    − 437,251

Round to the nearest thousand. Estimate.

11. 8,863
    − 1,529

12. 7,926
    − 2,397

13. 4,294
    − 3,487

14. 8,723
    − 6,821

Estimate.

15. Rudy picked 39 baskets of peaches in the morning and 22 baskets in the afternoon. How many baskets did Rudy pick?

Solve.

16. Mitchell had 7 bats. Judy gave him 4 bats. He gave Steve 3 bats. How many bats does Mitchell have left?

Addition and Subtraction Review

John read 23 pages in the morning. He read 36 pages in the afternoon.

How many pages did he read in all?

To find the total, *add*.

$$\begin{array}{r} 23 \\ +36 \\ \hline 59 \end{array}$$

He read 59 pages.

How many more pages did he read in the afternoon than in the morning?

To compare the numbers, *subtract*.

$$\begin{array}{r} 36 \\ -23 \\ \hline 13 \end{array}$$

He read 13 more pages in the afternoon.

EXERCISES *Find the sum or difference.*

1. $4 + 8$

2. $14 - 7$

3. $13 - 8$

4. $9 + 6$

5. $17 - 9$

6. $8 + 8$

7. $5 + 6$

8. $16 - 7$

9. $3 + 9$

10. $12 - 6$

11. $7 + 6$

12. $15 - 9$

13. $\begin{array}{r} 16 \\ + 3 \\ \hline \end{array}$

14. $\begin{array}{r} 57 \\ - 4 \\ \hline \end{array}$

15. $\begin{array}{r} 23 \\ +16 \\ \hline \end{array}$

16. $\begin{array}{r} 46 \\ -13 \\ \hline \end{array}$

17. $\begin{array}{r} 86 \\ -44 \\ \hline \end{array}$

18. $\begin{array}{r} 34 \\ -31 \\ \hline \end{array}$

19. $\begin{array}{r} 84 \\ +13 \\ \hline \end{array}$

20. $\begin{array}{r} 42 \\ +26 \\ \hline \end{array}$

21. $\begin{array}{r} 67 \\ -42 \\ \hline \end{array}$

22. $\begin{array}{r} 35 \\ +34 \\ \hline \end{array}$

Solve.

23. Carla delivers 34 papers in the morning. After school she delivers 53 papers. How many does she deliver in one day?

24. Mrs. Thomas wants to make 48 donuts. She has made 35. How many more does she need to make?

Addition with One or Two Renamings

When you add, sometimes you must rename.

Find the sum of 426 and 835.

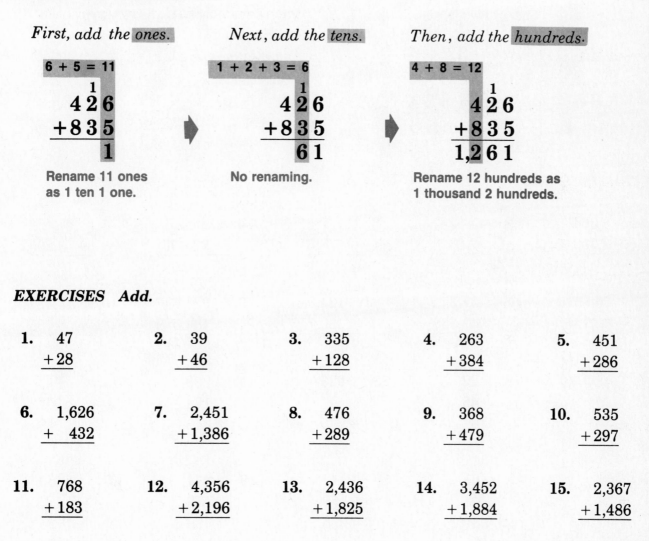

First, add the ones.

6 + 5 = 11

$$\begin{array}{r} 4\overset{1}{2}6 \\ +835 \\ \hline 1 \end{array}$$

Rename 11 ones
as 1 ten 1 one.

Next, add the tens.

1 + 2 + 3 = 6

$$\begin{array}{r} 4\overset{1}{2}6 \\ +835 \\ \hline 61 \end{array}$$

No renaming.

Then, add the hundreds.

4 + 8 = 12

$$\begin{array}{r} \overset{1}{4}26 \\ +835 \\ \hline 1{,}261 \end{array}$$

Rename 12 hundreds as
1 thousand 2 hundreds.

EXERCISES Add.

1. 47 +28	2. 39 +46	3. 335 +128	4. 263 +384	5. 451 +286
6. 1,626 + 432	7. 2,451 +1,386	8. 476 +289	9. 368 +479	10. 535 +297
11. 768 +183	12. 4,356 +2,196	13. 2,436 +1,825	14. 3,452 +1,884	15. 2,367 +1,486

Solve.

16. Debbie climbed up 356 steps. Then she climbed up 328 more steps. How many steps did she climb?

17. Jerry's coin collection has 267 pennies and 178 nickels. How many pennies and nickels does Jerry have?

Adding Greater Numbers,
Adding More Than Two Numbers

Study the example.

$4 + 0 + 4 = 8$	$6 + 2 + 5 = 13$	$1 + 2 + 3 + 8 = 14$	$1 + 3 + 2 + 3 = 9$
3,2 6 **4**	¹ 3,2 **6** 4	¹¹ 3,**2** 6 4	¹¹ **3**,2 6 4
2,3 2 **0**	2,3 **2** 0	2,**3** 2 0	**2**,3 2 0
+3,8 5 **4**	+3,8 **5** 4	+3,**8** 5 4	+**3**,8 5 4
8	**3** 8	**4** 3 8	**9,4** 3 8

EXERCISES Add.

1.	3,364	**2.**	4,823	**3.**	5,486	**4.**	26,451	**5.**	47,428
	+2,789		+2,359		+8,748		+13,896		+ 8,395

6.	56,657	**7.**	32,371	**8.**	124,384	**9.**	328,647	**10.**	13,467
	+82,746		+47,658		+ 89,756		+184,579		+ 8,796

11.	43	**12.**	22	**13.**	126	**14.**	258	**15.**	1,246
	25		45		47		174		2,354
	+36		+87		+225		+346		+3,549

16.	52	**17.**	61	**18.**	143	**19.**	274	**20.**	2,356
	34		48		56		153		1,483
	41		36		218		328		425
	+27		+55		+ 67		+162		+2,154

Solve.

21. Dr. Wilson gave toothbrushes to all the students in fourth grade classes. The students in the classes numbered 25, 31, 28, and 26. How many toothbrushes did he need?

22. The Daily News prints two papers in a day. In the morning, 263,457 papers are delivered. In the afternoon, 417,658 papers are delivered. What is the total number of papers delivered in a day?

Estimating Sums

When you do not need an exact answer, you can **estimate**.
You can also use estimation to check addition.

Estimate 376 + 647.

First, round each addend to its greatest place-value position. Then, add.

$$376 \rightarrow 400$$
$$+647 \rightarrow +600$$
$$\overline{1,000}$$

Now, find the actual sum.

$$376$$
$$+647$$
$$\overline{1,023}$$

Compare the estimate to the actual sum. Is the answer reasonable?

EXERCISES   Round to the greatest place-value position. Estimate.

1. 43 40
   +26 +30
        70

2. 56
   +31

3. 46
   +44

4. 71
   +69

5. 68
   +54

6. 326
   +572

7. 286
   +742

8. 493
   +816

9. 576
   +349

10. 821
    +299

11. 2,367
    +4,561

12. 3,869
    +7,275

13. 4,293
    +3,709

14. 5,876
    +6,113

Solve. Estimate the sum.

15. The North Town bus traveled 74 miles. The South Town bus traveled 57 miles. About how many miles did they both travel?

16. The highway crew painted 238 miles of lines on Monday. They painted 376 miles of lines on Tuesday. About how many miles of lines did they paint?

Problem Solving

Marcos buys a chili dog
and a medium root beer.
What is his total cost?

Menu	Cost
Chili dog	89¢
Hamburger	95¢
Fishburger	89¢
Root beer	35¢, 45¢, 55¢

Use the plan below to solve the problem.

Read
the problem. ▶ **Decide**
what to do. ▶ **Solve**
the problem. ▶ **Examine**
the solution.

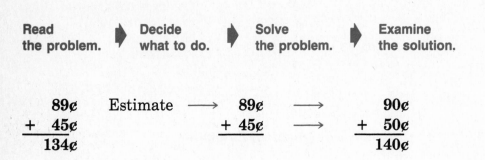

```
    89¢      Estimate ⟶     89¢    ⟶        90¢
 +  45¢                  +  45¢    ⟶     +  50¢
   134¢                                    140¢
```

The answer makes sense.

Estimate. Choose which answer makes sense.
Write a, b, or c. Use the menu above.

1. Melinda had a fishburger and
   a small root beer. Mary had a
   hamburger and a large root beer.
   What is the total cost?

   a. 150¢
   b. 374¢
   c. 274¢
   _____

2. Jack had a chili dog and a large
   root beer. Jeff had a hamburger
   and a medium root beer. Which
   one spent the most?

   a. Jack
   b. Jeff
   c. 284¢
   _____

3. Mike used 249 hamburger rolls
   on Saturday and 492 on Sunday.
   How many hamburger rolls did
   he use in two days?

   a. 492 > 249
   b. 741
   c. 249 < 492
   _____

Patterns in Computation: Even and Odd Numbers

The ones digit of an even number is 0, 2, 4, 6, or 8.
The ones digit of an odd number is 1, 3, 5, 7, or 9.
Study the pattern below.

0, 1, 2, 3, 4, 5, 6, 7, 8, 9, 10, 11, 12, 13, 14, 15, 16, 17, 18, 19, 20, ... means the
pattern goes on

Is the sum of two even numbers even or odd? Is the sum of
two odd numbers even or odd? Study the pattern below.

Write EVEN or ODD for each number.

1. 2	**2.** 7	**3.** 0	**4.** 14	**5.** 36	**6.** 85
7. 101	**8.** 299	**9.** 700	**10.** 1,000	**11.** 4,321	**12.** 9,999

Use the pattern to tell if the sum is EVEN or ODD. Then add.

13. 8 + 9	**14.** 7 + 7	**15.** 6 + 9	**16.** 24 + 5	**17.** 16 + 22
18. 95 + 71	**19.** 103 + 86	**20.** 342 + 489	**21.** 623 + 549	**22.** 804 + 390

Maintenance

Write the number named by each 6.

1. 367   **2.** 4,346   **3.** 16,825   **4.** 8,672

Fill in the circle with $<$, $>$, or $=$.

5. 328 ◯ 279   **6.** 453 ◯ 453   **7.** 1,253 ◯ 1,189   **8.** 3,974 ◯ 7,102

Round each number to its greatest place-value position.

9. 36   **10.** 2,187   **11.** 439   **12.** 8,651

Find the sum or difference.

13.   426
      +271

14.   573
      −341

15.   987
      −374

16.   364
      +283

17.   697
      −323

18.   3,468
      +8,796

19.   468
      277
      +234

20.   426
      359
      +571

Estimate each sum.

21.   623
      +285

22.   482
      +237

23.   549
      +376

24.   788
      +627

25.   2,474
      +6,806

26.   8,493
      +4,162

Solve.

27. If Steve has 70¢, how much more money does he need to have 98¢?

28. There were 683 visitors on Friday night. On Saturday, there were 572. About how many visitors were there both nights?

Subtraction with One or Two Renamings

When you subtract, sometimes you must rename.

Find the difference between 235 and 67.

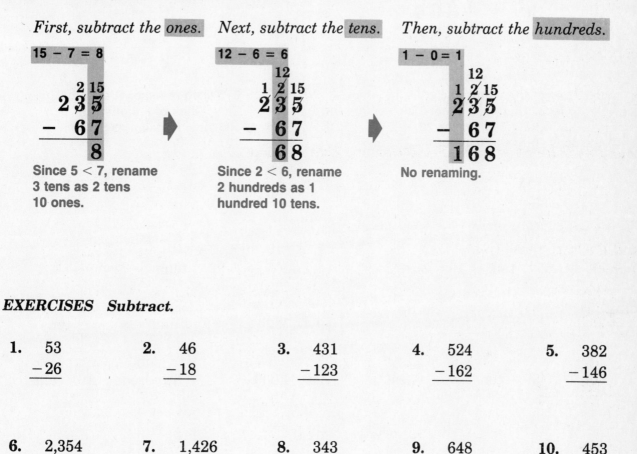

First, subtract the ones.

15 − 7 = 8

```
    2 15
  2 3 5
 −  6 7
      8
```

Since 5 < 7, rename
3 tens as 2 tens
10 ones.

Next, subtract the tens.

12 − 6 = 6

```
      12
  1  2 15
  2  3 5
 −   6 7
     6 8
```

Since 2 < 6, rename
2 hundreds as 1
hundred 10 tens.

Then, subtract the hundreds.

1 − 0 = 1

```
      12
  1  2 15
  2  3 5
 −   6 7
  1  6 8
```

No renaming.

EXERCISES *Subtract.*

1. 53 −26	2. 46 −18	3. 431 −123	4. 524 −162	5. 382 −146
6. 2,354 −1,622	7. 1,426 −1,284	8. 343 −167	9. 648 −283	10. 453 −378
11. 822 −368	12. 524 −268	13. 2,624 −1,248	14. 3,435 −1,681	15. 3,673 −2,898

Solve.

16. Mr. Betts is testing a car. He must drive 486 miles. He has traveled 258 miles. How much further must he drive?

17. Sue's family must drive 1,328 miles while on vacation. They have driven 978 miles so far. How many more miles must they drive?

Subtracting with Zeros

When you subtract numbers with zeros, you can rename in a different way.

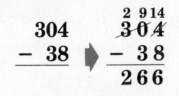

$$\begin{array}{r} 304 \\ -\ 38 \end{array}$$

$$\begin{array}{r} {\scriptstyle 2\ 9\ 14} \\ 3\,0\,4 \\ -\ 3\,8 \\ \hline 2\,6\,6 \end{array}$$

4 < 8, so rename. There are 0 tens. Think of 3 hundreds as 30 tens. Rename as 29 tens 10 ones. Subtract.

$$\begin{array}{r} {\scriptstyle 5\ 9\ 9\ 16} \\ 6{,}0\,0\,6 \\ -2{,}3\,4\,8 \\ \hline 3{,}6\,5\,8 \end{array}$$

6 < 8, so rename. There are 0 tens. Think of 6 thousands as 600 tens. Rename as 599 tens 10 ones. Subtract.

EXERCISES *Complete.*

1. 600 → __59__ tens __10__ ones

2. 300 → __29__ tens _____ ones

3. 400 → _____ tens __10__ ones

4. 700 → __6__ hundreds _____ tens

5. 1,000 → __99__ tens _____ ones

6. 4,000 → _____ hundreds __10__ tens

Subtract.

7. $\begin{array}{r} 40 \\ -26 \end{array}$

8. $\begin{array}{r} 500 \\ -327 \end{array}$

9. $\begin{array}{r} 302 \\ -146 \end{array}$

10. $\begin{array}{r} 410 \\ -256 \end{array}$

11. $\begin{array}{r} 5{,}300 \\ -2{,}743 \end{array}$

12. $\begin{array}{r} 8{,}000 \\ -7{,}463 \end{array}$

13. $\begin{array}{r} 4{,}006 \\ -2{,}579 \end{array}$

14. $\begin{array}{r} 3{,}003 \\ -1{,}487 \end{array}$

15. $\begin{array}{r} 5{,}070 \\ -2{,}484 \end{array}$

16. $\begin{array}{r} 6{,}060 \\ -5{,}372 \end{array}$

Solve.

17. A choir bought 2,000 records. They sold 1,423 records. How many are left?

18. The school wants to buy a projector for $1,004. They have raised $978. How much more do they need?

Subtracting Greater Numbers

Study the example.

Subtract ones.

$$\begin{array}{r} 3,1\overset{7}{\cancel{8}}\overset{14}{\cancel{4}} \\ -1,36\,7 \\ \hline 7 \end{array}$$

Rename 8 tens as 7 tens 10 ones.

Subtract tens.

$$\begin{array}{r} 3,1\overset{7}{\cancel{8}}\overset{14}{\cancel{4}} \\ -1,3\,6\,7 \\ \hline 1\,7 \end{array}$$

No renaming.

Subtract hundreds.

$$\begin{array}{r} \overset{2}{\cancel{3}},\overset{11}{\cancel{1}}\overset{7}{\cancel{8}}\overset{14}{\cancel{4}} \\ -1,3\,6\,7 \\ \hline 8\,1\,7 \end{array}$$

Rename 3 thousands as 2 thousands 10 hundreds.

Subtract thousands.

$$\begin{array}{r} \overset{2}{\cancel{3}},\overset{11}{\cancel{1}}\overset{7}{\cancel{8}}\overset{14}{\cancel{4}} \\ -1,3\,6\,7 \\ \hline 1,8\,1\,7 \end{array}$$

No renaming.

EXERCISES Subtract.

1. $\begin{array}{r} 4,236 \\ -1,354 \\ \hline \end{array}$

2. $\begin{array}{r} 3,651 \\ -1,783 \\ \hline \end{array}$

3. $\begin{array}{r} 6,174 \\ -2,839 \\ \hline \end{array}$

4. $\begin{array}{r} 5,654 \\ -4,275 \\ \hline \end{array}$

5. $\begin{array}{r} 9,483 \\ -8,576 \\ \hline \end{array}$

6. $\begin{array}{r} 31,257 \\ -\ 4,769 \\ \hline \end{array}$

7. $\begin{array}{r} 43,471 \\ -26,684 \\ \hline \end{array}$

8. $\begin{array}{r} 54,203 \\ -26,849 \\ \hline \end{array}$

9. $\begin{array}{r} 26,008 \\ -18,469 \\ \hline \end{array}$

10. $\begin{array}{r} 73,254 \\ -28,839 \\ \hline \end{array}$

11. $\begin{array}{r} 184,265 \\ -\ 36,472 \\ \hline \end{array}$

12. $\begin{array}{r} 230,046 \\ -\ 64,753 \\ \hline \end{array}$

13. $\begin{array}{r} 100,300 \\ -\ 43,043 \\ \hline \end{array}$

14. $\begin{array}{r} 387,254 \\ -289,476 \\ \hline \end{array}$

15. $\begin{array}{r} 750,624 \\ -274,586 \\ \hline \end{array}$

16. $\begin{array}{r} 483,453 \\ -294,856 \\ \hline \end{array}$

Solve.

17. The newspaper printed 634,257 copies of a special edition. They only sold 586,489. How many copies were left?

18. The baseball team sold 43,327 tickets for their game. Only 38,259 people came. How many people did not come?

Estimating Differences

When you do not need an exact answer, you can estimate.
You can also use estimation to check subtraction.

Estimate 642 − 385.

*First, round each number to
its greatest place-value
position. Then, subtract.*

Now, find the actual difference.

$$
\begin{array}{r}
624 \rightarrow 600 \\
-385 \rightarrow -400 \\
\hline
200
\end{array}
$$

$$
\begin{array}{r}
624 \\
-385 \\
\hline
239
\end{array}
$$

Compare the estimate
to the actual
difference. Is the
answer reasonable?

EXERCISES   Round to the greatest place-value position. Estimate.

1. $\begin{array}{r} 56 \\ -23 \\ \hline \end{array}$ $\begin{array}{r} 60 \\ -20 \\ \hline 40 \end{array}$

2. $\begin{array}{r} 42 \\ -27 \\ \hline \end{array}$

3. $\begin{array}{r} 76 \\ -44 \\ \hline \end{array}$

4. $\begin{array}{r} 83 \\ -47 \\ \hline \end{array}$

5. $\begin{array}{r} 77 \\ -49 \\ \hline \end{array}$

6. $\begin{array}{r} 527 \\ -369 \\ \hline \end{array}$

7. $\begin{array}{r} 391 \\ -160 \\ \hline \end{array}$

8. $\begin{array}{r} 750 \\ -401 \\ \hline \end{array}$

9. $\begin{array}{r} 636 \\ -568 \\ \hline \end{array}$

10. $\begin{array}{r} 471 \\ -186 \\ \hline \end{array}$

11. $\begin{array}{r} 5,364 \\ -2,671 \\ \hline \end{array}$

12. $\begin{array}{r} 4,837 \\ -2,498 \\ \hline \end{array}$

13. $\begin{array}{r} 6,192 \\ -2,877 \\ \hline \end{array}$

14. $\begin{array}{r} 8,603 \\ -6,257 \\ \hline \end{array}$

Solve. Estimate the difference.

15. Mrs. Smith wants to buy a T.V. set
for $439. She has saved $321. About
how much more does she need to
save?

16. The Jackson family planned to travel
5,843 miles in 14 days. In ten days
they have traveled 3,582 miles. About
how many more miles do they need
to go?

Problem Solving

Carl wrote 8 invitations in the morning and 9 in the afternoon. He needs one stamp for each invitation. If he has 10 stamps, how many more stamps does he need?

First Step
Add to find out how many stamps he needs.

Second Step
Subtract to find out how many more stamps he needs.

$$8 + 9 = 17$$

$$17 - 10 = 7$$

He needs 7 more stamps.

1. Read the problem.
2. Decide what to do.
3. Solve the problem.
4. Examine the solution.

Solve.

1. Mr. Wallace had a stack of 36 sheets of colored paper. The class used 18 sheets. Then he added 23 more sheets to the stack. How many sheets are in the stack?

2. Mrs. Jones bought 13 packages of hot dog buns and 18 packages of hamburger buns. She took 25 packages to a picnic. How many packages did she have left?

3. Mrs. Brown baked 36 chocolate chip cookies. She also baked 24 peanut butter cookies. Her children ate 15 cookies. How many cookies were left?

4. Jamie washed 23 desks in one room and 18 in another room. Mark washed 34 desks. How many more did Jamie wash than Mark?

5. The cook made 86 trays of food. A group of people took 58 of them. Then the cook made 25 more trays. How many trays are there now?

6. The janitor had 45 new light bulbs. He used 37 of them. Then he bought 45 more. How many does he have now?

Chapter 3 Test

Find the sum or difference.

1. 3,254
   +1,635

2. 4,758
   −2,416

3. 2,426
   +4,152

4. 5,143
   −3,021

5. 3,528
   +1,361

6. 2,456
   +1,837

7. 3,159
   +1,684

8. 46,284
   + 7,154

9. 36,841
   + 8,639

10. 72,489
    +46,354

11. 48,975
    +22,464

12. 2,261
    1,742
    +2,437

13. 16,375
    2,847
    +37,538

14. 3,451
    −1,673

15. 2,274
    −1,436

16. 32,184
    − 7,316

17. 62,456
    − 8,384

18. 50,663
    − 4,215

19. 33,543
    −28,716

20. 67,753
    −39,061

21. 48,354
    −39,186

Find the sum or difference. Check your answer using estimation.

22. 543
    +216

23. 3,643
    −1,358

24. 5,184
    +2,689

Solve.

25. Karen has 1,347 pennies saved. Bill has 896 pennies saved. How many pennies would they have if they combined their savings?

26. The Jones family is taking a 2,453 mile vacation. They have traveled 1,628 miles. How much farther will they travel?

Maintenance

Standardized Format

Directions Work each problem on your own paper. Choose the letter of the correct answer. If the correct answer is not given, choose the letter for *none of the above*. Make no marks on this test.

1. Add.	2. Subtract.	3. What is the missing addend?
7 + 8	13 − 6	3 + □ = 10
a 14	**e** 5	**a** 4
b 15	**f** 6	**b** 5
c 16	**g** 7	**c** 6
d *none of the above*	**h** *none of the above*	**d** *none of the above*

4. Complete the fact family.	5. Add. 348 +521	6. Subtract. 8,657 −4,236
4 + 9 = 13 9 + 4 = 13 13 − 4 = 9		
e 17 − 4 = 13	**a** 829	**e** 3,481
f 13 − 9 = 4	**b** 867	**f** 4,421
g 9 − 4 = 5	**c** 869	**g** 4,881
h *none of the above*	**d** *none of the above*	**h** *none of the above*

7. Compute.	8. Add.	9. What is the number?
7 − (5 − 2)	7 + 2 + 3 + 5	seven thousand, twelve
a 0	**e** 15	**a** 712
b 3	**f** 16	**b** 7,012
c 4	**g** 17	**c** 7,120
d *none of the above*	**h** *none of the above*	**d** *none of the above*

10. Which digit is in the thousands place? 84,563	11. Which number is greater than 2,009?	12. What is 76 rounded to the nearest ten?
e 4	**a** 2,000	**e** 75
f 5	**b** 2,008	**f** 85
g 8	**c** 2,010	**g** 95
h *none of the above*	**d** *none of the above*	**h** *none of the above*

13. Add.

$$\begin{array}{r} 3,589 \\ +4,697 \\ \hline \end{array}$$

a 8,272

b 8,286

c 8,295

d *none of the above*

14. Add.

196 + 415 + 278

e 868

f 889

g 899

h *none of the above*

15. Subtract.

$$\begin{array}{r} 483 \\ -195 \\ \hline \end{array}$$

a 288

b 312

c 317

d *none of the above*

---

16. Subtract.

$$\begin{array}{r} 8,275 \\ -2,793 \\ \hline \end{array}$$

e 5,482

f 6,062

g 6,522

h *none of the above*

17. Round to the nearest hundred. Then estimate.

$$\begin{array}{r} 724 \\ -175 \\ \hline \end{array}$$

a 400

b 600

c 800

d *none of the above*

18. Round to the nearest thousand. Then estimate.

$$\begin{array}{r} 3,801 \\ +4,563 \\ \hline \end{array}$$

e 7,000

f 8,000

g 9,000

h *none of the above*

---

19. The bar graph shows the number of points scored by each team. How many more points were scored by East than by North?

a 8

b 10

c 80

d *none of the above*

20. Mr. Brown bought 172 tomato plants. He planted 75 of them. How many more must he plant?

e 97

f 107

g 147

h *none of the above*

---

21. Diane spent $22 for a skirt and $13 for a sweater. How can you find how much more the skirt cost than the sweater?

a add $13 and $22

b round $13 and $22

c subtract $13 from $22

d *none of the above*

22. Dwayne has delivered 47 papers. He has 58 more papers to deliver. How many papers does he deliver in all?

e 11

f 105

g 110

h *none of the above*

Copyright © 1988 by Merrill Publishing Co. Columbus. Ohio 43216

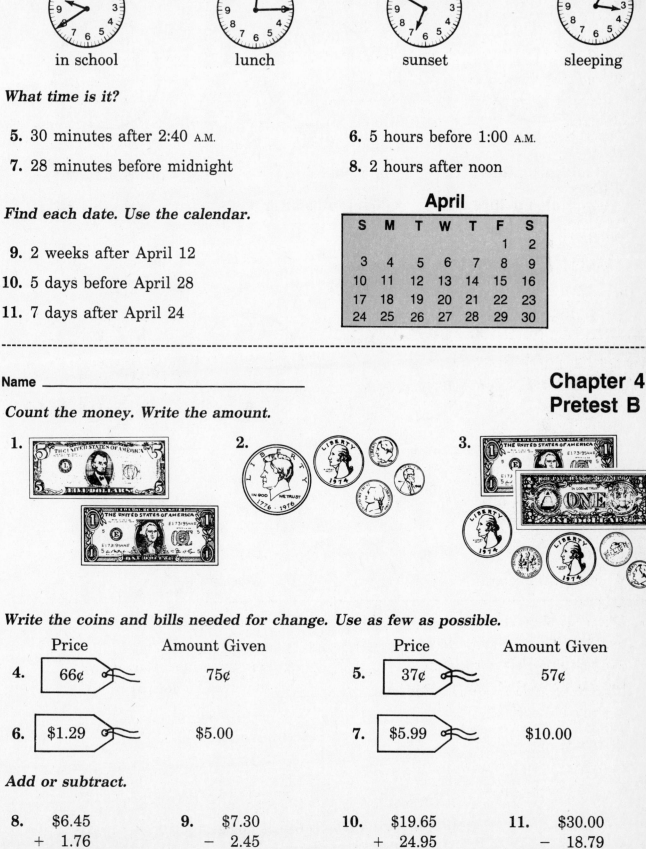

Name _____

Write each time. Use numerals and A.M. *or* P.M.

1.   2.   3.   4.

in school   lunch   sunset   sleeping

What time is it?

5. 30 minutes after 2:40 A.M.   6. 5 hours before 1:00 A.M.

7. 28 minutes before midnight   8. 2 hours after noon

Find each date. Use the calendar.

9. 2 weeks after April 12

10. 5 days before April 28

11. 7 days after April 24

April

S	M	T	W	T	F	S
					1	2
3	4	5	6	7	8	9
10	11	12	13	14	15	16
17	18	19	20	21	22	23
24	25	26	27	28	29	30

Name _____

Count the money. Write the amount.

1.   2.   3.

Write the coins and bills needed for change. Use as few as possible.

	Price	Amount Given		Price	Amount Given
4.	66¢	75¢	5.	37¢	57¢
6.	$1.29	$5.00	7.	$5.99	$10.00

Add or subtract.

8. $6.45
   + 1.76

9. $7.30
   − 2.45

10. $19.65
   + 24.95

11. $30.00
   − 18.79

Time

Here are some ways to write and say the time.

3:38

38 minutes after 3

22 minutes before 4

4:30

half past 4

30 minutes after 4

1:45

quarter till 2

45 minutes after 1

EXERCISES   *Write each time. Use numerals.*

1. ____ : ____

2. ____ : ____

3. ____ : ____

4. ____ : ____

Complete.

5. ____ : ____

half _____ _____

6. ____ : ____

quarter _____ _____

7. ____ : ____

_____ till _____

Match.

8. 2:45   half past 8

9. 8:30   20 minutes after 9

10. 5:15   quarter till 3

11. 9:20   quarter past 5

Write A.M. or P.M.

12. go to school   8:00 _____

13. practice ball   4:30 _____

14. do homework   6:30 _____

15. watch sunrise   6:00 _____

Using Time

Study these examples.

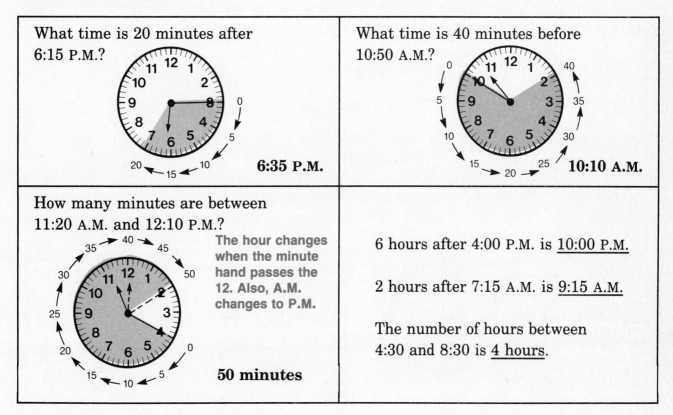

What time is 20 minutes after 6:15 P.M.?

6:35 P.M.

What time is 40 minutes before 10:50 A.M.?

10:10 A.M.

How many minutes are between 11:20 A.M. and 12:10 P.M.?

The hour changes when the minute hand passes the 12. Also, A.M. changes to P.M.

50 minutes

6 hours after 4:00 P.M. is 10:00 P.M.

2 hours after 7:15 A.M. is 9:15 A.M.

The number of hours between 4:30 and 8:30 is 4 hours.

EXERCISES   *What time is it?*

1. 15 minutes before 6:40 P.M. _____

2. 40 minutes after 5:05 A.M. _____

3. 6 hours before 10:30 A.M. _____

4. 4 hours after 8:15 P.M. _____

5. 25 minutes after 2:35 P.M. _____

6. 2 hours after 4:15 A.M. _____

7. 8 hours before 7:30 P.M. _____

8. 20 minutes before 12:10 A.M. _____

Write the number of minutes or hours between the two times.

9. 10:00 to 3:00

10. 6:00 to 6:20

11. 10:40 to 11:30

12. 3:00 to 6:00

13. 2:15 to 8:15

14. 8:20 to 8:55

Patterns in Computation: Clock Arithmetic

To tell time on a clock, we do not usually say that dinner is at 18 o'clock, or that bedtime is 21 o'clock. To tell time, we use **clock arithmetic**, or **arithmetic mod 12**. Study the examples below.

18 = 6 (mod 12)

18 − 12 = 6

21 = 9 (mod 12)

21 − 12 = 9

17 = 5 (mod 12)

17 − 12 = 5

When you add time, you are also using clock arithmetic. Study the problems below.

Janet goes to work at 9:00 A.M. Five hours later, she takes a break. At what time does Janet take a break?

9 + 5 = 2 (mod 12)

9 + 5 = 14 → 14 − 12 = 2

Janet takes a break at 2:00 P.M.

Alfonso ate brunch at 11:00 A.M. on Saturday. Twenty-three hours later, he ate brunch on Sunday. At what time did Alfonso eat brunch on Sunday?

11 + 23 = 10 (mod 12)

11 + 23 = 34 → 34 − 12 = 22 → 22 − 12 = 10

Alfonso ate brunch at 10:00 A.M.

What time is it? Use mod 12.

1. 13:00   **2.** 17:00   **3.** 19:00   **4.** 22:00   **5.** 24:00

Add. Use mod 12.

6. 11 + 5 = _____   **7.** 6 + 8 = _____

8. 9 + 13 = _____   **9.** 8 + 19 = _____

10. 12 + 7   **11.** 3 + 5   **12.** 5 + 13   **13.** 4 + 20

14. 2 + 23   **15.** 1 + 31   **16.** 10 + 32   **17.** 11 + 40

Solve. Use numerals and A.M. **or** P.M.

18. Conchita went shopping at 6:30 P.M. Three hours later, she came home. At what time did Conchita come home?

19. Joey went to school at 8:00 A.M. He met Kirk eight hours later. At what time did Joey meet Kirk?

Problem Solving

*Use the calendars at the
right to find each date below.*

	January					
S	M	T	W	T	F	S
		1	2	3	4	5
6	7	8	9	10	11	12
13	14	15	16	17	18	19
20	21	22	23	24	25	26
27	28	29	30	31		

	February					
S	M	T	W	T	F	S
					1	2
3	4	5	6	7	8	9
10	11	12	13	14	15	16
17	18	19	20	21	22	23
24	25	26	27	28		

1. one week after January 1

2. 2 weeks before January 31

3. 4 weeks after January 20

4. 5 days after January 15

5. 4 days before February 7

6. 10 days after January 29

7. 21 days after February 1

8. 14 days before February 6

Use the calendars above to solve each problem below.

9. Jay's sister will get her first pay check on January 3. After that, she will get paid every 2 weeks. How many paychecks will she get in January and February? List the dates.

10. The Franklins' electric meter is read the fourth Thursday of every month. On what dates will it be read in January and February?

11. The Wilsons are going on vacation. They stopped delivery of their newspaper for 12 days beginning on January 25. When is delivery to begin again?

12. The Hunters moved into their new house on January 15. Their new furniture will arrive in a week to 10 days. On what days might the furniture arrive?

Maintenance

Add or subtract.

1.   932
        +876

2.   5,148
        +1,884

3.   971
        −386

4.   15,800
        − 8,762

5.   3,692
        −1,872

6.   48,192
        +12,936

7.   75
         87
        +63

8.   372
         833
        +923

9. 7 + (10 − 3)

10. (3 + 4) − 2

11. 9 − (4 − 2)

Order the numbers from least to greatest.

12. 10, 8, 17, 15

13. 97, 100, 95, 102, 101

14. 97, 79, 709, 907

15. 3, 30, 33, 13, 31

Estimate.

16.   902
         +718

17.   886
         +492

18.   426
         −187

19.   150
         − 43

20.   82
          91
         +88

21.   37
          72
         +48

22.   6,792
          4,091
         +2,983

23.   9,782
         −8,204

Solve.

24. Tanya must go to bed at 8:30. She has one hour of homework. What is the latest time she can start her homework to have time to finish?

25. Bill started raking leaves at 4:15. He raked for two hours. What time was it when he finished?

Money

How much money is shown?

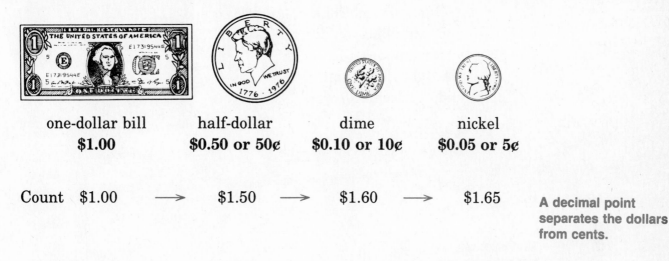

one-dollar bill
$1.00

half-dollar
$0.50 or 50¢

dime
$0.10 or 10¢

nickel
$0.05 or 5¢

Count $1.00 → $1.50 → $1.60 → $1.65

A decimal point separates the dollars from cents.

EXERCISES   Count the money. Use the dollar sign and a decimal point to write the amount.

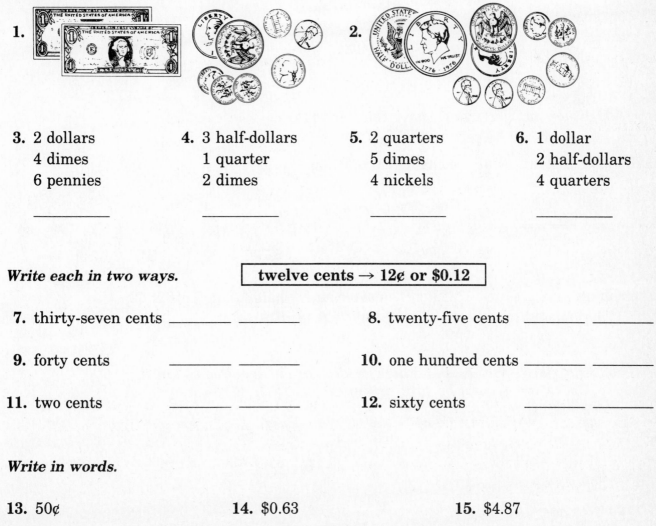

1.

2.

3. 2 dollars
4 dimes
6 pennies

_____

4. 3 half-dollars
1 quarter
2 dimes

_____

5. 2 quarters
5 dimes
4 nickels

_____

6. 1 dollar
2 half-dollars
4 quarters

_____

Write each in two ways. | twelve cents → 12¢ or $0.12 |

7. thirty-seven cents _____ _____

8. twenty-five cents _____ _____

9. forty cents _____ _____

10. one hundred cents _____ _____

11. two cents _____ _____

12. sixty cents _____ _____

Write in words.

13. 50¢

14. $0.63

15. $4.87

Adding and Subtracting with Money, Making Change

Add or subtract dollars and cents like you do whole numbers. Then place the dollar sign and the decimal point in the answer.

Add $2.25 and $1.87.

$$\begin{array}{r} \$2.25 \rightarrow 225 \\ +\ 1.87 \rightarrow +187 \\ \hline 412 \rightarrow \$4.12 \end{array}$$

EXERCISES *Add or subtract.*

1. $3.67
   + 2.84

2. $6.27
   − 2.53

3. $4.06
   − 1.27

4. $2.81
   + 1.47

5. $5.06
   + 3.74

6. $3.21
   − 1.64

7. $5.00
   − 3.48

8. $2.56
   + 4.85

9. $8.54
   − 2.31

10. $4.27
    + 1.06

Ted bought a pencil for 18¢. He gave the clerk $1.00.
What change should he get?

Start with 18¢ and count the change up to $1.00.

The change is: 2 pennies, 1 nickel, 1 quarter, and 1 half-dollar. This is 82¢.
Check the amount by subtracting.   **$1.00 − 0.18 = $0.82**

EXERCISES *Write the coins and bills needed for change. Use as few as possible. Check the amount by subtracting.*

Price	Amount Given		Price	Amount Given

11. $.21 ⊙— $1.00

12. $.33 ⊙— $1.00

13. $1.55 ⊙— $5.00

14. $1.76 ⊙— $5.00

Patterns in Computation: Counting Money

Counting is often used when making change. Study the example below.

Janice buys a note pad for $0.41. If she gives the clerk $1.00, she will get back at least 6 coins in change ($0.59). But Janice does not want to get pennies back in change. So she gives the clerk a dollar and a penny ($1.01).

Janice only gets 2 coins back.

$0.41 → $0.51 → $1.01

Study the following pattern.

Price	Amount Given	Change
$0.33	$1.03	$1.03 − $0.33 = $0.70
$0.79	$1.04	$1.04 − $0.79 = $0.25
$1.44	$2.04	$2.04 − $1.44 = $0.60

Use the pattern to complete the following.

Price	Amount Given	Change	Coins
$1.17	1. _____	$0.10	1 dime
$0.23	$1.03	2. _____	1 half-dollar, 1 quarter, 1 nickel
$1.77	3. _____	$0.25	4. _____
$1.28	$2.03	5. _____	6. _____
$0.59	$1.04	7. _____	8. _____
$1.13	9. _____	10. _____	1 dime, 1 nickel

Problem Solving

Listed below each problem are the facts you need to solve it.
Check (√) the ones you know.

1. Chuck bought a radio. How much change did he get from $20?
   a. cost of radio
   b. amount of money given

2. Ali sold some stamps for $6.00. How much did she receive for each stamp?
   a. number of stamps sold
   b. amount of money received

3. Charna arrived at her uncle's home at 6 P.M. How long did it take her to drive there?
   a. time she left
   b. time she arrived

4. Jeff put the cake in the oven at 2:15 P.M. It is to bake for 50 minutes. When can he take the cake out of the oven?
   a. time put in the oven
   b. amount of time to bake

5. Lenny jogged for 40 minutes in the morning and 70 minutes in the afternoon. How long did he jog that day?
   a. minutes jogged in morning
   b. minutes jogged in afternoon

6. Norma won the race. Karen finished 8 seconds behind Norma. How long did it take Karen to run the race?
   a. time it took Norma
   b. additional time it took Karen

7. Suzy had $8.36. After she got paid for delivering her papers, she had enough money to buy a blouse. How much did she get paid?
   a. amount of money Suzy had
   b. cost of blouse

8. Ellie had saved some money. After she bought a toy for her baby sister, she had $12.75 left. How much money had Ellie saved?
   a. cost of toy
   b. amount of money left

Chapter 4 Test

Write each time. Use numerals and A.M. or P.M.

1.

baby's nap

2.

breakfast

3.

start school

Write the number of minutes between the two times.

4. 1:50 A.M. and 2:40 A.M.

5. 4:07 P.M. and 4:47 P.M.

Find each date. Use the calendar.

6. 15 days before April 19

7. 8 days after April 13

APRIL	S	M	T	W	T	F	S
			1	2	3	4	5
	6	7	8	9	10	11	12
	13	14	15	16	17	18	19
	20	21	22	23	24	25	26
	27	28	29	30			

Write the total amount of money. Use the dollar sign and a decimal point.

8. 3 quarters
2 dimes

9. 2 quarters
4 dimes
4 nickels

10. 3 dollars
2 quarters
5 nickels

Add or subtract.

11. $3.52
+ 1.64

12. $2.87
+ 3.49

13. $6.57
− 3.24

14. $2.53
+ 1.47

15. $4.81
− 2.78

16. $8.43
− 2.59

17. $4.06
+ 2.87

18. $3.72
− 1.68

19. $6.14
− 3.07

20. $4.86
+ 1.59

Multiply.

1. 4×7 **2.** 2×9 **3.** 5×6 **4.** 3×9

5. 7×3 **6.** 8×1 **7.** 6×6 **8.** 9×8

Complete.

9. $7 \times 4 = \square \times 7$ **10.** $3 \times 9 = 9 \times \square$ **11.** $1 \times 6 = \square$

12. $8 \times 0 = \square$ **13.** $4 \times \square = 16$ **14.** $5 \times \square = 45$

Divide.

1. $9 \div 1$ **2.** $32 \div 4$ **3.** $35 \div 5$ **4.** $18 \div 2$

5. $56 \div 8$ **6.** $36 \div 9$ **7.** $45 \div 9$ **8.** $24 \div 3$

Write the first five multiples of each number.   *Write EVEN or ODD.*

9. 5   **10.** 8   **11.** 9   **12.** 24   **13.** 63

Write the fact family for each group of numbers.

14. 8, 16, 2   **15.** 48, 6, 8   **16.** 1, 4, 4

Solve.

17. Kimi jogs 26 miles each week. She jogs 4 miles each day for 6 days. How many miles does she jog on the seventh day?

18. Alfonso painted 14 mailbox posts. Jackie painted 16 posts. They have 28 posts left to paint. How many posts will they paint in all?

Meaning of Multiplication

Mrs. Baker had 5 plates. She placed 3 cookies on each plate.
How many cookies did she have?

Each plate has the same number of cookies.
To find the total, you can add or multiply.

Addition $\qquad$ $3 + 3 + 3 + 3 + 3 = 15$

Multiplication $\qquad$ $5 \times 3 = 15$

There are 15 cookies in all.

EXERCISES *Complete the multiplication.*

1. xxx
   xxx
   xxx

   3 rows of 3

   $3 \times 3 =$ _____

2. xxxx
   xxxx

   2 rows of 4

   $2 \times 4 =$ _____

3.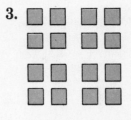

   4 groups of 4

   $4 \times 4 =$ _____

4. xxxxx
   xxxxx
   xxxxx
   xxxxx

   $4 \times 5 =$ _____

5.

   $3 \times 6 =$ _____

6.

   $7 \times 2 =$ _____

7.

   $3 \times 4 =$ _____

8.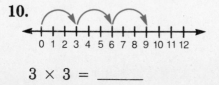

   4×2 _____

9.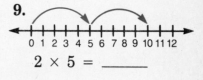

   $2 \times 5 =$ _____

10.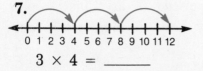

    $3 \times 3 =$ _____

11.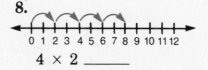

    $2 \times 4 =$ _____

12.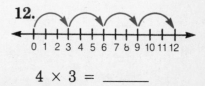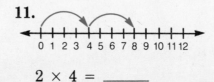

    $4 \times 3 =$ _____

Name _____

Multiplying by 2, 3, 4, and 5

Tom has two stacks of cards. Each stack has 7 cards.
The total number of cards is 2 × 7. He has 14 cards in all.

The numbers that you multiply are called **factors**.
The answer is called the **product**.
There are two ways to show multiplication.

$$2 \times 7 = 14$$
factors   product

$$\begin{array}{r} 7 \leftarrow \text{factors} \\ \times 2 \leftarrow \\ \hline 14 \leftarrow \text{product} \end{array}$$

EXERCISES   *Complete the multiplication.*

1. xxx   2 rows
   xxx   of 3

   2. xxxxxx   3 rows
      xxxxxx   of 7
      xxxxxx

   3. xxxxx   2 rows
      xxxxx   of 5

2 × 3 = _____   3 × 7 = _____   2 × 5 = _____

2 + 2 + 2 + 2 = 8   3 + 3 + 3 = 9   6 + 6 = 12   5 + 5 + 5 + 5 = 20

4. 4 × 2 = _____   **5.** 3 × 3 = _____   **6.** 2 × 6 = _____   **7.** 4 × 5 = _____

8. 3 × 9 = _____   **9.** 2 × 8 = _____   **10.** 4 × 7 = _____   **11.** 4 × 6 = _____

12. $\begin{array}{r} 4 \\ \times 3 \\ \hline \end{array}$ **13.** $\begin{array}{r} 7 \\ \times 5 \\ \hline \end{array}$ **14.** $\begin{array}{r} 9 \\ \times 2 \\ \hline \end{array}$ **15.** $\begin{array}{r} 8 \\ \times 4 \\ \hline \end{array}$ **16.** $\begin{array}{r} 9 \\ \times 4 \\ \hline \end{array}$

Match. Write the letter.

17. 5 × 6 _____   **a.** 2 + 2

18. 3 × 6 _____   **b.** 8 + 8 + 8

19. 2 × 5 _____   **c.** 5 + 5 + 5

20. 2 × 2 _____   **d.** 4 + 4 + 4 + 4

21. 3 × 5 _____   **e.** 5 + 5

22. 3 × 8 _____   **f.** 6 + 6 + 6 + 6 + 6

23. 4 × 4 _____   **g.** 6 + 6 + 6

Solve.

24. Mr. Bently works eight hours each day. He worked 5 days last week. How many hours did he work last week?

Name _____

Properties of Multiplication, Missing Factors

Study the properties under the examples.

$3 \times 4 = 12$ $0 \times 3 = 0$ $1 \times 6 = 6$
$4 \times 3 = 12$ $3 \times 0 = 0$ $6 \times 1 = 6$

The order of the factors does not change the product.

If 0 is a factor, the product is 0.

If 1 is a factor, the product is the other factor.

Sometimes you know the product and only one of the factors.
To find the other factor, think of a multiplication fact.

$3 \times \square = 27$ 3 times what number is 27?
$3 \times \boxed{9} = 27$ The missing factor is 9.

EXERCISES **Complete.**

1. $5 \times 2 = 10$ 2. $4 \times 6 = 24$ 3. $1 \times 4 = 4$ 4. $2 \times 0 = 0$
   $2 \times 5 = \square$ $6 \times 4 = \square$ $4 \times 1 = \square$ $0 \times 2 = \square$

5. $3 \times 6 = 18$ 6. $8 \times 0 = 0$ 7. $4 \times 8 = \square$ 8. $5 \times 9 = \square$
   $6 \times 3 = \square$ $0 \times 8 = \square$ $8 \times 4 = \square$ $9 \times 5 = \square$

9. $5 \times 6 = \square$ 10. $3 \times 8 = \square$ 11. $7 \times 1 = \square$ 12. $0 \times 5 = \square$
   $6 \times 5 = \square$ $8 \times 3 = \square$ $1 \times 7 = \square$ $5 \times 0 = \square$

13. $3 \times \square = 3$ 14. $\square \times 6 = 0$ 15. $\square \times 7 = 14$ 16. $\square \times 7 = 28$

17. $\square \times 9 = 27$ 18. $\square \times 4 = 16$ 19. $5 \times \square = 25$ 20. $3 \times \square = 21$

21. $3 \times \square = 18$ 22. $5 \times \square = 40$ 23. $\square \times 6 = 12$ 24. $4 \times \square = 4$

Solve.

25. What number times 7 is 35?   26. Four times what number is eight?

55

Meaning of Division

Twelve children were placed on four teams.
How many were on each team?
You need to *divide* 12 by 4.
Division is like finding a missing factor.

total number of children	number of groups	number in each group
12 ÷	**4** =	☐ $4 \times ? = 12$
12 ÷	**4** =	**3**

There were 3 children on each team.

Division can be used to find the size of each group or the number of groups.

EXERCISES   *Complete.*

1. ✗✗✗✗✗✗
✗✗✗✗✗✗

$2 \times 7 = 14$

$14 \div 2 = $ ☐

2. ▲▲▲▲▲
▲▲▲▲▲
▲▲▲▲▲

$3 \times 5 = 15$

$15 \div 3 = $ ☐

3. ⊙⊙ ⊙⊙
⊙⊙ ⊙⊙ ⊙⊙
⊙⊙ ⊙⊙

$5 \times 4 = 20$

$20 \div 5 = $ ☐

4. $2 \times 6 = 12$

$12 \div 2 = $ ☐

5. $3 \times 7 = 21$

$21 \div 3 = $ ☐

6. $5 \times 8 = 40$

$40 \div 5 = $ ☐

7. $4 \times 9 = 36$

$36 \div 4 = $ ☐

8. $3 \times 8 = 24$

$24 \div 3 = $ ☐

9. $3 \times 6 = 18$

$18 \div 3 = $ ☐

10.

☐ $\times 2 = 10$

$10 \div 2 = $ ☐

11.

☐ $\times 4 = 16$

$16 \div 4 = $ ☐

12.

☐ $\times 3 = 27$

$27 \div 3 = $ ☐

13. ☐ $\times 5 = 30$

$30 \div 5 = $ ☐

14. ☐ $\times 4 = 28$

$28 \div 4 = $ ☐

15. ☐ $\times 5 = 25$

$25 \div 5 = $ ☐

16. ☐ $\times 9 = 18$

$18 \div 9 = $ ☐

17. ☐ $\times 8 = 32$

$32 \div 8 = $ ☐

18. ☐ $\times 2 = 8$

$8 \div 2 = $ ☐

Division by 1, 2, 3, 4, and 5

Doug collects toy cars. He can keep 5 cars in a shoe box. How many boxes will he need to keep 30 cars?

To find out, divide 30 by 5.

There are two ways to show division.

$$30 \div 5 = 6$$
dividend   divisor   quotient

$$\begin{array}{r} 6 \leftarrow \text{quotient} \\ \text{divisor} \rightarrow 5\overline{)30} \leftarrow \text{dividend} \end{array}$$

Doug needs **6** boxes.

EXERCISES *Divide.*

1. $15 \div 3 =$ _____ **2.** $28 \div 4 =$ _____ **3.** $14 \div 2 =$ _____

4. $24 \div 3 =$ _____ **5.** $18 \div 2 =$ _____ **6.** $16 \div 4 =$ _____

7. $2 \div 1 =$ _____ **8.** $12 \div 2 =$ _____ **9.** $20 \div 5 =$ _____

10. $5 \div 5 =$ _____ **11.** $21 \div 3 =$ _____ **12.** $45 \div 5 =$ _____

13. $4\overline{)12}$ **14.** $5\overline{)35}$ **15.** $5\overline{)25}$ **16.** $1\overline{)8}$ **17.** $3\overline{)18}$

18. $2\overline{)16}$ **19.** $1\overline{)6}$ **20.** $4\overline{)32}$ **21.** $5\overline{)10}$ **22.** $3\overline{)27}$

Solve.

23. Mr. Rice's class needs to have 4 teams. There are 36 children in the class. How many should be on each team?

24. Four children are blowing up balloons. There are 24 balloons to blow up. How many balloons does each child need to blow up?

Name _____

Maintenance

Complete.

1. $6 + \boxed{} = 9$
2. $5 + \boxed{} = 8$
3. $\boxed{} + 3 = 7$
4. $\boxed{} + 6 = 14$

5. $8 + \boxed{} = 8$
6. $\boxed{} + 9 = 14$
7. $8 + \boxed{} = 15$
8. $0 + \boxed{} = 7$

Add or subtract.

9.
```
  732
  618
+ 284
```

10.
```
  55
  41
+ 35
```

11.
```
  4,392
-   508
```

12.
```
  15,496
- 12,088
```

13.
```
  9,862
+ 8,497
```

14.
```
  48,484
+ 76,937
```

15.
```
  5,080
- 1,764
```

16.
```
  17,000
-  5,631
```

17.
```
  905
+ 496
```

18.
```
  422
- 188
```

Write the number named by each 8.

19. 83,496
20. 108,461
21. 4,378
22. 6,836

Add or subtract.

23.
```
  $10.87
+  23.65
```

24.
```
  $8.98
   4.98
+  1.15
```

25.
```
  $5.00
-  1.39
```

26.
```
  $25.75
-  21.58
```

Multiply or divide.

27.
```
  8
× 4
```

28.
```
  6
× 5
```

29.
```
  9
× 3
```

30. $5\overline{)25}$
31. $4\overline{)16}$
32. $3\overline{)24}$

Solve.

33. August 17 was on Wednesday. What is the date 2 weeks later? (Hint: make a calendar.)

34. Jill saved 5¢ each day for five days. How much money did she save?

58

Name _____

Multiplying by 6, 7, 8, and 9

The band is marching in a parade. There are 6 students in each of the 8 rows. How many band members are there?

Multiply.

$$8 \times 6 = 48$$

There are **48** band members.

EXERCISES *Complete the multiplication.*

1.
```
XXXXX
XXXXX
XXXXX
XXXXX
XXXXX
XXXXX
XXXXX
```
$7 \times 6 =$ _____

2.
```
OOOOOOOOO
OOOOOOOOO
OOOOOOOOO
OOOOOOOOO
OOOOOOOOO
OOOOOOOOO
```
$6 \times 9 =$ _____

3.
```
XXXXXXX
XXXXXXX
XXXXXXX
XXXXXXX
XXXXXXX
XXXXXXX
XXXXXXX
```
$7 \times 8 =$ _____

Multiply.

4.	5.	6.	7.	8.	9.
4 $\times 9$	5 $\times 6$	2 $\times 8$	3 $\times 6$	5 $\times 7$	4 $\times 6$

10.	11.	12.	13.	14.	15.
1 $\times 7$	2 $\times 9$	4 $\times 8$	3 $\times 7$	1 $\times 6$	7 $\times 9$

16.	17.	18.	19.	20.	21.
4 $\times 7$	3 $\times 8$	2 $\times 7$	5 $\times 9$	3 $\times 9$	5 $\times 8$

Solve.

22. Mr. Wills worked on his project for 6 days. He worked 8 hours each day. How many hours did he work?

23. Jack broke his leg. He wore a cast on his leg for exactly six weeks. How many days did he wear a cast?

Multiples

EXERCISES **Complete the tables. The left column shows what number to multiply by.**

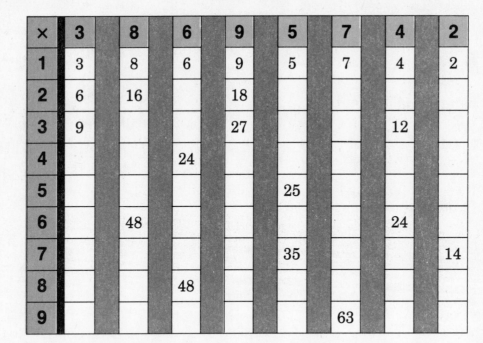

×	3	8	6	9	5	7	4	2
1	3	8	6	9	5	7	4	2
2	6	16		18				
3	9			27			12	
4			24					
5					25			
6		48					24	
7					35			14
8			48					
9						63		

Write the numbers. Use the tables.

1. a common multiple of 5 and 7

2. two common multiples of 3 and 4

3. three common multiples of 2 and 6

4. four common multiples of 3 and 6

Write EVEN or ODD. Remember, even numbers are multiples of 2.

5. 19 _____

6. 12 _____

7. 64 _____

8. 37 _____

9. 44 _____

10. 73 _____

11. 240 _____

12. 306 _____

13. 188 _____

14. 577 _____

15. 111 _____

16. 99 _____

Division by 6, 7, 8, and 9
More Division

Gary is stocking shelves with cereal.
He has 42 boxes to put on 6 shelves.
How many boxes will be on each shelf?

Divide.

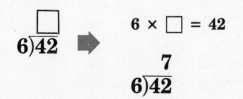

He will put 7 boxes on each shelf.

Remember these rules.

> **When you divide a number by 1, the quotient is the number.**
>
> **When you divide a number by itself, the quotient is 1.**
>
> **When you divide 0 by any number, the quotient is 0.**
>
> **You cannot divide by 0.**

EXERCISES Divide.

1. $24 \div 8 =$ _____   **2.** $18 \div 9 =$ _____   **3.** $30 \div 6 =$ _____   **4.** $56 \div 8 =$ _____

5. $81 \div 9 =$ _____   **6.** $0 \div 7 =$ _____   **7.** $18 \div 6 =$ _____   **8.** $48 \div 8 =$ _____

9. $0 \div 9 =$ _____   **10.** $49 \div 7 =$ _____   **11.** $64 \div 8 =$ _____   **12.** $24 \div 6 =$ _____

13. $9\overline{)63}$ **14.** $6\overline{)6}$ **15.** $9\overline{)54}$ **16.** $7\overline{)14}$ **17.** $8\overline{)0}$ **18.** $7\overline{)28}$

19. $7\overline{)35}$ **20.** $6\overline{)0}$ **21.** $8\overline{)72}$ **22.** $9\overline{)9}$ **23.** $6\overline{)36}$ **24.** $8\overline{)40}$

Solve.

25. Mrs. Page's kindergarten class has 45 blocks. Nine children are sharing the blocks. How many blocks does each child have?

26. Mr. Clark's room has 32 desks. He wants 8 desks in each row. How many rows will he have?

Patterns in Computation: Divisibility

Barbara is playing a game with two children. She wants to give each child an equal number of cards. She has 14 cards. Can she do it without having any cards left over?

The number 14 can be divided by 2 with a remainder of 0. So, we say that 14 is **divisible** by 2.

> A number is divisible by:
> - 2 if its ones digit is 0, 2, 4, 6, or 8.
> - 5 if its ones digit is 0 or 5.
> - 3 if the sum of the digits is divisible by 3.

State whether each number is divisible by 2, 3, or 5.

	ones digit	by 2?	by 5?	sum of digits	by 3?
184	4	yes	no	$1 + 8 + 4 = 13$	no
255	5	no	yes	$2 + 5 + 5 = 12$	yes
3,357	7	no	no	$3 + 3 + 5 + 7 = 18$	yes

Write whether each number is divisible by 2, 3, or 5.

1. 9   2. 18   3. 21   4. 25

5. 65   6. 72   7. 150   8. 80

9. 123   10. 64   11. 125   12. 216

13. 330   14. 632   15. 675   16. 1,986

17. If a number is divisible by 10, is it always divisible by 5?

18. If a number is divisible by 3, is it always divisible by 9?

19. State a rule for divisibility by 10.

Related Facts

You can write four different facts using the numbers **5**, **3**, and **15**.

$$5 \times 3 = 15 \qquad 3 \times 5 = 15$$
$$15 \div 3 = 5 \qquad 15 \div 5 = 3$$

You can write two different facts using **7, 7**, and **49**.

$$7 \times 7 = 49$$
$$49 \div 7 = 7$$

EXERCISES *Write the fact family for each group of numbers.*

1. 5, 7, 35

2. 4, 8, 32

3. 3, 27, 9

4. 30, 6, 5

5. 2, 1, 2

6. 3, 7, 21

7. 4, 16, 4

8. 5, 1, 5

9. 9, 6, 54

10. 3, 12, 4

11. 5, 4, 20

12. 63, 7, 9

13. 6, 42, 7

14. 25, 5, 5

15. 1, 4, 4

16. 45, 9, 5

Problem Solving

Add	Subtract	Multiply	Divide
join together	separate or compare	join together groups of the same number	separate into smaller groups of the same number

Use the plan below to solve problems.

Read the problem. ▸ **Decide** what to do. ▸ **Solve** the problem. ▸ **Examine** the solution.

Decide what to do. Write ADD, SUBTRACT, MULTIPLY, or DIVIDE. Then solve.

1. Kate has $17.00. She spends $3.00. How much money does she have left?

2. Lee has $25.00. He buys 6 softballs at $4.00 each. How much change does he get?

3. Chuck gives boat rides to 10 people. He takes 2 people at a time. How many rides does he give?

4. The City Hotel has 81 rooms. There are 9 rooms on each floor. How many floors does the hotel have?

5. Kyle has 5 plants in a planter. How many planters does she need for 36 plants? How many plants remain?

6. There are 35 dogs registered for the dog show but 3 dogs do not attend. Each show area can handle 8 dogs. How many show areas are needed?

Problem Solving

Trudy buys 4 tickets to the musical. The tickets are $8.00 each. How much change does she receive from $40.00?

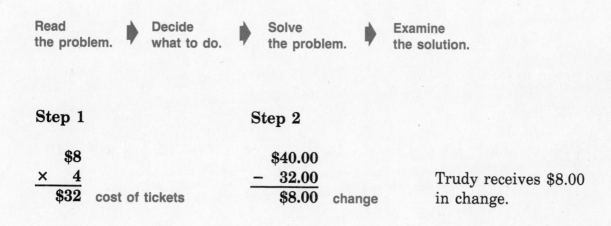

Read the problem. ➤ **Decide what to do.** ➤ **Solve the problem.** ➤ **Examine the solution.**

Step 1

$$\begin{array}{r} \$8 \\ \times\ \ 4 \\ \hline \$32 \end{array}$$ cost of tickets

Step 2

$$\begin{array}{r} \$40.00 \\ -\ 32.00 \\ \hline \$8.00 \end{array}$$ change

Trudy receives $8.00 in change.

Solve.

1. The Nelsons travel 386 miles one day and 427 miles the second day. It is 1,100 miles to their cottage. How many more miles do they have to travel?

2. Ernie saved $3.25 last week and $5.75 this week. How much more money does he need to buy a baseball glove that costs $15.00?

3. Jeff and his father buy baseball tickets for $8.50 each. The bus ride costs $7.00. How much does it cost to attend the game?

4. The market sells peaches in bags of 6 for $1.00. If mother buys 4 bags, how much change will she receive from $5.00?

5. The school cafeteria uses 5 cases of white bread and 4 cases of rye bread each day. How many cases are used in one week?

6. The janitor carried 4 boxes of tablets upstairs on Monday and 3 boxes on Tuesday. Each box contained 9 tablets. How many tablets did he carry upstairs?

Chapter 5 Test

Multiply.

1.	3	2.	6	3.	4	4.	7	5.	5	6.	6
	$\times 5$		$\times 5$		$\times 4$		$\times 3$		$\times 8$		$\times 8$

7. 7×7 **8.** 9×4 **9.** 6×7 **10.** 8×8 **11.** 7×2

Write the missing factor.

12. $6 \times \boxed{} = 36$ **13.** $\boxed{} \times 8 = 24$ **14.** $3 \times \boxed{} = 18$ **15.** $\boxed{} \times 8 = 16$

Divide.

16. $7\overline{)42}$ **17.** $9\overline{)63}$ **18.** $5\overline{)5}$ **19.** $3\overline{)27}$ **20.** $4\overline{)36}$ **21.** $3\overline{)15}$

22. $30 \div 6$ **23.** $9 \div 1$ **24.** $21 \div 3$ **25.** $20 \div 5$ **26.** $9 \div 3$

Write the first five multiples of each number.

27. 7   **28.** 3   **29.** 6

Write EVEN or ODD.

30. 6 _____   **31.** 23 _____   **32.** 74 _____   **33.** 65 _____

Write the fact family for each group of numbers.

34. 9, 45, 5   **35.** 2, 9, 18   **36.** 63, 9, 7   **37.** 48, 6, 8

_____   _____   _____   _____

_____   _____   _____   _____

_____   _____   _____   _____

_____   _____   _____   _____

Multiply.

1. 7 × 400

2. 5 × 80

3. 9 × 60

4. 8 × 4,000

5. 8 × 2 × 7

6. 5 × 4 × 3

7. 6 × 7 × 4

8. 9 × 2 × 6

9. 3 × 65

10. 4 × 12

11. 55 × 8

12. 89 × 2

13. 74 × 4

14. 168 × 6

15. 243 × 7

16. 9 × 1,643

Solve.

17. A plane can travel 185 miles in one hour. How far can it travel in 7 hours?

18. There are 365 days in a year. How many days are there in 3 years?

Estimate.

1.   346
    × 4

2.   49
    × 9

3. $42.95
    × 5

4.   2,147
    × 4

Multiply.

5. $0.17 × 2

6. $0.95 × 5

7. $8.40 × 7

8. $82.45 × 6

Solve. If there are not enough facts, write the facts you need.

9. There are 8 hot dog buns in a package. How many hot dog buns are there in 5 packages?

10. It takes Toshiro 7 hours to read a book. It takes Alice 5 hours to read the same book. After 2 hours, how many more pages does Alice read than Toshiro?

Multiplying Tens, Hundreds, and Thousands, Multiplying 2-Digit Numbers

Study these examples.

| Multiply 30 × 3. | Multiply 500 × 8. | Multiply 32 × 3. |

Multiply 30 × 3.

$$\begin{array}{r} \mathbf{30} \\ \times\ \mathbf{3} \\ \hline \mathbf{90} \end{array}$$ 3 tens

9 tens

Multiply 500 × 8.

$$\begin{array}{r} \mathbf{500} \\ \times\ \mathbf{8} \\ \hline \mathbf{4,000} \end{array}$$ 5 hundreds

40 hundreds

Multiply 32 × 3.

Multiply the ones.

$$\begin{array}{r} \mathbf{32} \\ \times\ \mathbf{3} \\ \hline \mathbf{6} \end{array}$$ 3 × 2 ones

Multiply the tens.

$$\begin{array}{r} \mathbf{32} \\ \times\ \mathbf{3} \\ \hline \mathbf{96} \end{array}$$ 3 × 3 tens

EXERCISES Multiply.

1. 5 × 1

2. 5 × 10

3. 5 × 100

4. 5 × 1,000

5. 3 × 7

6. 3 × 70

7. 3 × 700

8. 3 × 7,000

9. 8 × 4

10. 8 × 40

11. 8 × 400

12. 8 × 4,000

13. 5 × 6

14. 5 × 60

15. 5 × 600

16. 5 × 6,000

17.
$$\begin{array}{r} 10 \\ \times\ 4 \\ \hline \end{array}$$

18.
$$\begin{array}{r} 100 \\ \times\ 4 \\ \hline \end{array}$$

19.
$$\begin{array}{r} 1,000 \\ \times\ 4 \\ \hline \end{array}$$

20.
$$\begin{array}{r} 600 \\ \times\ 7 \\ \hline \end{array}$$

21.
$$\begin{array}{r} 70 \\ \times\ 8 \\ \hline \end{array}$$

22.
$$\begin{array}{r} 400 \\ \times\ 3 \\ \hline \end{array}$$

23.
$$\begin{array}{r} 9,000 \\ \times\ 4 \\ \hline \end{array}$$

24.
$$\begin{array}{r} 6,000 \\ \times\ 4 \\ \hline \end{array}$$

25.
$$\begin{array}{r} 33 \\ \times\ 2 \\ \hline \end{array}$$

26.
$$\begin{array}{r} 11 \\ \times\ 5 \\ \hline \end{array}$$

27.
$$\begin{array}{r} 40 \\ \times\ 2 \\ \hline \end{array}$$

28.
$$\begin{array}{r} 31 \\ \times\ 2 \\ \hline \end{array}$$

29.
$$\begin{array}{r} 23 \\ \times\ 3 \\ \hline \end{array}$$

30.
$$\begin{array}{r} 10 \\ \times\ 7 \\ \hline \end{array}$$

31.
$$\begin{array}{r} 14 \\ \times\ 2 \\ \hline \end{array}$$

32.
$$\begin{array}{r} 43 \\ \times\ 2 \\ \hline \end{array}$$

33.
$$\begin{array}{r} 11 \\ \times\ 6 \\ \hline \end{array}$$

34.
$$\begin{array}{r} 30 \\ \times\ 2 \\ \hline \end{array}$$

35.
$$\begin{array}{r} 12 \\ \times\ 4 \\ \hline \end{array}$$

36.
$$\begin{array}{r} 10 \\ \times\ 3 \\ \hline \end{array}$$

Multiplying with Renaming

Study these examples.

Multiply the ones.	*Multiply the tens.*	*Multiply the ones.*	*Multiply the tens.*
$\overset{2}{2}8$	$\overset{2}{2}8$	$\overset{1}{6}4$	$\overset{1}{6}4$
$\times\ 3$	$\times\ 3$	$\times\ 4$	$\times\ 4$
4	84	6	256

$3 \times 8 = 24$	3×2 tens = 6 tens	$4 \times 4 = 16$	4×6 tens = 24 tens
Rename 24 as	6 tens + 2 tens =	Rename 16 as	24 tens + 1 ten = 25 tens
2 tens 4 ones.	8 tens	1 ten 6 ones.	25 tens = 2 hundreds 5 tens

EXERCISES **Multiply.**

1. 15 × 6	**2.** 17 × 4	**3.** 17 × 5	**4.** 18 × 3	**5.** 35 × 2
6. 43 × 6	**7.** 53 × 6	**8.** 36 × 7	**9.** 66 × 4	**10.** 73 × 5
11. 16 × 6	**12.** 14 × 5	**13.** 29 × 3	**14.** 18 × 5	**15.** 19 × 3
16. 15 × 4	**17.** 47 × 2	**18.** 84 × 6	**19.** 96 × 4	**20.** 38 × 8
21. 76 × 4	**22.** 88 × 5	**23.** $94 × 8	**24.** $55 × 9	**25.** $86 × 7
26. 72 × 6	**27.** $47 × 8	**28.** 37 × 5	**29.** $49 × 7	**30.** 65 × 4

Multiplying Three or More Factors

Sometimes you need to find the product of three or more numbers. Multiply any two numbers at a time.

Here are two ways to multiply $2 \times 3 \times 4$.

$$\underbrace{(2 \times 3)}_{6} \times 4 \qquad \begin{array}{r} 6 \\ \times\ 4 \\ \hline 24 \end{array} \text{ product} \qquad \bigg| \qquad 2 \times \underbrace{(3 \times 4)}_{12} \qquad \begin{array}{r} 12 \\ \times\ 2 \\ \hline 24 \end{array} \text{ product}$$

Notice that the products are the same.

This shows the **grouping property** of multiplication. That is, the way factors are grouped does not change the product.

EXERCISES Find each product in two different ways.

1. $5 \times 2 \times 0$ **2.** $6 \times 1 \times 1$ **3.** $1 \times 3 \times 3$ **4.** $2 \times 5 \times 1$

5. $7 \times 1 \times 5$ **6.** $2 \times 2 \times 7$ **7.** $4 \times 4 \times 2$ **8.** $4 \times 7 \times 2$

9. $3 \times 9 \times 2$ **10.** $5 \times 5 \times 3$ **11.** $8 \times 8 \times 1$ **12.** $5 \times 9 \times 2$

13. $2 \times 5 \times 8$ **14.** $4 \times 4 \times 4$ **15.** $2 \times 8 \times 2$ **16.** $9 \times 2 \times 4$

17. $4 \times 7 \times 5$ **18.** $8 \times 5 \times 5$ **19.** $8 \times 0 \times 3$ **20.** $5 \times 9 \times 8$

21. $2 \times 2 \times 2 \times 2$ **22.** $2 \times 3 \times 2 \times 5$ **23.** $7 \times 4 \times 0 \times 6$

Multiplying 3-Digit Numbers

For a relay race, each person on a team ran 148 feet. Each team had 4 members. What was the total distance run by each team?

Multiply 148 by 4.

Multiply the ones.

$$\begin{array}{r} \overset{3}{148} \\ \times\ 4 \\ \hline 2 \end{array}$$

4 × 8 = 32
32 ones =
3 tens 2 ones

Multiply the tens.

$$\begin{array}{r} \overset{13}{148} \\ \times\ 4 \\ \hline 92 \end{array}$$

(4 × 4) + 3 = 19
19 tens =
1 hundred 9 tens

Multiply the hundreds.

$$\begin{array}{r} \overset{13}{148} \\ \times\ 4 \\ \hline 592 \end{array}$$

(4 × 1) + 1 = 5
5 hundreds

Each team ran 592 feet.

EXERCISES Multiply.

1.
$$\begin{array}{r} 236 \\ \times\ 2 \\ \hline \end{array}$$

2.
$$\begin{array}{r} 174 \\ \times\ 4 \\ \hline \end{array}$$

3.
$$\begin{array}{r} 308 \\ \times\ 3 \\ \hline \end{array}$$

4.
$$\begin{array}{r} 263 \\ \times\ 3 \\ \hline \end{array}$$

5.
$$\begin{array}{r} 478 \\ \times\ 2 \\ \hline \end{array}$$

6.
$$\begin{array}{r} 137 \\ \times\ 7 \\ \hline \end{array}$$

7.
$$\begin{array}{r} 107 \\ \times\ 9 \\ \hline \end{array}$$

8.
$$\begin{array}{r} 245 \\ \times\ 4 \\ \hline \end{array}$$

9.
$$\begin{array}{r} 163 \\ \times\ 2 \\ \hline \end{array}$$

10.
$$\begin{array}{r} 163 \\ \times\ 5 \\ \hline \end{array}$$

11.
$$\begin{array}{r} 104 \\ \times\ 8 \\ \hline \end{array}$$

12.
$$\begin{array}{r} 132 \\ \times\ 6 \\ \hline \end{array}$$

13.
$$\begin{array}{r} 274 \\ \times\ 3 \\ \hline \end{array}$$

14.
$$\begin{array}{r} 154 \\ \times\ 5 \\ \hline \end{array}$$

15.
$$\begin{array}{r} 144 \\ \times\ 6 \\ \hline \end{array}$$

Solve.

16. Billy delivered 146 fliers on Monday, Wednesday, and Friday. How many did he deliver in all?

17. Mrs. Clark took two trips last month. She traveled 238 miles on each trip. How many miles did she travel?

Name _____

Maintenance

Add or subtract.

1. 14,692
   − 8,488

2. 6,374
   + 7,838

3. 12,910
   + 82,846

4. 90,406
   − 72,728

5. 15,000
   4,981
   + 12,672

Write in standard form.

6. fourteen thousand, six hundred two

7. eighty-eight thousand, forty-three

8. four hundred sixty-two thousand, seven hundred ninety-one

Replace each circle with <, >, or =.

9. 403 ◯ 304

10. 201 ◯ 210

11. 4,988 ◯ 4,989

Write each time. Use numerals.

12.

13.

14.

Multiply or divide.

15. 23
    × 3

16. 9
    × 5

17. 400
    × 7

18. 184
    × 5

19. 7)42

20. 9)45

21. 8)48

22. 3)24

Solve.

23. Vicki earned $5 weeding. She spent $3.79. How much does she have left?

24. A cupcake pan will hold nine cupcakes. How many times will the pan have to be filled to get 36 cupcakes?

72

More Multiplying

The movie theater has 564 seats. All the seats were filled for 7 showings. If each person bought a ticket, how many tickets were sold?

Multiply 564 × 7.

Multiply the ones.

$$\begin{array}{r} 2 \\ 564 \\ \times\ 7 \\ \hline 8 \end{array}$$

4 × 7 = 28
28 ones =
2 tens 8 ones

Multiply the tens.

$$\begin{array}{r} 42 \\ 564 \\ \times\ 7 \\ \hline 48 \end{array}$$

(7 × 6) + 2 = 44
44 tens =
4 hundreds 4 tens

Multiply the hundreds.

$$\begin{array}{r} 42 \\ 564 \\ \times\ 7 \\ \hline 3,948 \end{array}$$

(7 × 5) + 4 = 39
39 hundreds =
3 thousands
9 hundreds

3,948 tickets were sold.

EXERCISES Multiply.

1. $\begin{array}{r} 326 \\ \times\ 5 \\ \hline \end{array}$

2. $\begin{array}{r} 243 \\ \times\ 7 \\ \hline \end{array}$

3. $\begin{array}{r} 534 \\ \times\ 3 \\ \hline \end{array}$

4. $\begin{array}{r} 402 \\ \times\ 9 \\ \hline \end{array}$

5. $\begin{array}{r} 859 \\ \times\ 2 \\ \hline \end{array}$

6. $\begin{array}{r} 760 \\ \times\ 4 \\ \hline \end{array}$

7. $\begin{array}{r} 618 \\ \times\ 8 \\ \hline \end{array}$

8. $\begin{array}{r} 971 \\ \times\ 6 \\ \hline \end{array}$

9. $\begin{array}{r} 185 \\ \times\ 5 \\ \hline \end{array}$

10. $\begin{array}{r} 797 \\ \times\ 3 \\ \hline \end{array}$

11. $\begin{array}{r} 7,249 \\ \times\ 2 \\ \hline \end{array}$

12. $\begin{array}{r} 2,910 \\ \times\ 9 \\ \hline \end{array}$

13. $\begin{array}{r} 6,065 \\ \times\ 4 \\ \hline \end{array}$

14. $\begin{array}{r} 3,871 \\ \times\ 7 \\ \hline \end{array}$

15. $\begin{array}{r} 5,348 \\ \times\ 6 \\ \hline \end{array}$

Solve.

16. The theater pays each worker $460 a month. How much does the theater pay to 8 workers?

17. The theater pays $1,432 each week to rent a film. How much does it cost to rent the film for 4 weeks?

Estimating Products, Multiplying with Money

Tickets for a bus trip cost $27.40 for each person. How much would it cost for a family of 4 to take the bus trip?

To find the cost, *multiply.*

Estimate the cost.

- *Round to the greatest place.*
- *Then multiply.*

$$\begin{array}{r} \$27.40 \\ \times \quad 4 \\ \hline \end{array} \qquad \begin{array}{r} \$30 \\ \times \quad 4 \\ \hline \$120 \end{array}$$

The cost is *about* $120.

Find the actual cost.

- *Remember to place the dollar sign and a decimal point in the product.*

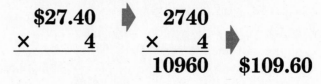

$$\begin{array}{r} \$27.40 \\ \times \quad 4 \\ \hline \end{array} \quad\blacktriangleright\quad \begin{array}{r} 2740 \\ \times \quad 4 \\ \hline 10960 \end{array} \quad\blacktriangleright\quad \$109.60$$

The cost is $109.60.

EXERCISES *Place the dollar sign and a decimal point in each product.*

1.	2.	3.	4.	5.
$3.14	$6.00	$4.06	$30.46	$56.83
× 3	× 7	× 8	× 6	× 5
942	4200	3248	18276	28415

Multiply. Then estimate to see if the product is reasonable.

6. $4.63 $5
   ×   7   ×7

7. $22.95
   ×   9

8. $28.43
   ×   8

9. 346
   × 4

10. 583
    × 6

11. 4,637
    ×   5

12. 7,028
    ×   3

13. 6,238
    ×   2

14. 5,354
    ×   6

15. $15.98 × 4

16. 8,423 × 8

Patterns in Computation: Multiplying Whole Numbers

If you know basic multiplication facts, you can multiply numbers that have 4 or more digits. Think of each step as a separate multiplication fact. Study the pattern below.

2	20	200	400	4,000	40,000
× 4	× 4	× 4	× 2	× 2	× 2
8	80	800	800	8,000	80,000

Sometimes you must rename.

	^{2}	$^{3\,2}$	$^{3\,2}$	$^{3\,3\,2}$	$^{3\,3\,3\,2}$
7	77	777	444	4,444	44,444
× 4	× 4	× 4	× 7	× 7	× 7
28	308	3,108	3,108	31,108	311,108

Notice that 777 × 4 = 444 × 7 and that 200 × 4 = 400 × 2.
Does 999 × 3 = 333 × 9?

Use the pattern to complete the following.

1. 6,000 × 7 _____ 7,000 × 6

2. 14,000 × 7 = _____ × 14

3. 222 × 8 = _____ × 2

4. 3,333 × _____ = 2,222 × 33

Multiply. Use the pattern.

5.	6.	7.	8.	9.
3	33	222	2,222	22,222
× 2	× 2	× 3	× 3	× 3

10.	11.	12.	13.	14.
9	99	999	5,555	55,555
× 5	× 5	× 5	× 9	× 9

Problem Solving

There are 6 plastic balls
in one package. How many
balls are there in 4 packages?

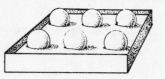

Use the plan below to solve the problem.

Read   **Decide**   **Solve**   **Examine**
the problem.   what to do.   the problem.   the solution.

4 × 6 = 24

Check by adding.   6 + 6 + 6 + 6 = 24 ✔   The answer checks.

Solve.

1. There are 5 students in one
   row. How many students are
   in 5 rows?

2. There are 7 cars parked in a
   row. How many cars are there
   in 3 rows?

3. There are 4 pictures in a row
   on a table. How many pictures
   are there in 8 rows?

4. There are 9 pieces of paper in
   a tablet. How many pieces of
   paper are there in 3 tablets?

Answer each question. Use the bar graph.

5. How many students pick birds
   and hamsters?

6. How many students pick dogs,
   cats, and fish?

7. How many students have
   favorite pets?

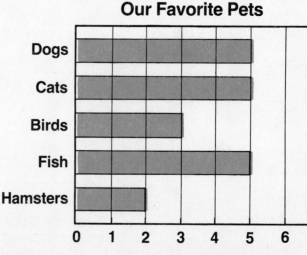

Our Favorite Pets

Problem Solving

There are 5,086 people at the rodeo. How many more people attend the rodeo this year than last year?

Are there enough facts?

No, you need to know last year's attendance before you can subtract.

Solve. If there are not enough facts, write the facts you need.

1. Southside School's basketball team scores 62 points. Elm Park School's team scored more points. How many points do they score together?

   _____

2. The school auditorium has 915 seats. There are 768 people in attendance. How many seats are empty?

   _____

3. The third grade mothers save 826 coupons. The second grade mothers save 592 coupons. How many more coupons do the third grade mothers have?

   _____

4. There are 1,005 dogs, cats, and horses at the art show. There are 783 dogs. How many cats are at the show?

   _____

5. The PTA raises $982 from auctions and $569 from bake sales. How much money do they raise all together?

   _____

6. There are 5,086 people in attendance at the rodeo. There were 4,912 in attendance last year. How many people attend the rodeo both years?

   _____

77

Chapter 6 Test

Multiply.

1. 300
    × 4

2. 70
    × 6

3. 4,000
    × 2

4. 100
    × 9

5. 60
    × 5

6. 43
    × 3

7. 82
    × 4

8. 413
    × 3

9. 44
    × 4

10. 371
    × 8

11. $7.51
    × 5

12. 4,216
    × 6

13. 708
    × 8

14. $10.25
    × 9

15. 6,874
    × 9

16. 400 × 8

17. $703 × 6

18. 4,192 × 5

Find each product.

19. 3 × 6 × 2

20. 20 × 4 × 6

21. 7 × 8 × 9

Estimate.

22. 742
    × 8

23. 6,871
    × 3

24. 906
    × 7

25. 88
    × 8

Solve.

26. Track clips for the race track are 69¢ per package. Joan and Bud need six packages. How much will they spend?

27. Jan's photo album has 48 pages. There are eight photos on each page. How many photos are there?

28. A class has four groups of six students. How many students are there?

29. There are 400 sticks in a box of craft sticks. How many sticks are in seven boxes?

Multiply.

1. 10 × 86
2. 10 × 90
3. 40 × 550
4. 50 × 600

5. $32
   × 70

6.   73
   × 14

7.   86
   × 18

8. $79
   × 67

9.   674
   × 36

10.   188
   × 29

11.   435
   × 10

12.   330
   × 70

Multiply.

1. $3.99
   × 45

2. $4.73
   × 27

3. $15.38
   × 40

4. $9.41
   × 62

5. 1,364
   × 55

6. 4,306
   × 74

7. 5,323
   × 90

8. 8,780
   × 36

Estimate.

9.   89
   × 37

10.   66
   × 12

11. $54
   × 26

12. $773
   × 58

Solve.

13. One bicycle costs $69. Find the cost of 22 bicycles.

14. One plant costs $3.28. Find the cost of 14 plants.

Multiplying by 10–19

These examples show how to multiply by 10.

$$\begin{array}{r} 6 \\ \times 10 \\ \hline 60 \end{array} \qquad \begin{array}{r} 38 \\ \times 10 \\ \hline 380 \end{array} \qquad \begin{array}{r} 50 \\ \times 10 \\ \hline 500 \end{array}$$

This example shows how to multiply by a number between 10 and 20.

Multiply by the ones.	*Multiply by the tens.*	*Add.*
$\begin{array}{r} 36 \\ \times 14 \\ \hline 144 \end{array}$ 4 × 36	$\begin{array}{r} 36 \\ \times 14 \\ \hline 144 \\ 360 \end{array}$ 1 ten × 36	$\begin{array}{r} 36 \\ \times 14 \\ \hline 144 \\ +360 \\ \hline 504 \end{array}$

EXERCISES Multiply.

1. $\begin{array}{r} 3 \\ \times 10 \\ \hline \end{array}$
2. $\begin{array}{r} 7 \\ \times 10 \\ \hline \end{array}$
3. $\begin{array}{r} 14 \\ \times 10 \\ \hline \end{array}$
4. $\begin{array}{r} 76 \\ \times 10 \\ \hline \end{array}$
5. $\begin{array}{r} 60 \\ \times 10 \\ \hline \end{array}$
6. $\begin{array}{r} 247 \\ \times\ 10 \\ \hline \end{array}$

7. $\begin{array}{r} 46 \\ \times 12 \\ \hline 92 \end{array}$ 2 × 46
   1 ten × 46
8. $\begin{array}{r} 83 \\ \times 16 \\ \hline 498 \end{array}$ 6 × 83
   1 ten × 83
9. $\begin{array}{r} 54 \\ \times 13 \\ \hline \end{array}$ 3 × 54
   1 ten × 54
10. $\begin{array}{r} 64 \\ \times 17 \\ \hline \end{array}$ 7 × 64
    1 ten × 64

11. $\begin{array}{r} 72 \\ \times 14 \\ \hline \end{array}$
12. $\begin{array}{r} 36 \\ \times 18 \\ \hline \end{array}$
13. $\begin{array}{r} 78 \\ \times 11 \\ \hline \end{array}$
14. $\begin{array}{r} 95 \\ \times 15 \\ \hline \end{array}$
15. $\begin{array}{r} 27 \\ \times 19 \\ \hline \end{array}$

16. $\begin{array}{r} 69 \\ \times 18 \\ \hline \end{array}$
17. $\begin{array}{r} 84 \\ \times 13 \\ \hline \end{array}$
18. $\begin{array}{r} 57 \\ \times 16 \\ \hline \end{array}$
19. $\begin{array}{r} 35 \\ \times 14 \\ \hline \end{array}$
20. $\begin{array}{r} 46 \\ \times 17 \\ \hline \end{array}$

Multiplying by Tens, Multiplying by 2-Digit Numbers

This example shows how to multiply by tens.

$$
\begin{array}{r}
42 \\
\times\ 2 \quad \text{tens} \\
\hline
84 \quad \text{tens}
\end{array}
\quad\blacktriangleright\quad
\begin{array}{r}
42 \\
\times 20 \\
\hline
840
\end{array}
$$

This example shows how to multiply by any 2-digit number.

Multiply by the ones.

$$
\begin{array}{r}
38 \\
\times 26 \\
\hline
228
\end{array}
\quad 6 \times 38
$$

$\blacktriangleright$

Multiply by the tens.

$$
\begin{array}{r}
38 \\
\times 26 \\
\hline
228 \\
760
\end{array}
\quad 2 \text{ tens} \times 38
$$

$\blacktriangleright$

Add.

$$
\begin{array}{r}
38 \\
\times 26 \\
\hline
228 \\
+760 \\
\hline
988
\end{array}
$$

EXERCISES Multiply.

1. $\begin{array}{r} 13 \\ \times 30 \\ \hline \end{array}$
　　2. $\begin{array}{r} 34 \\ \times 70 \\ \hline \end{array}$
　　3. $\begin{array}{r} 90 \\ \times 20 \\ \hline \end{array}$
　　4. $\begin{array}{r} 45 \\ \times 50 \\ \hline \end{array}$
　　5. $\begin{array}{r} 73 \\ \times 80 \\ \hline \end{array}$
　　6. $\begin{array}{r} 660 \\ \times\ 40 \\ \hline \end{array}$

7. $\begin{array}{r} 87 \\ \times 75 \\ \hline \end{array}$

5×87

$6090 \quad 7 \text{ tens} \times 87$

8. $\begin{array}{r} 28 \\ \times 59 \\ \hline \end{array}$

9×28

$5 \text{ tens} \times 28$

9. $\begin{array}{r} 56 \\ \times 33 \\ \hline \end{array}$

3×56

$3 \text{ tens} \times 56$

10. $\begin{array}{r} 46 \\ \times 97 \\ \hline \end{array}$

7×46

$9 \text{ tens} \times 46$

11. $\begin{array}{r} 14 \\ \times 48 \\ \hline \end{array}$
　　12. $\begin{array}{r} 68 \\ \times 84 \\ \hline \end{array}$
　　13. $\begin{array}{r} 39 \\ \times 62 \\ \hline \end{array}$
　　14. $\begin{array}{r} 62 \\ \times 57 \\ \hline \end{array}$
　　15. $\begin{array}{r} 75 \\ \times 83 \\ \hline \end{array}$

16. $\begin{array}{r} 53 \\ \times 28 \\ \hline \end{array}$
　　17. $\begin{array}{r} 95 \\ \times 66 \\ \hline \end{array}$
　　18. $\begin{array}{r} 81 \\ \times 39 \\ \hline \end{array}$
　　19. $\begin{array}{r} 27 \\ \times 74 \\ \hline \end{array}$
　　20. $\begin{array}{r} 54 \\ \times 45 \\ \hline \end{array}$

Patterns in Computation: Relating Addition and Multiplication

Addition and multiplication are related. Study the pattern below.

Find 13×8. Recall that
$13 \times 8 = (10 \times 8) + (3 \times 8)$.

$$
\begin{array}{rcr}
10 \times 8 = & & 80 \\
+\ 3 \times 8 = & + & 24 \\
\hline
& & 104
\end{array}
$$

Find 34×23. Recall that
$34 \times 23 = (34 \times 20) + (34 \times 3)$.

$$
\begin{array}{rcl}
34 \times 20 = 340 + 340 & = & 680 \\
+\ 34 \times\ 3 = 34 + 34 + 34 & = & +\ 102 \\
\hline
34 \times 23 \qquad\qquad & = & 782
\end{array}
$$

Complete.

1.
$$
\begin{array}{r}
10 \times 21 = \underline{\hspace{1cm}} \\
+\ 1 \times 21 = \underline{\hspace{1cm}} \\
\hline
11 \times 21 = \underline{\hspace{1cm}}
\end{array}
$$

2.
$$
\begin{array}{r}
10 \times 98 = \underline{\hspace{1cm}} \\
10 \times 98 = \underline{\hspace{1cm}} \\
10 \times 98 = \underline{\hspace{1cm}} \\
+\ 1 \times 98 = \underline{\hspace{1cm}} \\
\hline
31 \times 98 = \underline{\hspace{1cm}}
\end{array}
$$

3.
$$
\begin{array}{r}
39 \times 10 = \underline{\hspace{1cm}} \\
39 \times\ 1 = \underline{\hspace{1cm}} \\
+\ 39 \times\ 1 = \underline{\hspace{1cm}} \\
\hline
39 \times 12 = \underline{\hspace{1cm}}
\end{array}
$$

4.
$$
\begin{array}{r}
46 \times 10 = \underline{\hspace{1cm}} \\
46 \times 10 = \underline{\hspace{1cm}} \\
46 \times 10 = \underline{\hspace{1cm}} \\
46 \times\ 1 = \underline{\hspace{1cm}} \\
+\ 46 \times\ 1 = \underline{\hspace{1cm}} \\
\hline
46 \times 32 = \underline{\hspace{1cm}}
\end{array}
$$

5.
$$
\begin{array}{r}
64 \times 10 = \underline{\hspace{1cm}} \\
64 \times\ 1 = \underline{\hspace{1cm}} \\
64 \times\ 1 = \underline{\hspace{1cm}} \\
+\ 64 \times\ 1 = \underline{\hspace{1cm}} \\
\hline
64 \times 13 = \underline{\hspace{1cm}}
\end{array}
$$

6.
$$
\begin{array}{r}
100 \times 57 = \underline{\hspace{1cm}} \\
10 \times 57 = \underline{\hspace{1cm}} \\
+\ 1 \times 57 = \underline{\hspace{1cm}} \\
\hline
111 \times 57 = \underline{\hspace{1cm}}
\end{array}
$$

Use the pattern to find each product.

7. 54×23

8. 73×42

9. 65×31

10. 329×14

Maintenance

Order from least to greatest.

1. 88, 48, 84, 46, 50

2. 3,133, 3,313, 1,333, 3,331

3. 79, 46, 82, 50, 49

4. 742, 402, 740, 247

Add or subtract.

5. 7,634
   + 4,781

6. 12,936
   + 92,844

7. 79,347
   − 42,678

8. $15.00
   −   9.87

What time is it?

9. 8 hours before 7:30 A.M.

10. 3 hours after 8:30 A.M.

11. 4 hours after 6:00 P.M.

12. 12 hours before 7:00 P.M.

Multiply or divide.

13. 7 × 9

14. 8)48

15. 9)45

16. 6 × 7

Multiply.

17. 700
    ×   7

18. $83
    ×   6

19. 718
    ×   4

20. 6,127
    ×   5

21. 37
    × 10

Solve. Use the bar graph.

22. If Edna sells five more tickets, will she have sold more than Caron?

23. Don has sold two more tickets that are not shown on the chart. How many tickets has he sold?

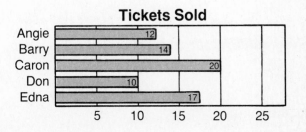

Tickets Sold

Angie 12
Barry 14
Caron 20
Don 10
Edna 17

5   10   15   20   25

Multiplying Greater Numbers, More Estimating Products

Multiply 263 by 23.

When you multiply with money, remember to put the dollar sign and a decimal point in the product.

Multiply by the ones.	*Multiply by the tens.*	*Add.*
263 × 23 789 3 × 263	263 × 23 789 5260 2 tens × 263	263 × 23 789 +5260 6,049

EXERCISES **Multiply.**

1. 343
 × 34
 	
   4 × 343
   3 tens × 343
	2. $4.86
	   × 42
		3. 251
		 × 96
			4. 138
			 × 75

5. $6.14
   × 83
	6. 869
	 × 57
		7. 592
		 × 26
			8. $7.25
			   × 38

9. 977 × 64

10. 2,814
  × 42
	11. $73.27
	   × 35
		12. 3,460
		  × 57
			13. 4,155
			  × 29
				14. $36.82
				   × 64

Round each factor to its greatest place-value position. Then estimate the product.

15. 73 ×32	16. 96 ×86	17. 142 × 48	18. 315 × 97

Problem Solving

When solving word problems,
remember to follow the steps.

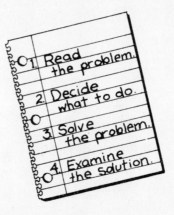

1. Read the problem.
2. Decide what to do.
3. Solve the problem.
4. Examine the solution.

EXERCISES Solve. Use the chart.

1. The art teacher ordered 23 packages of construction paper. Find the total cost.

School Supplies Store	
Box of 100 pencils	$3.59
Package of 500 sheets of writing paper	$4.07
Box of 20 crayons	$1.35
Package of 50 sheets of construction paper	$6.50

2. Mr. Sesher ordered 30 packages of writing paper. How many sheets will he get?

3. The student council ordered 40 boxes of pencils to sell. How many pencils were ordered?

4. The kindergarten teacher needed to buy 18 boxes of crayons. Find the total cost.

5. Find the cost of 28 packages of writing paper.

6. How many crayons would the school have if 40 boxes were ordered?

7. The school ordered a package of construction paper for each of the 200 students. How many sheets would that be?

8. Find the cost of 16 boxes of pencils.

Chapter 7 Test

Multiply.

1. 72
    × 10

2. 41
    × 30

3. 492
    × 50

4. 704
    × 70

5. 589
    × 40

6. 81
    × 12

7. 33
    × 33

8. 74
    × 26

9. 82
    × 71

10. 52
    × 67

11. 308
    × 56

12. 483
    × 27

13. 816
    × 72

14. 3,987
    × 45

15. $32.99
    × 25

16. $0.99 × 12

17. $8.40 × 23

18. 35 × $12.72

Estimate.

19. 847
    × 76

20. 83
    × 32

21. 482
    × 48

22. 806
    × 43

23. 548
    × 29

Solve.

24. Jamie delivers 57 papers each day. How many papers does Jamie deliver in 21 days?

25. A checker board has 12 rows of 12 squares. How many squares are on a checker board?

26. Mr. Kim bakes 24 cookies on a cookie sheet. How many cookies can he bake on 25 cookie sheets?

27. Carol earns $4.75 each hour. How much does she earn in 37 hours?

Maintenance

Standardized Format

Directions Work each problem on your own paper. Choose the letter of the correct answer. If the correct answer is not given, choose the letter for *none of the above*. Make no marks on this test.

1. Add.

$8 + 3 + 6 + 2$

a 7

b 18

c 19

d *none of the above*

2. What is the missing addend?

$12 = \Box + 7$

e 4

f 5

g 6

h *none of the above*

3. What number does the 5 name?

365,147

a 500

b 5,000

c 50,000

d *none of the above*

4. What is 4,437 rounded to the nearest thousand?

e 4,000

f 5,000

g 5,500

h *none of the above*

5. Add.

$\begin{array}{r} 39,157 \\ +23,489 \end{array}$

a 62,646

b 63,732

c 66,526

d *none of the above*

6. Subtract.

$61,072 - 6,385$

e 2,683

f 2,778

g 54,687

h *none of the above*

7. What is the time?

a 5:40

b 6:45

c 8:25

d *none of the above*

8. How much money is shown?

e $3.50

f $11.15

g $15.05

h *none of the above*

9. Subtract.

$\begin{array}{r} \$37.25 \\ -\ 14.67 \end{array}$

a $22.52

b $43.42

c $51.92

d *none of the above*

10. Multiply.

7×6

e 42

f 44

g 48

h *none of the above*

11. What is the missing factor?

$4 \times \Box = 32$

a 7

b 8

c 9

d *none of the above*

12. Divide.

$3\overline{)27}$

e 7

f 8

g 9

h *none of the above*

13. Which number is a multiple of 9?

   a 72

   b 19

   c 12

   d *none of the above*

14. Complete the fact family.

$6 \times 9 = 54$
$54 \div 6 = 9$
$54 \div 9 = 6$

   e $6 + 9 = 15$

   f $9 - 6 = 3$

   g $9 \times 6 = 54$

   h *none of the above*

15. Multiply.

$\$23 \times 3$

   a $56

   b $66

   c $69

   d *none of the above*

16. Multiply.

$$\begin{array}{r} 3{,}109 \\ \times\quad 6 \\ \hline \end{array}$$

   e 18,604

   f 18,654

   g 18,904

   h *none of the above*

17. Multiply.

$$\begin{array}{r} 476 \\ \times\quad 30 \\ \hline \end{array}$$

   a 1,428

   b 14,208

   c 14,280

   d *none of the above*

18. Multiply.

283×54

   e 15,282

   f 19,364

   g 25,477

   h *none of the above*

19. Choose the best estimate.

86×32

   a 2,400

   b 2,700

   c 3,200

   d *none of the above*

20. What is Joan's change?

slacks	$14.99
shirt	$ 9.99
tie	$ 4.99

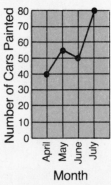

   e $10.03

   f $11.10

   g $12.28

   h *none of the above*

21. There are 24 hours in one day. How many hours are there in two weeks?

   a 240

   b 336

   c 360

   d *none of the above*

22. The line graph shows the number of cars Mr. Wagner painted during a four-month period. During which month did he paint 50 cars?

   e April

   f May

   g June

   h *none of the above*

Divide.

1. 7)63   2. 8)32   3. 4)30   4. 6)40   5. 8)76

6. 2)86   7. 3)63   8. 5)55   9. 2)74   10. 9)92

11. 7)91   12. 6)84   13. 3)88   14. 5)72   15. 6)87

Find the average.

16. 22, 38, 33   17. 9, 12, 6, 3, 15   18. 16, 20, 24, 27, 18

Divide.

1. 2)184   2. 5)420   3. 7)504   4. 3)502   5. 4)705

6. 6)444   7. 4)230   8. 9)908   9. 8)515   10. 6)792

Solve.

11. Sabra needs 26 pounds of lawn seed. How many 5-pound bags of seed should she buy?

12. The sum of two numbers is 35. The difference is 7. Find the two numbers.

Division Facts, Remainders

Find quotients by thinking of missing factors.

Divide 12 by 6.

Think:
6 × [2] = 12

2 ← quotient
divisor → 6)12 ← dividend

Divide 23 by 3.

Think:
3 × [7] = 21
3 × [8] = 24

7 R2
3)23
21
2   remainder

EXERCISES   Divide. Write the quotient and remainder, if any.

1. 5)10

2. 8)24

3. 8)46

4. 9)77

5. 4)0

6. 6)25

7. 5)23

8. 7)56

9. 6)6

10. 9)70

11. 1)3

12. 2)8

13. 9)50

14. 5)5

15. 4)32

16. 8)23

17. 7)45

18. 2)0

19. 4)16

20. 4)39

Solve.

21. August has 31 days. How many weeks does August have? How many days are left over?

22. Fifteen shoes are in a box. How many pairs could there be?

2-Digit Quotients

The school band has 42 students. The band director wants to place the same number of students on each of two buses. How many should go on each bus? To find the answer, divide 42 by 2.

42 = 4 tens 2 ones

Divide the tens.

$$\begin{array}{r} 2 \\ 2\overline{)4\,2} \\ -4 \\ \hline 0 \end{array}$$

2 × 2 tens
= 4 tens

Divide the ones.

$$\begin{array}{r} 2\;1 \\ 2\overline{)4\,2} \\ -4\downarrow \\ \hline 0\,2 \\ -2 \\ \hline 0 \end{array}$$

2 × 1 = 2

EXERCISES   Divide.

1. $3\overline{)63}$ 2. $2\overline{)24}$ 3. $7\overline{)70}$ 4. $3\overline{)69}$ 5. $2\overline{)44}$

6. $2\overline{)68}$ 7. $6\overline{)66}$ 8. $3\overline{)99}$ 9. $2\overline{)48}$ 10. $7\overline{)77}$

11. $6\overline{)60}$ 12. $2\overline{)64}$ 13. $8\overline{)88}$ 14. $2\overline{)84}$ 15. $4\overline{)80}$

Solve.

16. Forty-eight couples went to a square dance. It takes 4 couples to make a square. How many squares will there be?

17. Eight children are going to make 80 name tags. How many should each child make?

Patterns in Computation: Dividing Whole Numbers

If you know basic division facts, you can divide whole
numbers with 4 or more digits. Think of each step as a
separate division fact. Study the pattern below.

$\frac{4}{2)8}$ | $\frac{4 \text{ tens}}{2)8 \text{ tens}} \longrightarrow \frac{40}{2)80}$ | $\frac{4 \text{ thousands}}{2)8 \text{ thousands}} \longrightarrow \frac{4,000}{2)8,000}$

$\frac{44}{2)88}$ | $\frac{404}{2)808}$ | $\frac{4,004}{2)8,008}$ | $\frac{40,040}{2)80,080}$

Divide. Use the pattern.

1. $3)\overline{6}$

2. $3)\overline{6 \text{ tens}}$

3. $3)\overline{60}$

4. $3)\overline{6 \text{ hundreds}}$

5. $3)\overline{600}$

6. $3)\overline{9}$

7. $3)\overline{9 \text{ hundreds}}$

8. $3)\overline{900}$

9. $3)\overline{990}$

10. $3)\overline{9,000}$

11. $5)\overline{5}$

12. $5)\overline{50}$

13. $5)\overline{500}$

14. $5)\overline{5,000}$

15. $5)\overline{5,050}$

16. $2)\overline{6}$

17. $2)\overline{66}$

18. $2)\overline{6,000}$

19. $2)\overline{6,600}$

20. $2)\overline{6,606}$

21. $4)\overline{8}$

22. $4)\overline{808}$

23. $4)\overline{888}$

24. $4)\overline{8,000}$

25. $4)\overline{8,008}$

Division with Renaming

When you divide, you may need to rename tens as ones.

Divide 34 by 2.

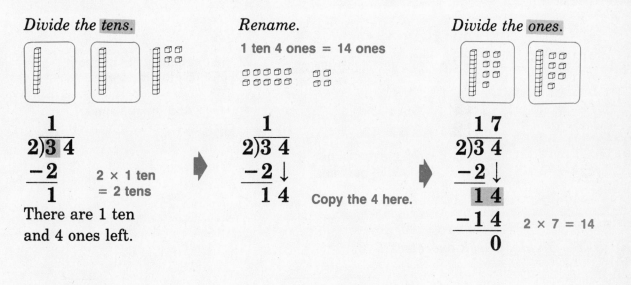

Divide the tens.

$$\begin{array}{r} 1 \\ 2\overline{)3\ 4} \\ -2 \\ \hline 1 \end{array}$$

2 × 1 ten
= 2 tens

There are 1 ten
and 4 ones left.

Rename.

1 ten 4 ones = 14 ones

$$\begin{array}{r} 1 \\ 2\overline{)3\ 4} \\ -2\downarrow \\ \hline 1\ 4 \end{array}$$

Copy the 4 here.

Divide the ones.

$$\begin{array}{r} 1\ 7 \\ 2\overline{)3\ 4} \\ -2\downarrow \\ \hline 1\ 4 \\ -1\ 4 \\ \hline 0 \end{array}$$

2 × 7 = 14

EXERCISES Divide.

1. $\begin{array}{r} 2 \\ 3\overline{)8\ 4} \\ \hline \\ 4 \\ \hline \end{array}$

2. $\begin{array}{r} 1 \\ 5\overline{)8\ 5} \\ \hline \\ 5 \\ \hline \end{array}$

3. $\begin{array}{r} 2 \\ 2\overline{)5\ 2} \\ \hline \\ 2 \\ \hline \end{array}$

4. $\begin{array}{r} 1 \\ 4\overline{)7\ 2} \\ \hline \\ 2 \\ \hline \end{array}$

5. $8\overline{)96}$

6. $2\overline{)76}$

7. $5\overline{)65}$

8. $6\overline{)78}$

9. $3\overline{)78}$

10. $4\overline{)96}$

11. $6\overline{)84}$

12. $5\overline{)75}$

13. $3\overline{)45}$

14. $7\overline{)98}$

More 2-Digit Quotients

Divide 95 by 4.

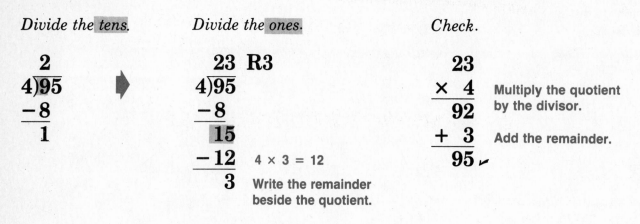

Divide the tens.

```
   2
4)95
 -8
   1
```

Divide the ones.

```
   23 R3
4)95
 -8
   15
  -12      4 × 3 = 12
    3      Write the remainder
           beside the quotient.
```

Check.

```
   23
 ×  4      Multiply the quotient
   92      by the divisor.
 +  3      Add the remainder.
   95 ✓
```

EXERCISES **Divide. Check exercises 1–3.**

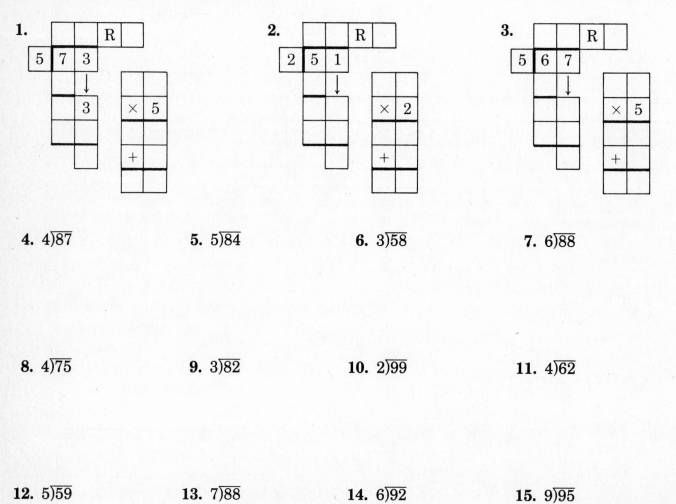

1.
```
5 7 3  R
    3   × 5
        +
```

2.
```
2 5 1  R
        × 2
        +
```

3.
```
5 6 7  R
        × 5
        +
```

4. 4)87   5. 5)84   6. 3)58   7. 6)88

8. 4)75   9. 3)82   10. 2)99   11. 4)62

12. 5)59   13. 7)88   14. 6)92   15. 9)95

Finding Averages

Find the average of 2, 5, 3, 2, 3.

Add the numbers.

$$2 + 5 + 3 + 2 + 3 = 15$$

5 addends

*Divide by the
number of addends.*

$$15 \div 5 = 3$$

The average is 3.

EXERCISES *Find the average.*

1.   8
    6
    7   4)28
 +7
  28

2.   9
  11
 + 4

3.   11
   5
   6
 +10

4.   7
  5
  6
  5
 +7

5.   23
  15
  21
 +17

6.   30
  17
  25
 +12

7.   14
  16
  11
  23
 +16

8.   20
  30
  24
 +22

9.   24
  29
 +25

10.   11
  16
  10
  19
 +14

11.   13
  19
   6
 +26

Solve.

12. Three children collected cans. Andy picked up 18, Sally picked up 12, and Bill picked up 15. What was their average?

13. Karen earned $28 for completing two different jobs. What was the average for each job?

Maintenance

Add or subtract.

1. 97,438
   − 73,692

2. $43.89
   + 90.63

3. 58,272
   + 38,467

4. 17,410
   − 12,836

Compute.

5. 14 + (62 − 41)

6. (76 + 13) − 48

7. 100 − (50 + 12)

Multiply or divide.

8. 6 × 5

9. 7 × 8

10. 9 × 4

11. 3)18

12. 6)42

13. 82 × 7

14. 3)48

15. $27 × 10

16. 5)90

17. 36
   × 8

18. 27
   × 81

19. 108
   × 35

20. 7)99

21. 4)67

22. 8)90

23. 3)78

Solve. Use the line graph.

24. How many weeks did Melinda spell 18 or more words correctly?

25. In which week did she have her lowest score?

26. Find the average number of words spelled correctly for the first 5 weeks.

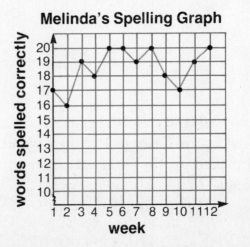

Melinda's Spelling Graph

Dividing 3-Digit Numbers

Divide 374 by 5.

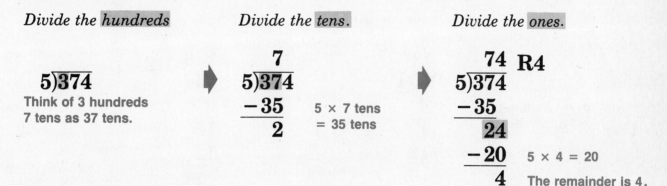

Divide the hundreds

5)374

Think of 3 hundreds 7 tens as 37 tens.

Divide the tens.

$$\begin{array}{r} 7 \\ 5\overline{)374} \\ -35 \\ \hline 2 \end{array}$$

5 × 7 tens = 35 tens

Divide the ones.

$$\begin{array}{r} 74 \text{ R4} \\ 5\overline{)374} \\ -35 \\ \hline 24 \\ -20 \\ \hline 4 \end{array}$$

5 × 4 = 20

The remainder is 4.

EXERCISE **Divide.**

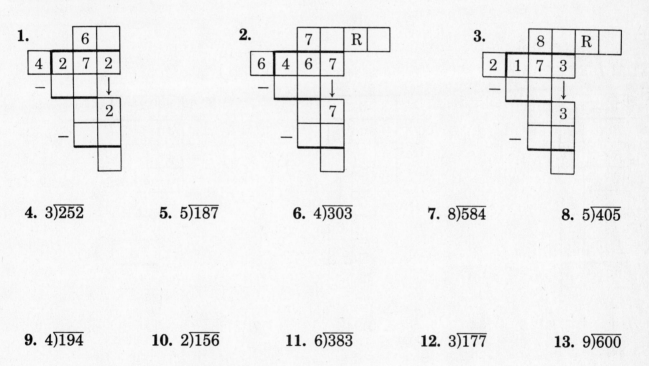

1.
2.
3.

4. 3)252   **5.** 5)187   **6.** 4)303   **7.** 8)584   **8.** 5)405

9. 4)194   **10.** 2)156   **11.** 6)383   **12.** 3)177   **13.** 9)600

Solve.

14. How many teams of 4 can be formed with 172 people?

15. There are 5 boys and 480 papers. If each boy delivers the same number of papers, how many papers will each boy deliver?

3-Digit Quotients

Divide 554 by 4.

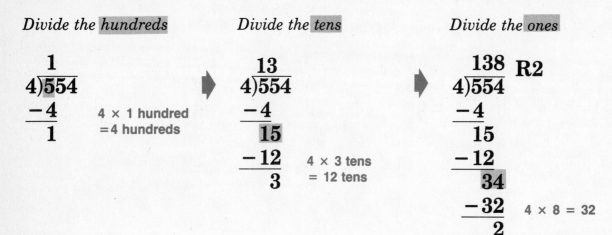

Divide the hundreds

$$\begin{array}{r} 1 \\ 4\overline{)554} \\ -4 \\ \hline 1 \end{array}$$

4 × 1 hundred
= 4 hundreds

Divide the tens

$$\begin{array}{r} 13 \\ 4\overline{)554} \\ -4 \\ \hline 15 \\ -12 \\ \hline 3 \end{array}$$

4 × 3 tens
= 12 tens

Divide the ones

$$\begin{array}{r} 138 \\ 4\overline{)554} \\ -4 \\ \hline 15 \\ -12 \\ \hline 34 \\ -32 \\ \hline 2 \end{array} \text{R2}$$

4 × 8 = 32

EXERCISES *Divide.*

1.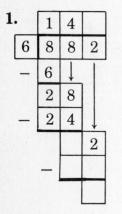

2.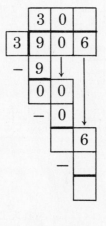

3.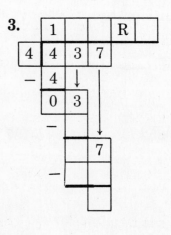

4. 7)890

5. 4)744

6. 9)949

7. 3)854

8. 8)968

Solve.

9. There are 652 school papers to pass out. How many should each of the 4 delivery people take?

10. There are 9 committees and 117 students. What is the average number of students on each committee?

Problem Solving

Apples are priced 4 for 79¢.
How much does 1 apple cost?

$$\begin{array}{r} 19 \text{ R3} \rightarrow 20 \\ 4\overline{)79} \\ -4 \\ \hline 39 \\ -36 \\ \hline 3 \end{array}$$

When the remainder is not 0, the
quotient is rounded up. Most
stores use this rule in pricing.
Store computers are programed
to round up.

One apple will
cost 20¢.

EXERCISES   Solve.

1. The cost of five green peppers is $1.29
   (129¢). What is the cost of one green
   pepper?

2. The cost of six pears is $1.89 (189¢).
   What is the cost of one pear?

3. Raisins are priced 8 packs for $1.98
   (198¢). What is the cost of one pack?

4. Almonds are priced 3 bags for $2.65
   (265¢). What is the cost of one bag?

5. Three packages of ready-to-pop popcorn
   cost $1.47 (147¢). What is the cost of
   one package?

6. Six cans of soup cost $1.81 (181¢).
   What is the cost of one can?

7. Tonia is buying 9 items at the store.
   The total cost is $9.26. What is the
   average cost of each item?

8. Marsha is buying 8 packages of
   chicken. The total cost is $17.43. What
   is the average cost of each package?

Problem Solving

Hector buys 10 stamps at the post office. He spends $1.78. How many of each does he buy?

Use the table at the right to find your answer.

22¢	8¢	Total Spent
0	10	$0.80
1	9	$0.94
2	8	$1.08
3	7	$1.22

Use the plan below to solve the problem.

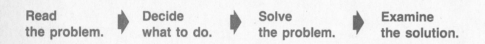

Read the problem. **Decide** what to do. **Solve** the problem. **Examine** the solution.

Hector buys seven 22¢ stamps and three 8¢ stamps.

Solve. Use guess and check.

1. Gloria spends $2.94 at the Hobby Shop. She buys yarn for 49¢ a roll and patterns for 98¢ each. How many of each does she buy?

2. I am thinking of two numbers. Their sum is 11. Their product is 24 and their difference is 5. What are the two numbers?

3. Put the numbers 2, 3, 4, 5, 6, 7, 8, 9 into two groups. No number can be the sum of two other numbers in that same group.

4. ☐1 ☐5 ☐3
   ☐2 ☐4 ☐6

   Arrange the blocks so each pair will have a sum of 7.

5. Think of a number greater than 40 and less than 50. The sum of its factors is 14 and their difference is 4. What is the number?

6. Suppose Hector buys 10 stamps at the post office. He spends $2.06. How many of each stamp does he buy? (Use the table at the top.)

Chapter 8 Test

Divide.

1. $8\overline{)64}$ 2. $7\overline{)42}$ 3. $9\overline{)76}$ 4. $4\overline{)92}$ 5. $3\overline{)63}$

6. $7\overline{)84}$ 7. $5\overline{)76}$ 8. $6\overline{)192}$ 9. $5\overline{)255}$ 10. $3\overline{)309}$

11. $8\overline{)872}$ 12. $4\overline{)896}$ 13. $5\overline{)376}$ 14. $6\overline{)787}$ 15. $7\overline{)807}$

Find the average.

16. 30, 18, 12, 26, 24   17. 9, 15, 16, 12

Solve.

18. A page in Bert's photo album holds 8 photos. How many pages will he need to hold 96 photos?

19. The sum of 2 numbers is 16. The product is 63. What are the numbers.?

20. There are 19 people who want to cross the creek. Each boat carries 4 people. How many boats do they need?

21. It snowed for 2 hours on Monday, 6 hours on Tuesday and 1 hour on Wednesday. What was the average number of hours it snowed?

Name _____

Name each figure.

1.

A

B   C

2.

X

W

3.

N

R

4.

S

T

Is each pair of figures congruent? Write YES or NO.

5.

6.

7.

- -

Name _____

Answer each question. Use the figures at the right.

1. Which figures are triangles?

2. Which figures are quadrilaterals?

3. Which figures are parallelograms?

4. How many lines of symmetry does figure D have?

A   B   C

D   E   F

Name each shape below.

5.

6.

7.

8.

Name the point for each number pair.

9. (3, 5)   10. (4, 2)

11. (2, 1)   12. (5, 3)

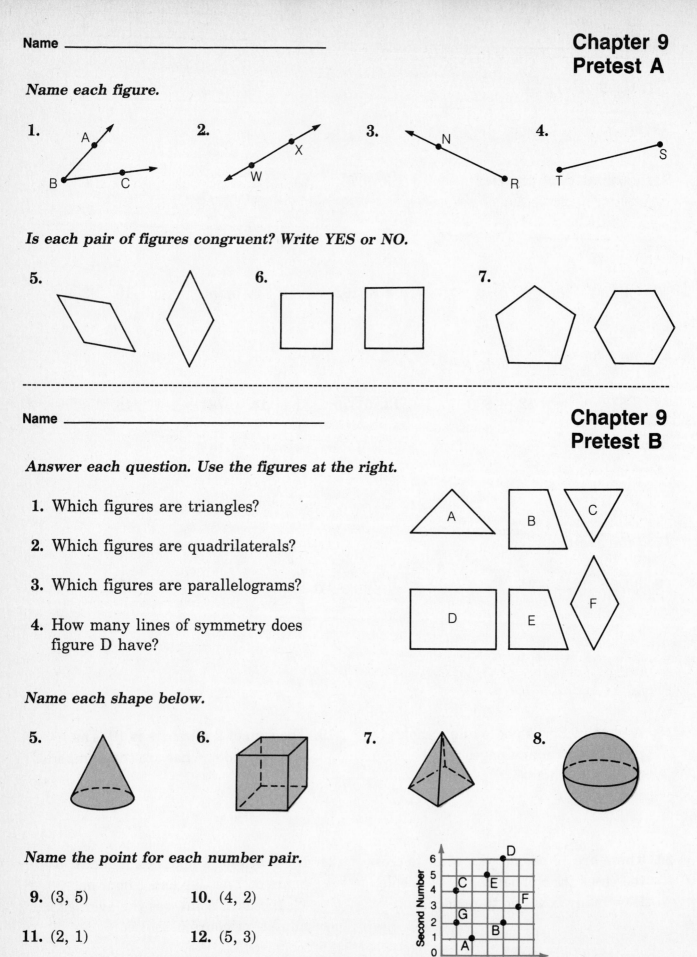

Plane Figures

A **plane** is a flat surface that goes on and on.

A **closed plane** figure has an inside and an outside.

A **polygon** is a closed plane figure with straight sides.

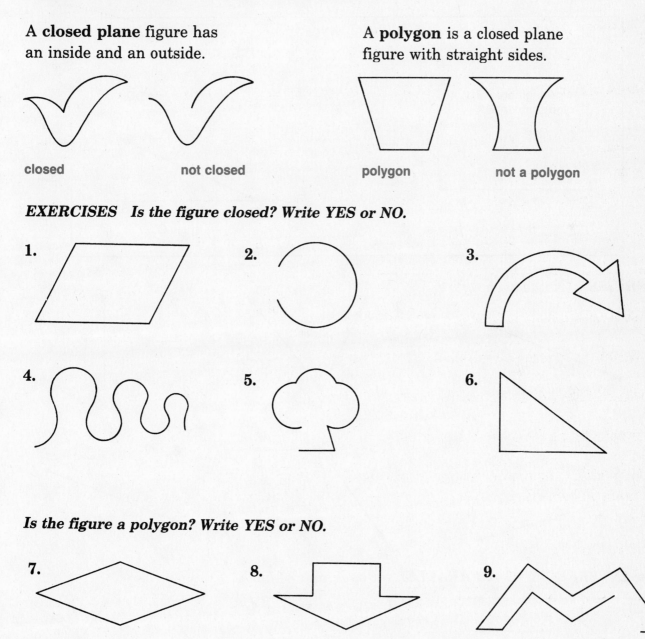

closed   not closed   polygon   not a polygon

EXERCISES Is the figure closed? Write YES or NO.

1.

2.

3.

4.

5.

6.

Is the figure a polygon? Write YES or NO.

7.

8.

9.

10.

11.

12.

Segments, Lines, Rays, and Angles

Study the ways to name each figure.

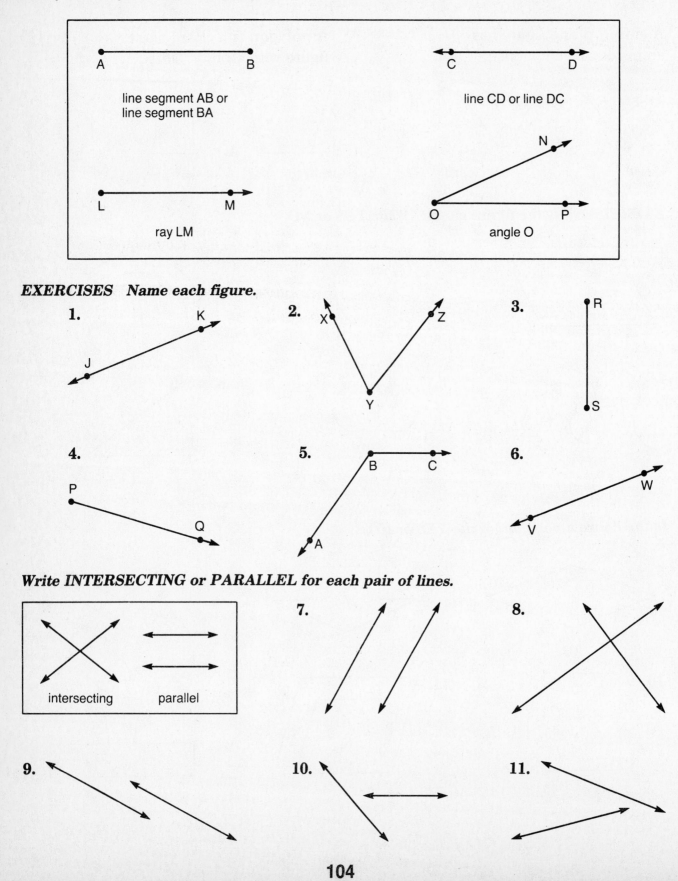

A •————————• B

line segment AB or
line segment BA

C ◄•————————•► D

line CD or line DC

L •————————•——► M

ray LM

angle O

EXERCISES Name each figure.

1.

2.

3.

4.

5.

6.

Write INTERSECTING or PARALLEL for each pair of lines.

intersecting   parallel

7.

8.

9.

10.

11.

Patterns in Geometry: Tessellations

A **tessellation,** or tiling, is a complete covering of a flat
surface by figures. No gaps or overlapping is allowed.
You see tessellations in floor tiles, fabrics, and wallpaper.
Tessellations can be made up of polygons, or other shapes.

Study the pattern below.

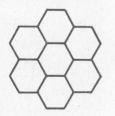

1 type of polygon

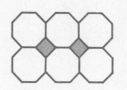

2 types of polygons

not **polygons**

Use the pattern above to draw a tessellation of each figure.
Use 6 of each shape in your drawing.

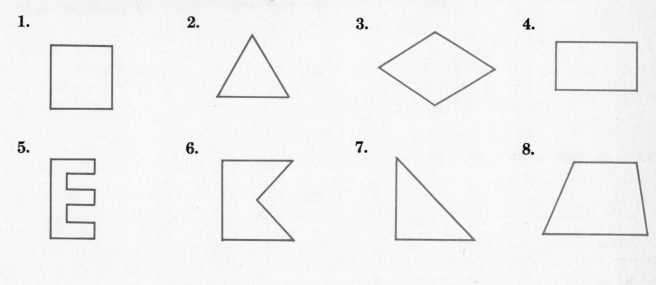

1.

2.

3.

4.

5.

6.

7.

8.

Can these shapes form tessellations? Write YES or NO.

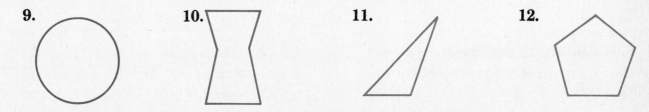

9.

10.

11.

12.

Maintenance

Write each of the following in expanded form.

1. 48   **2.** 671   **3.** 1,409   **4.** 18,235

Add or subtract.

5.
$$7,149 + 672$$

6.
$$6,930 - 5,915$$

7.
$$56,441 + 23,074$$

8.
$$42,828 - 14,582$$

9.
$$466 + 248 + 6,414$$

Multiply or divide.

10. 4×8 **11.** $3\overline{)27}$ **12.** 8×7 **13.** $9\overline{)63}$

14. 42×4 **15.** $4\overline{)66}$ **16.** 312×8 **17.** $6\overline{)156}$

18. $7 \times 3 \times 4$ **19.** $2\overline{)433}$ **20.** 53×12 **21.** $8\overline{)536}$

Name the sides of each polygon.

22.

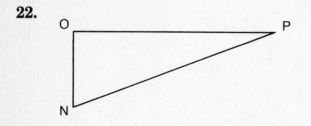

23.

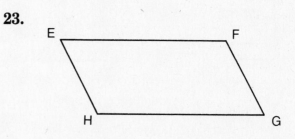

Solve.

24. Pete delivers 18 newspapers each day. How many papers does he deliver in 5 days?

25. Lisa bought a skirt that cost $12 and a sweater that cost $18. How much did she spend in all?

Name _____

Congruent Figures and Polygons

Congruent figures are the same size and shape.

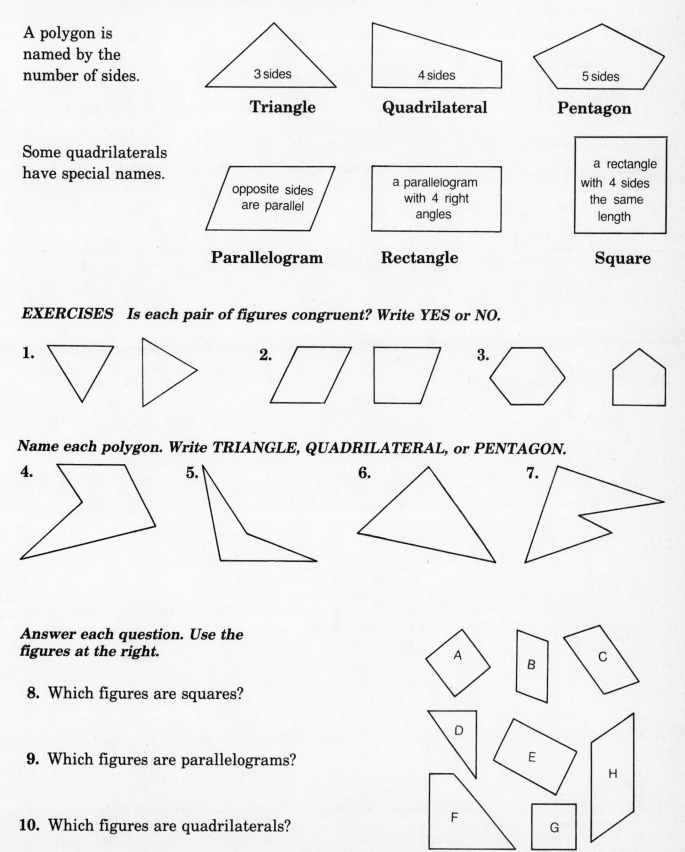

A polygon is
named by the
number of sides.

3 sides

Triangle

4 sides

Quadrilateral

5 sides

Pentagon

Some quadrilaterals
have special names.

opposite sides
are parallel

Parallelogram

a parallelogram
with 4 right
angles

Rectangle

a rectangle
with 4 sides
the same
length

Square

EXERCISES *Is each pair of figures congruent? Write YES or NO.*

1.

2.

3.

Name each polygon. Write TRIANGLE, QUADRILATERAL, or PENTAGON.

4.

5.

6.

7.

*Answer each question. Use the
figures at the right.*

A   B   C

D   E   H

8. Which figures are squares?

9. Which figures are parallelograms?

10. Which figures are quadrilaterals?

F   G

Name _____

Solid Figures

Study the solid figures shown below.

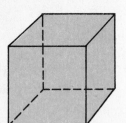
Cube

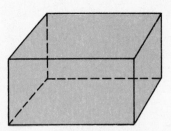
Rectangular Prism

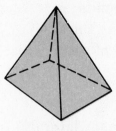
Pyramid

Cylinder

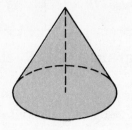
Cone

Sphere

EXERCISES *Name each shape.*

1.
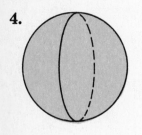

2.
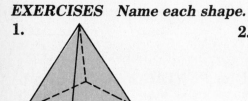

3.
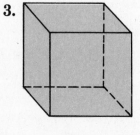

4.
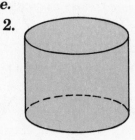

5.
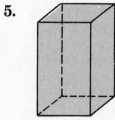

6.
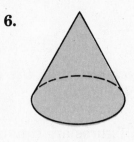

7.
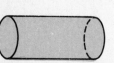

8.
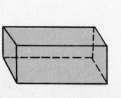

9.
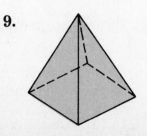

Copyright © 1988 by Merrill Publishing Co., Columbus, Ohio 43216

108

Symmetry

Symmetric figures can be folded in half so the two halves match exactly. A **line of symmetry** separates the two matching halves.

The figures below are symmetric.

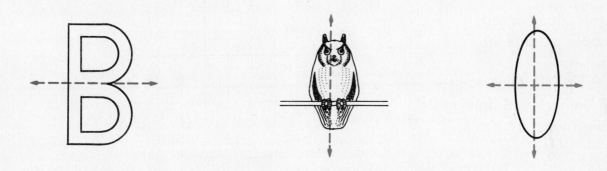

EXERCISES.   Is each dashed line a line of symmetry? Write YES or NO.

1.   2.   3.   4.

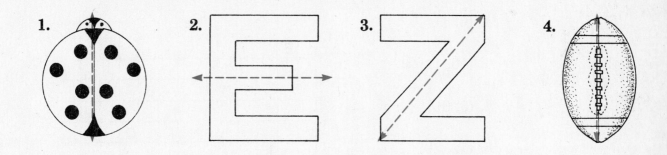

How many lines of symmetry does each figure have? Draw them.

5.   6.   7.   8.

9.   10.   11.   12.

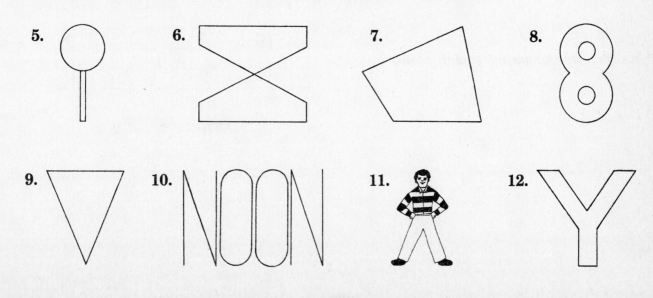

Points on a Grid

A **number pair** can be used to locate a point on a grid.

In a number pair, the *first* number tells the number of units to the right of zero.

The *second* number tells the number of units up.

The number pair (3, 5) locates point R. Point R is 3 units to the right of zero and 5 units up.

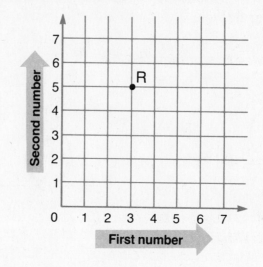

EXERCISES *Name the point for each number pair.*

1. (10, 5)   2. (8, 9)

3. (2, 6)   4. (0, 4)

5. (5, 2)   6. (10, 11)

7. (9, 0)   8. (3, 9)

9. (9, 7)   10. (12, 2)

11. (1, 11)   12. (4, 10)

Write the number pair for each point.

13. A   14. L

15. C   16. F

17. H   18. M

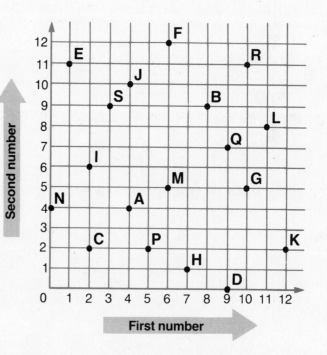

Name _____

Chapter 9 Test

Is the figure a polygon? Write YES or NO.

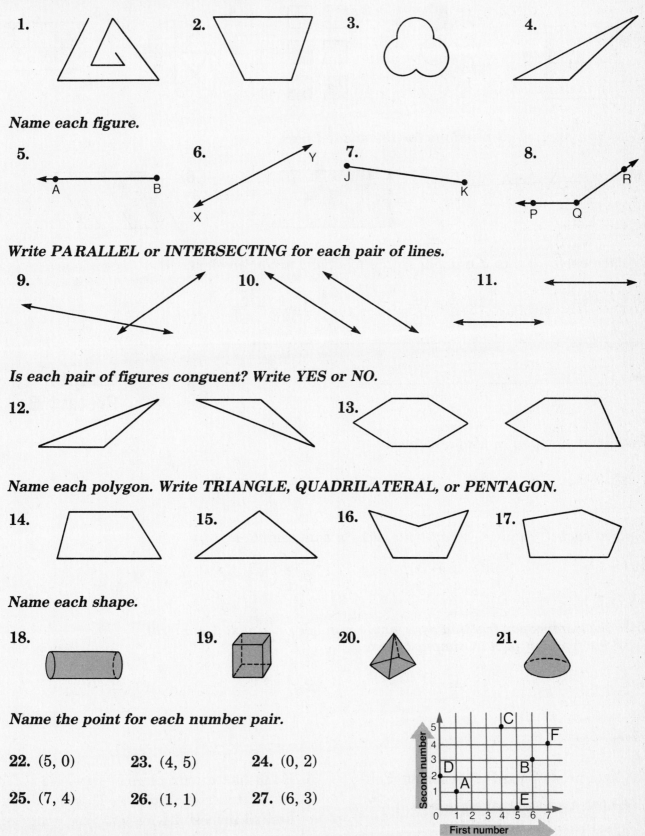

1.

2.

3.

4.

Name each figure.

5.

6.

7.

8.

Write PARALLEL or INTERSECTING for each pair of lines.

9.

10.

11.

Is each pair of figures conguent? Write YES or NO.

12.

13.

Name each polygon. Write TRIANGLE, QUADRILATERAL, or PENTAGON.

14.

15.

16.

17.

Name each shape.

18.

19.

20.

21.

Name the point for each number pair.

22. (5, 0)

23. (4, 5)

24. (0, 2)

25. (7, 4)

26. (1, 1)

27. (6, 3)

Write a fraction for the shaded part.

1.   2.   3.   4.   5.

Write two equivalent fractions for the shaded part.

6.   7.   8.

Replace each ☐ with a number so the fractions are equivalent.

9. $\frac{3}{5} = \frac{\square}{15}$

10. $\frac{4}{9} = \frac{8}{\square}$

11. $\frac{9}{27} = \frac{\square}{9}$

12. $\frac{7}{8} = \frac{21}{\square}$

- -

Write each fraction in simplest form.

1. $\frac{6}{20}$

2. $\frac{8}{18}$

3. $\frac{6}{9}$

4. $\frac{5}{15}$

5. $\frac{12}{16}$

Replace each ◯ with <, >, or = to make a true sentence.

6. $\frac{1}{3} \bigcirc \frac{2}{3}$

7. $\frac{3}{5} \bigcirc \frac{3}{8}$

8. $\frac{1}{2} \bigcirc \frac{4}{8}$

9. $\frac{1}{3} \bigcirc \frac{2}{9}$

*Write each improper fraction as a whole number or a mixed numeral.
Write the fraction part in simplest form.*

10. $\frac{14}{6}$

11. $\frac{12}{5}$

12. $\frac{9}{9}$

13. $\frac{37}{7}$

Solve.

14. Carla needs $\frac{5}{8}$ yard of ribbon to make a bow. Can she make the bow if she has $\frac{3}{4}$ yard of ribbon?

15. Kang had a long piece of wire. He cut off two 8-inch pieces. Then he had 25 inches of wire left. How long was the wire when he began?

Fractions, Regions, and Sets

Fractions can *represent* part of a region or part of a set.

2 parts shaded

3 parts in all

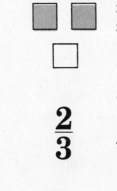

2 blocks shaded

3 blocks in all

$\dfrac{2}{3}$

The numerator tells the number of parts used.

The denominator tells the number of parts in the whole.

$\dfrac{2}{3}$

The numerator tells the number of objects used.

The denominator tells the number of objects in the set.

EXERCISES   *Write a fraction for the shaded part.*

1.

☐ –parts shaded

☐ –parts in whole

2.

☐ –shaded flags

☐ –total flags

3.

4.

5.

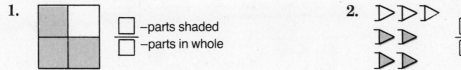

6.

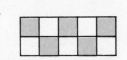

7.

8.

9.

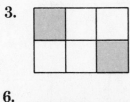

10.

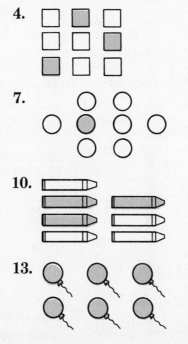

11.

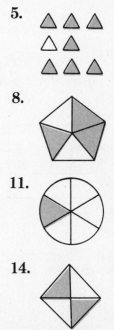

12.

13.

14.

Equivalent Fractions

More than one fraction can name the same amount.
Fractions that name the same amount are **equivalent.**
Study the following examples.

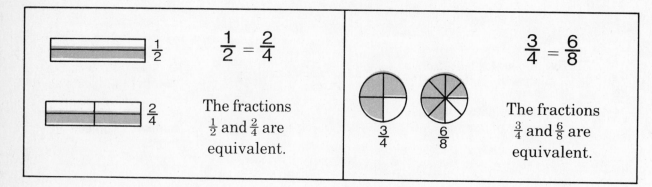

$$\frac{1}{2} \qquad \frac{1}{2} = \frac{2}{4}$$

$$\frac{2}{4}$$

The fractions
$\frac{1}{2}$ and $\frac{2}{4}$ are
equivalent.

$$\frac{3}{4} = \frac{6}{8}$$

$$\frac{3}{4} \qquad \frac{6}{8}$$

The fractions
$\frac{3}{4}$ and $\frac{6}{8}$ are
equivalent.

EXERCISES *Use the pictures to write equivalent fractions.*

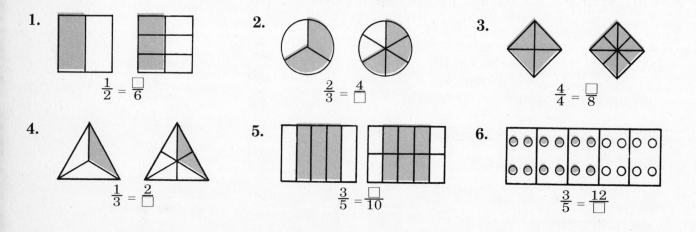

1. $\frac{1}{2} = \frac{\square}{6}$

2. $\frac{2}{3} = \frac{4}{\square}$

3. $\frac{4}{4} = \frac{\square}{8}$

4. $\frac{1}{3} = \frac{2}{\square}$

5. $\frac{3}{5} = \frac{\square}{10}$

6. $\frac{3}{5} = \frac{12}{\square}$

Choose two equivalent fractions for the shaded part.

7.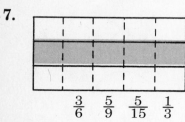

$$\frac{3}{6} \qquad \frac{5}{9} \qquad \frac{5}{15} \qquad \frac{1}{3}$$

8.

$$\frac{3}{4} \qquad \frac{12}{16} \qquad \frac{4}{8} \qquad \frac{4}{12}$$

9.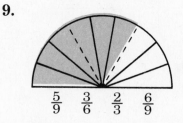

$$\frac{5}{9} \qquad \frac{3}{6} \qquad \frac{2}{3} \qquad \frac{6}{9}$$

Write two equivalent fractions for each.

10. Todd had 3 nickels and
3 dimes. What fraction of
the coins are nickels?

11. Linda picked two yellow roses
and 4 red roses. What fraction
of the roses are not red?

More on Equivalent Fractions

To find an equivalent fraction, multiply the numerator
and denominator of a fraction by the same number (not zero).

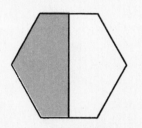

$$\frac{1}{2} = \frac{1 \times 2}{2 \times 2} = \frac{2}{4}$$ Multiply the numerator by 2.

Multiply the denominator by 2.

The fractions $\frac{1}{2}$ and $\frac{2}{4}$ are equivalent.

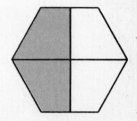

EXERCISES *Fill in each* □ *with a number so that the*
fractions are equivalent.

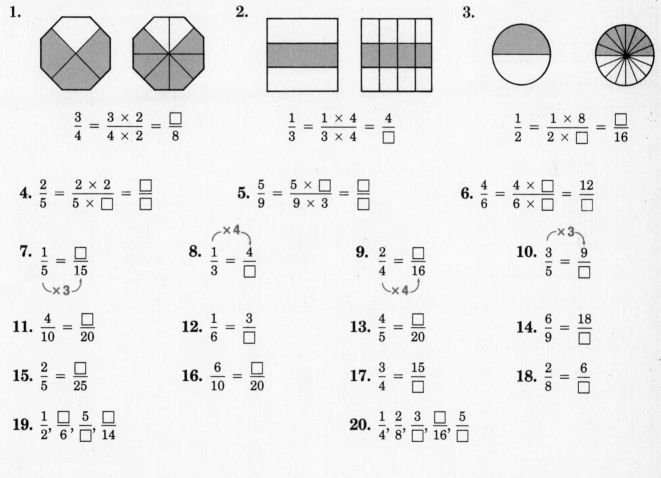

1.

$$\frac{3}{4} = \frac{3 \times 2}{4 \times 2} = \frac{\square}{8}$$

2.

$$\frac{1}{3} = \frac{1 \times 4}{3 \times 4} = \frac{4}{\square}$$

3.

$$\frac{1}{2} = \frac{1 \times 8}{2 \times \square} = \frac{\square}{16}$$

4. $\dfrac{2}{5} = \dfrac{2 \times 2}{5 \times \square} = \dfrac{\square}{\square}$

5. $\dfrac{5}{9} = \dfrac{5 \times \square}{9 \times 3} = \dfrac{\square}{\square}$

6. $\dfrac{4}{6} = \dfrac{4 \times \square}{6 \times \square} = \dfrac{12}{\square}$

7. $\dfrac{1}{5} = \dfrac{\square}{15}$ (×3)

8. $\dfrac{1}{3} = \dfrac{4}{\square}$ (×4)

9. $\dfrac{2}{4} = \dfrac{\square}{16}$ (×4)

10. $\dfrac{3}{5} = \dfrac{9}{\square}$ (×3)

11. $\dfrac{4}{10} = \dfrac{\square}{20}$

12. $\dfrac{1}{6} = \dfrac{3}{\square}$

13. $\dfrac{4}{5} = \dfrac{\square}{20}$

14. $\dfrac{6}{9} = \dfrac{18}{\square}$

15. $\dfrac{2}{5} = \dfrac{\square}{25}$

16. $\dfrac{6}{10} = \dfrac{\square}{20}$

17. $\dfrac{3}{4} = \dfrac{15}{\square}$

18. $\dfrac{2}{8} = \dfrac{6}{\square}$

19. $\dfrac{1}{2}, \dfrac{\square}{6}, \dfrac{5}{\square}, \dfrac{\square}{14}$

20. $\dfrac{1}{4}, \dfrac{2}{8}, \dfrac{3}{\square}, \dfrac{\square}{16}, \dfrac{5}{\square}$

Solve.

21. Jack read $\dfrac{2}{3}$ of his book.

How many ninths did he read?

22. Donna walked $\dfrac{3}{4}$ of a mile.

How many twelfths is this?

Dividing to Find Equivalent Fractions

You can find an equivalent fraction by dividing the numerator
and denominator by a common factor greater than 1.

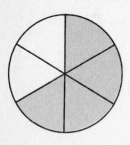

$$\frac{4}{6} = \frac{4 \div 2}{6 \div 2} = \frac{2}{3}$$

Divide the numerator by 2.
Divide the denominator by 2.

The fractions $\frac{4}{6}$ and $\frac{2}{3}$ are equivalent.

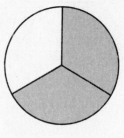

EXERCISES *Fill in each* ☐ *with a number so that the*
fractions are equivalent.

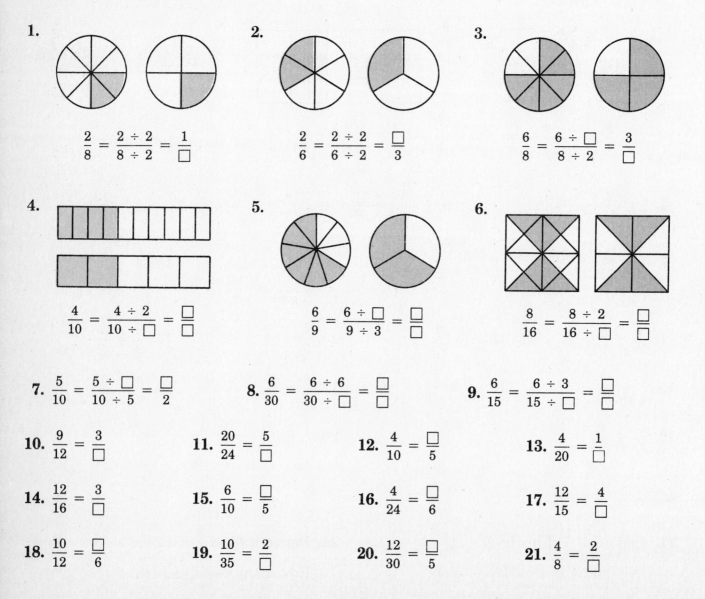

1.

$$\frac{2}{8} = \frac{2 \div 2}{8 \div 2} = \frac{1}{\square}$$

2.

$$\frac{2}{6} = \frac{2 \div 2}{6 \div 2} = \frac{\square}{3}$$

3.

$$\frac{6}{8} = \frac{6 \div \square}{8 \div 2} = \frac{3}{\square}$$

4.

$$\frac{4}{10} = \frac{4 \div 2}{10 \div \square} = \frac{\square}{\square}$$

5.

$$\frac{6}{9} = \frac{6 \div \square}{9 \div 3} = \frac{\square}{\square}$$

6.

$$\frac{8}{16} = \frac{8 \div 2}{16 \div \square} = \frac{\square}{\square}$$

7. $\frac{5}{10} = \frac{5 \div \square}{10 \div 5} = \frac{\square}{2}$

8. $\frac{6}{30} = \frac{6 \div 6}{30 \div \square} = \frac{\square}{\square}$

9. $\frac{6}{15} = \frac{6 \div 3}{15 \div \square} = \frac{\square}{\square}$

10. $\frac{9}{12} = \frac{3}{\square}$

11. $\frac{20}{24} = \frac{5}{\square}$

12. $\frac{4}{10} = \frac{\square}{5}$

13. $\frac{4}{20} = \frac{1}{\square}$

14. $\frac{12}{16} = \frac{3}{\square}$

15. $\frac{6}{10} = \frac{\square}{5}$

16. $\frac{4}{24} = \frac{\square}{6}$

17. $\frac{12}{15} = \frac{4}{\square}$

18. $\frac{10}{12} = \frac{\square}{6}$

19. $\frac{10}{35} = \frac{2}{\square}$

20. $\frac{12}{30} = \frac{\square}{5}$

21. $\frac{4}{8} = \frac{2}{\square}$

Patterns in Computation: Equivalent Fractions

There are many fractions that name the number 1.

$$1 = \frac{1}{1} = \frac{4}{4} = \frac{52}{52} = \frac{341}{341} = \frac{2,581}{2,581} \text{ and so on.}$$

When you multiply a number by 1, the product is that number. Study the pattern below.

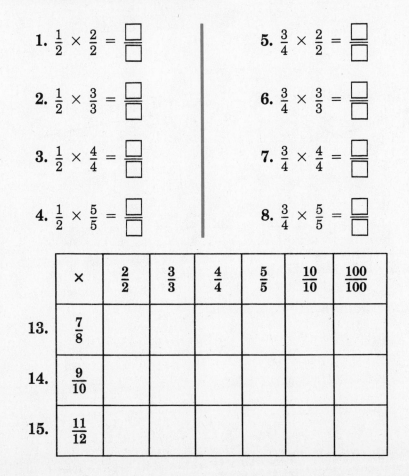

$$\frac{1}{3} \times \frac{1}{1} = \frac{1}{3} \qquad \frac{1}{3} \times \frac{2}{2} = \frac{2}{6} \qquad \frac{1}{3} \times \frac{3}{3} = \frac{3}{9}$$

$$\frac{2}{3} \times \frac{1}{1} = \frac{2}{3} \qquad \frac{2}{3} \times \frac{2}{2} = \frac{4}{6} \qquad \frac{2}{3} \times \frac{3}{3} = \frac{6}{9}$$

Complete. Use the pattern.

1. $\frac{1}{2} \times \frac{2}{2} = \frac{\square}{\square}$

2. $\frac{1}{2} \times \frac{3}{3} = \frac{\square}{\square}$

3. $\frac{1}{2} \times \frac{4}{4} = \frac{\square}{\square}$

4. $\frac{1}{2} \times \frac{5}{5} = \frac{\square}{\square}$

5. $\frac{3}{4} \times \frac{2}{2} = \frac{\square}{\square}$

6. $\frac{3}{4} \times \frac{3}{3} = \frac{\square}{\square}$

7. $\frac{3}{4} \times \frac{4}{4} = \frac{\square}{\square}$

8. $\frac{3}{4} \times \frac{5}{5} = \frac{\square}{\square}$

9. $\frac{10}{11} \times \frac{2}{2} = \frac{\square}{\square}$

10. $\frac{10}{11} \times \frac{3}{3} = \frac{\square}{\square}$

11. $\frac{10}{11} \times \frac{4}{4} = \frac{\square}{\square}$

12. $\frac{10}{11} \times \frac{5}{5} = \frac{\square}{\square}$

	×	$\frac{2}{2}$	$\frac{3}{3}$	$\frac{4}{4}$	$\frac{5}{5}$	$\frac{10}{10}$	$\frac{100}{100}$
13.	$\frac{7}{8}$						
14.	$\frac{9}{10}$						
15.	$\frac{11}{12}$						

Maintenance

Fill each ◯ with <, >, or = to make a true sentence.

1. 629 ◯ 647

2. 5,382 ◯ 5,328

3. $0.75 ◯ 75¢

Write the fact family for each group of numbers.

4. 6, 30, 5

5. 1, 9, 9

6. 36, 9, 4

Multiply or divide.

7. 452 × 8

8. 6)‾84‾

9. 32 × 48

10. 4)‾514‾

11. 3,000 × 6

12. 7)‾75‾

Estimate.

13. 227
    + 681

14. 6,250
    − 4,824

15. 716
    ×   5

16. 391
    × 22

Write a name for each figure.

17.

18.

19.

Name a fraction for the shaded part.

20.

21.

22.

Fill in each ☐ with a number so that the fractions are equivalent.

23. $\frac{2}{3} = \frac{2 \times \square}{3 \times \square} = \frac{\square}{12}$

24. $\frac{10}{12} = \frac{10 \div 2}{12 \div \square} = \frac{\square}{6}$

25. $\frac{8}{16} = \frac{8 \div \square}{16 \div \square} = \frac{1}{\square}$

Solve.

26. Notebook paper costs 99¢. Karen had 9 pennies, 7 nickels,
    and 5 dimes. Does she have enough money to buy the paper?

Fractions in Simplest Form

A fraction is in **simplest form** when the numerator and denominator have no common factors greater than 1.

You can write the simplest form of $\frac{18}{24}$ as follows.

Divide the numerator and denominator by a common factor.

$$\frac{18}{24} = \frac{18 \div 3}{24 \div 3} = \frac{6}{8} \quad \blacktriangleright \quad \frac{6}{8} = \frac{6 \div 2}{8 \div 2} = \frac{3}{4}$$

To save time, you could have divided by the greatest common factor.

$$\frac{18}{24} = \frac{18 \div 6}{24 \div 6} = \frac{3}{4}$$

EXERCISES *Is the fraction in simplest form? Write YES or NO.*

1. $\frac{12}{18}$

2. $\frac{15}{25}$

3. $\frac{7}{12}$

4. $\frac{6}{21}$

5. $\frac{3}{15}$

6. $\frac{9}{14}$

7. $\frac{25}{30}$

8. $\frac{9}{81}$

Write an equivalent fraction in simplest form.

9. $\frac{9}{15}$

10. $\frac{8}{36}$

11. $\frac{5}{20}$

12. $\frac{8}{12}$

13. $\frac{6}{14}$

14. $\frac{4}{24}$

15. $\frac{4}{20}$

16. $\frac{20}{36}$

17. $\frac{15}{40}$

18. $\frac{12}{21}$

19. $\frac{20}{25}$

20. $\frac{6}{9}$

21. $\frac{3}{15}$

22. $\frac{4}{14}$

23. $\frac{9}{72}$

24. $\frac{10}{100}$

Solve. Write each answer in simplest form.

25. Mark has 3 red pens and 9 blue pens. What fraction of his pens are blue?

26. A class has 15 girls and 15 boys. What fraction of the students are girls?

Comparing and Ordering Fractions

To compare fractions with the same denominator, compare the numerator.

Compare $\frac{4}{7}$ and $\frac{3}{7}$.

Since $4 > 3$, then $\frac{4}{7} > \frac{3}{7}$.

Use equivalent fractions to compare fractions with different denominators.

Compare $\frac{2}{5}$ and $\frac{5}{15}$.

$$\frac{2}{5} = \frac{2 \times 3}{5 \times 3} = \frac{6}{15}$$

Since $\frac{6}{15} > \frac{5}{15}$, then $\frac{2}{5} > \frac{5}{15}$.

EXERCISES *Fill in each* $\bigcirc$ *with* $<, >,$ *or* $=$ *to make a true sentence.*

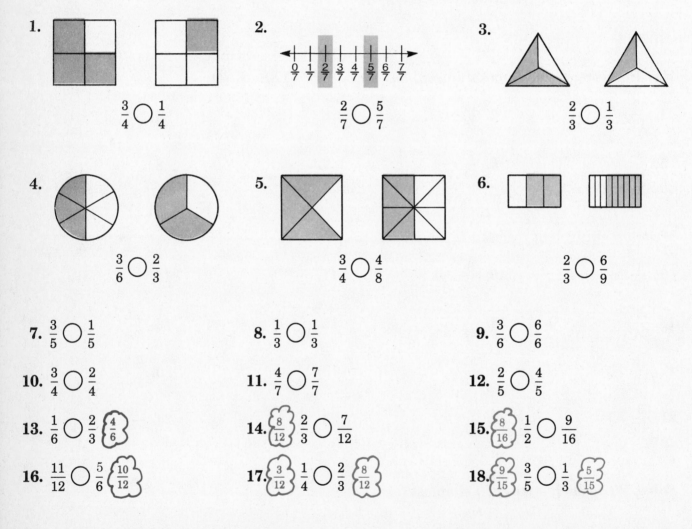

1. $\frac{3}{4} \bigcirc \frac{1}{4}$

2. $\frac{2}{7} \bigcirc \frac{5}{7}$

3. $\frac{2}{3} \bigcirc \frac{1}{3}$

4. $\frac{3}{6} \bigcirc \frac{2}{3}$

5. $\frac{3}{4} \bigcirc \frac{4}{8}$

6. $\frac{2}{3} \bigcirc \frac{6}{9}$

7. $\frac{3}{5} \bigcirc \frac{1}{5}$

8. $\frac{1}{3} \bigcirc \frac{1}{3}$

9. $\frac{3}{6} \bigcirc \frac{6}{6}$

10. $\frac{3}{4} \bigcirc \frac{2}{4}$

11. $\frac{4}{7} \bigcirc \frac{7}{7}$

12. $\frac{2}{5} \bigcirc \frac{4}{5}$

13. $\frac{1}{6} \bigcirc \frac{2}{3} \left\{\frac{4}{6}\right\}$

14. $\left\{\frac{8}{12}\right\} \frac{2}{3} \bigcirc \frac{7}{12}$

15. $\left\{\frac{8}{16}\right\} \frac{1}{2} \bigcirc \frac{9}{16}$

16. $\frac{11}{12} \bigcirc \frac{5}{6} \left\{\frac{10}{12}\right\}$

17. $\left\{\frac{3}{12}\right\} \frac{1}{4} \bigcirc \frac{2}{3} \left\{\frac{8}{12}\right\}$

18. $\left\{\frac{9}{15}\right\} \frac{3}{5} \bigcirc \frac{1}{3} \left\{\frac{5}{15}\right\}$

Order the fraction from least to greatest.

19. $\frac{6}{11}, \frac{8}{11}, \frac{3}{11}, \frac{10}{11}$

20. $\frac{1}{6}, \frac{5}{12}, \frac{5}{6}, \frac{7}{12}$

Mixed Numerals and Fractions

Fractions like $\frac{5}{3}$, $\frac{4}{2}$, and $\frac{3}{3}$ are called **improper fractions**. The numerator is greater than or equal to the denominator.

A **mixed numeral**, such as $2\frac{2}{3}$, has a whole number part and a fractional part.

Improper fractions and mixed numerals can be shown on a number line.

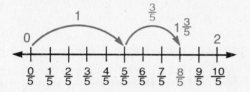

The number line shows both $1\frac{3}{5}$ and $\frac{8}{5}$.

To change an improper fraction to a mixed numeral, divide the numerator by the denominator. Write the remainder as a fraction.

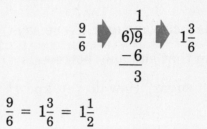

$$\frac{9}{6} = 1\frac{3}{6} = 1\frac{1}{2}$$

EXERCISES   *Fill in each $\bigcirc$ with <, >, or = to make a true sentence.*

1. $\frac{5}{2} \bigcirc 1$ 2. $\frac{2}{3} \bigcirc 1$ 3. $\frac{12}{8} \bigcirc 1$ 4. $\frac{6}{6} \bigcirc 1$

Write the letter for each of the following.

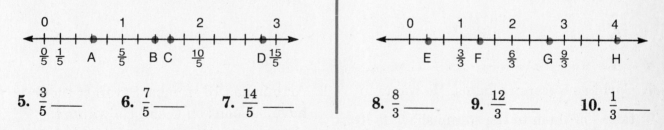

5. $\frac{3}{5}$ ____   6. $\frac{7}{5}$ ____   7. $\frac{14}{5}$ ____   8. $\frac{8}{3}$ ____   9. $\frac{12}{3}$ ____   10. $\frac{1}{3}$ ____

Write each improper fraction as a whole number or a mixed numeral.
Write the fraction part in simplest form.

11. $\frac{13}{5}$ 12. $\frac{14}{4}$ 13. $\frac{5}{3}$ 14. $\frac{11}{4}$

15. $\frac{12}{8}$ 16. $\frac{18}{6}$ 17. $\frac{22}{5}$ 18. $\frac{28}{3}$

Problem Solving

***EXERCISES Solve. You may wish to draw a picture to
help solve each problem.***

1. Joe has 8 cars. Four of them are blue.
   What fraction of Joe's cars are blue?

2. Harold walks $\frac{1}{2}$ mile to school. Tony rides
   his bike $\frac{5}{10}$ mile to school. Do they live
   the same distance from school? How
   do you know?

3. Helen needs $\frac{1}{2}$ cup of sugar. Steve says
   he has $\frac{2}{4}$ cup that she may borrow. Is
   that enough sugar? How do you know?

4. A piece of board was $\frac{3}{8}$ inches too long
   for the shelf. Tina decided to saw off
   $\frac{3}{4}$ inch. Did she saw off the correct
   amount? How do you know?

5. Three of Joe's six sweat shirts needed
   to be washed. He said that $\frac{1}{2}$ of his
   sweat shirts were dirty. Was he
   correct? How do you know?

6. Sue bought a new roll of film. Now she
   can take 24 photos. She said she will
   take photos of her dog with $\frac{1}{3}$ of them.
   How many photos will Sue take of her
   dog?

7. Carl has 8 stamp albums. He wants to
   take $\frac{3}{4}$ of them to the stamp show. Is it
   possible to do that? How many albums
   will he take?

8. Arthur has 16 stamps. Seven of them
   have balloons on them. He wants to
   trade so that $\frac{1}{2}$ of his stamps will have
   balloons. How many stamps must he
   trade?

Problem Solving

Sometimes you have to work backwards to solve problems.

Li Chen gave Patty $2.00. Then he gave Peter half of the money that he had left. Now Li Chen has $3.00. How much money did Li Chen start with?

Use the plan below to solve the problem.

Read the problem.	▶	Decide what to do.	▶	Solve the problem.	▶	Examine the solution.

$3.00 + $3.00 = $6.00

$3.00 was one-half of Li Chen's money. So he had $6.00 before he gave money to Peter.

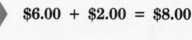 **$6.00 + $2.00 = $8.00**

Li Chen gave $2.00 to Patty.

He started with $8.00.

Solve.

1. Arlo found some shells on the beach. Andy gave him 7 more shells. Now, Arlo has 13 shells. How many shells did Arlo find on the beach?

2. Mrs. Otis bought some apples at the store. Cara and her friends ate 4 apples. Now Mrs. Otis has 8 apples left. How many apples did Mrs. Otis buy?

3. Heather had some stickers. She divided the stickers among her 5 best friends. Each friend received 7 stickers. How many stickers did Heather start with?

4. Ten students bought a plant for their teacher. The plant cost $5. The cost was divided among the students. How much did each student pay?

5. Ned is buying an eraser. He gives the clerk 50¢. The clerk gives Ned 11¢ in change. What is the price of the eraser?

6. Mr. Frederick made meatballs. He gave each of the 5 family members 2 meatballs. There are 3 meatballs left over. How many meatballs did Mr. Frederick make?

Chapter 10 Test

Write a fraction for the shaded part.

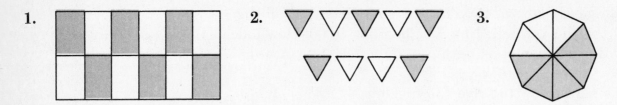

1. 2. 3.

Fill in the ☐ with a number so that the fractions are equivalent.

4. $\dfrac{1}{5} = \dfrac{\square}{15}$ 5. $\dfrac{9}{18} = \dfrac{3}{\square}$ 6. $\dfrac{3}{8} = \dfrac{12}{\square}$ 7. $\dfrac{10}{16} = \dfrac{\square}{8}$

8. $\dfrac{15}{20} = \dfrac{3}{\square}$ 9. $\dfrac{8}{10} = \dfrac{\square}{5}$ 10. $\dfrac{2}{3} = \dfrac{8}{\square}$ 11. $\dfrac{2}{9} = \dfrac{\square}{27}$

Write each fraction in simplest form.

12. $\dfrac{6}{10}$ 13. $\dfrac{8}{13}$ 14. $\dfrac{9}{18}$

Order the fractions from least to greatest.

15. $\dfrac{4}{6}, \dfrac{3}{6}, \dfrac{5}{6}, \dfrac{2}{6}$ 16. $\dfrac{3}{4}, \dfrac{3}{8}, \dfrac{1}{4}, \dfrac{7}{8}$

Write each improper fraction as a whole number or a mixed numeral. Write the fraction part in simplest form.

17. $\dfrac{5}{2}$ 18. $\dfrac{25}{10}$ 19. $\dfrac{19}{4}$ 20. $\dfrac{21}{21}$

Solve. Write each answer in simplest form.

21. Sam has 6 pairs of black socks and 9 pairs of blue socks. What fraction of his socks are blue?

22. Tammy cut some sandwiches into halves. She had 8 pieces. How many whole sandwiches did she have at the beginning?

Add or subtract. Write each answer in simplest form.

1. $\frac{1}{5} + \frac{1}{5}$

2. $\frac{1}{8} + \frac{5}{8}$

3. $\frac{2}{10} + \frac{3}{10}$

4. $\frac{7}{12} + \frac{2}{12}$

5. $\frac{6}{7} - \frac{3}{7}$

6. $\frac{7}{9} - \frac{4}{9}$

7. $\frac{11}{12} - \frac{3}{12}$

8. $\frac{9}{10} - \frac{1}{10}$

Add or subtract. Write each answer in simplest form.

1. $\frac{1}{2} + \frac{3}{8}$

2. $\frac{5}{12} - \frac{1}{4}$

3. $\frac{1}{3} + \frac{1}{6}$

4. $\frac{2}{3} - \frac{1}{4}$

5. $\frac{4}{5} - \frac{3}{10}$

6. $\frac{1}{4} + \frac{3}{8}$

7. $\frac{3}{4} - \frac{3}{8}$

8. $\frac{9}{16} + \frac{1}{4}$

9. $\frac{3}{10} + \frac{1}{5}$

10. $\frac{8}{9} - \frac{5}{6}$

11. $\frac{3}{4} + \frac{1}{6}$

12. $\frac{1}{2} - \frac{1}{6}$

Complete.

13. $\frac{1}{6}$ of 12 = ☐

14. $\frac{2}{3}$ of 15 = ☐

15. $\frac{4}{9}$ of 27 = ☐

16. $\frac{2}{7}$ of 28 = ☐

Solve.

17. Mrs. Kline spent $\frac{1}{3}$ hour reading and $\frac{1}{3}$ hour planting flowers. How much time did she spend reading and planting flowers?

18. Andy needs $\frac{3}{4}$ cup milk to make a sauce. He has $\frac{1}{4}$ cup milk. How much more milk does he need?

Adding Fractions with Same Denominators

Find the sum of $\frac{9}{16}$ and $\frac{3}{16}$. The fractions have the same denominator.

First, add the numerators.

Next, write the sum over the denominator.

Then, write the fraction in simplest form.

$$\frac{9}{16} + \frac{3}{16} \Rightarrow \frac{9+3}{16} \Rightarrow \frac{12}{16} \Rightarrow \frac{12 \div 4}{16 \div 4} = \frac{3}{4}$$

EXERCISES *Complete.*

1.

$\frac{2}{5} + \frac{1}{5} = \frac{2+1}{5} = \frac{\square}{5}$

2.

$\frac{3}{8} + \frac{2}{8} = \frac{3+2}{8} = \frac{\square}{8}$

3.

$\frac{1}{6} + \frac{4}{6} = \frac{1+4}{6} = \frac{\square}{6}$

4.

$\frac{2}{6} + \frac{1}{6} + \frac{3}{6}$ or $\frac{\square}{\square}$

5.

$\frac{4}{12} + \frac{6}{12} = \frac{\square}{12}$ or $\frac{5}{\square}$

6.

$\frac{1}{4} + \frac{1}{4} = \frac{\square}{4}$ or $\frac{\square}{\square}$

Add. Write each sum in simplest form.

7. $\frac{1}{3} + \frac{1}{3}$

8. $\frac{5}{8} + \frac{2}{8}$

9. $\frac{6}{7} + \frac{3}{7}$

10. $\frac{2}{5} + \frac{3}{5}$

11. $\frac{1}{4} + \frac{2}{4}$

12. $\frac{4}{6} + \frac{4}{6}$

13. $\frac{5}{12} + \frac{5}{12}$

14. $\frac{3}{10} + \frac{8}{10}$

15. $\frac{4}{9}$ $+\frac{3}{9}$

16. $\frac{3}{12}$ $+\frac{9}{12}$

17. $\frac{3}{4}$ $+\frac{2}{4}$

18. $\frac{3}{6}$ $+\frac{3}{6}$

19. $\frac{1}{6}$ $+\frac{2}{6}$

20. $\frac{4}{8}$ $+\frac{7}{8}$

Subtracting Fractions with Same Denominators

Subtract $\frac{3}{9}$ from $\frac{6}{9}$. These fractions have the same denominator.

First, subtract the numerators.

$$\frac{6}{9} - \frac{3}{9} = \frac{6-3}{9}$$

Next, write the difference over the denominator.

$$\frac{3}{9}$$

Then, write the fraction in simplest form.

$$\frac{3 \div 3}{9 \div 3} = \frac{1}{3}$$

EXERCISES *Complete.*

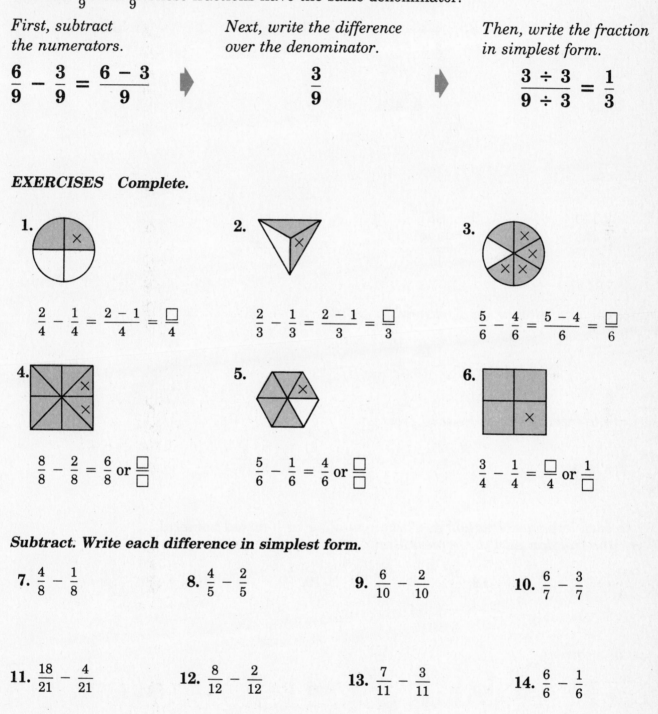

1. $\frac{2}{4} - \frac{1}{4} = \frac{2-1}{4} = \frac{\square}{4}$

2. $\frac{2}{3} - \frac{1}{3} = \frac{2-1}{3} = \frac{\square}{3}$

3. $\frac{5}{6} - \frac{4}{6} = \frac{5-4}{6} = \frac{\square}{6}$

4. $\frac{8}{8} - \frac{2}{8} = \frac{6}{8}$ or $\frac{\square}{\square}$

5. $\frac{5}{6} - \frac{1}{6} = \frac{4}{6}$ or $\frac{\square}{\square}$

6. $\frac{3}{4} - \frac{1}{4} = \frac{\square}{4}$ or $\frac{1}{\square}$

Subtract. Write each difference in simplest form.

7. $\frac{4}{8} - \frac{1}{8}$

8. $\frac{4}{5} - \frac{2}{5}$

9. $\frac{6}{10} - \frac{2}{10}$

10. $\frac{6}{7} - \frac{3}{7}$

11. $\frac{18}{21} - \frac{4}{21}$

12. $\frac{8}{12} - \frac{2}{12}$

13. $\frac{7}{11} - \frac{3}{11}$

14. $\frac{6}{6} - \frac{1}{6}$

15. $\frac{15}{16}$
    $-\frac{3}{16}$

16. $\frac{16}{18}$
    $-\frac{9}{18}$

17. $\frac{5}{6}$
    $-\frac{2}{6}$

18. $\frac{11}{12}$
    $-\frac{3}{12}$

19. $\frac{10}{15}$
    $-\frac{6}{15}$

20. $\frac{13}{14}$
    $-\frac{6}{14}$

Maintenance

Add, subtract, multiply, or divide.

1. $93.25
    + 52.88

2. 6,284
    − 2,376

3. 5,912
    × 8

4. 6)58

5. $8.15 × 21

6. 428 + 631 + 98

7. 10 × 5 × 3

Estimate.

8. 2,743
    +5,485

9. 951
    −439

10. 298
     × 9

11. 63
     ×47

Write each fraction in simplest form.

12. $\frac{6}{8}$

13. $\frac{10}{12}$

14. $\frac{12}{18}$

Order the fractions from least to greatest.

15. $\frac{6}{8}, \frac{7}{8}, \frac{4}{8}, \frac{3}{8}$

16. $\frac{9}{10}, \frac{2}{5}, \frac{6}{10}$

Write each improper fraction as a whole number or a mixed numeral. Write the fraction part in simplest form.

17. $\frac{18}{4}$

18. $\frac{15}{5}$

19. $\frac{22}{7}$

20. $\frac{24}{12}$

Add or subtract.

21. $\frac{2}{8} + \frac{3}{8}$

22. $\frac{8}{9} - \frac{3}{9}$

23. $\frac{1}{3} + \frac{1}{3}$

24. $\frac{11}{12} - \frac{6}{12}$

Solve.

25. Maria lives $\frac{1}{4}$ mile from her school. How far does Maria walk

to and from school in one day?

Adding Fractions with Different Denominators

Find the sum of $\frac{1}{2}$ and $\frac{1}{3}$. These fractions have different denominators.

First, find a common denominator.   *Write equivalent fractions.*   *Add.*

$$\frac{1}{2}$$ multiples of 2: 2, 4, 6, 8, . . .

$$+\frac{1}{3}$$ multiples of 3: 3, 6, 9, . . .

$$\frac{1}{2} = \frac{3}{6}$$
$$+\frac{1}{3} = \frac{2}{6}$$

$$\frac{3}{6}$$
$$+\frac{2}{6}$$
$$\frac{5}{6}$$

Is the answer in simplest form?

EXERCISES   Complete. Then add.

1. $\frac{1}{3} = \frac{\square}{15}$
    $+\frac{2}{5} = \frac{\square}{15}$

2. $\frac{1}{2} = \frac{\square}{4}$
    $+\frac{1}{4} = \frac{1}{4}$

3. $\frac{2}{5} = \frac{\square}{10}$
    $+\frac{1}{2} = \frac{\square}{10}$

4. $\frac{1}{7} = \frac{\square}{21}$
    $+\frac{2}{3} = \frac{\square}{21}$

Add. Write each sum in simplest form.

5. $\frac{1}{10}$
    $+\frac{1}{2}$

6. $\frac{2}{3}$
    $+\frac{1}{9}$

7. $\frac{5}{16}$
    $+\frac{1}{4}$

8. $\frac{5}{6}$
    $+\frac{1}{12}$

9. $\frac{2}{3}$
    $+\frac{4}{5}$

10. $\frac{1}{3}$
    $+\frac{5}{12}$

11. $\frac{1}{3}$
    $+\frac{2}{4}$

12. $\frac{2}{5}$
    $+\frac{6}{10}$

13. $\frac{2}{7}$
    $+\frac{12}{21}$

14. $\frac{2}{3}$
    $+\frac{1}{6}$

15. $\frac{1}{4}$
    $+\frac{5}{12}$

16. $\frac{3}{4}$
    $+\frac{3}{16}$

Patterns in Computation: Adding Fractions

You can use models to add fractions with different denominators.
Study the pattern below.

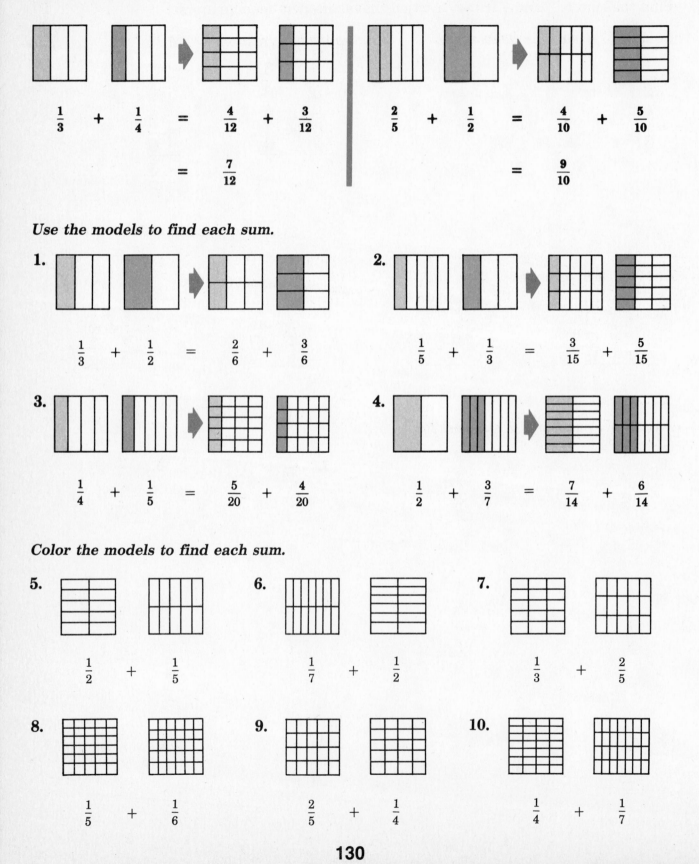

$$\frac{1}{3} + \frac{1}{4} = \frac{4}{12} + \frac{3}{12}$$

$$= \frac{7}{12}$$

$$\frac{2}{5} + \frac{1}{2} = \frac{4}{10} + \frac{5}{10}$$

$$= \frac{9}{10}$$

Use the models to find each sum.

1. $\frac{1}{3} + \frac{1}{2} = \frac{2}{6} + \frac{3}{6}$

2. $\frac{1}{5} + \frac{1}{3} = \frac{3}{15} + \frac{5}{15}$

3. $\frac{1}{4} + \frac{1}{5} = \frac{5}{20} + \frac{4}{20}$

4. $\frac{1}{2} + \frac{3}{7} = \frac{7}{14} + \frac{6}{14}$

Color the models to find each sum.

5. $\frac{1}{2} + \frac{1}{5}$

6. $\frac{1}{7} + \frac{1}{2}$

7. $\frac{1}{3} + \frac{2}{5}$

8. $\frac{1}{5} + \frac{1}{6}$

9. $\frac{2}{5} + \frac{1}{4}$

10. $\frac{1}{4} + \frac{1}{7}$

Subtracting Fractions with Different Denominators

Subtract $\frac{1}{2}$ from $\frac{3}{5}$. These fractions have different denominators.

First, find a common denominator.   *Write equivalent fractions.*   *Subtract.*

$\frac{3}{5}$ multiples of 5: 5, 10, 15, . . .

$-\frac{1}{2}$ multiples of 2: 2, 4, 6, 8, 10 . . .

$\frac{3}{5} = \frac{6}{10}$

$-\frac{1}{2} = \frac{5}{10}$

$\frac{6}{10}$

$-\frac{5}{10}$

$\frac{1}{10}$ Is the answer in simplest form?

EXERCISES   Complete. Then subtract.

1. $\frac{4}{5} = \frac{\square}{15}$
   $-\frac{2}{3} = \frac{\square}{15}$

2. $\frac{3}{4} = \frac{\square}{12}$
   $-\frac{1}{6} = \frac{\square}{12}$

3. $\frac{4}{5} = \frac{\square}{10}$
   $-\frac{1}{10} = \frac{\square}{10}$

4. $\frac{1}{2} = \frac{\square}{6}$
   $-\frac{1}{3} = \frac{\square}{6}$

Subtract. Write each difference in simplest form.

5. $\frac{3}{4}$
   $-\frac{1}{12}$

6. $\frac{1}{2}$
   $-\frac{3}{8}$

7. $\frac{5}{6}$
   $-\frac{1}{3}$

8. $\frac{2}{3}$
   $-\frac{4}{15}$

9. $\frac{4}{5}$
   $-\frac{1}{2}$

10. $\frac{2}{3}$
    $-\frac{1}{2}$

11. $\frac{7}{10}$
    $-\frac{2}{5}$

12. $\frac{3}{4}$
    $-\frac{1}{3}$

13. $\frac{7}{8}$
    $-\frac{1}{4}$

14. $\frac{9}{16}$
    $-\frac{1}{2}$

15. $\frac{1}{2}$
    $-\frac{1}{6}$

16. $\frac{3}{8}$
    $-\frac{1}{16}$

Fraction of a Number

Find $\frac{3}{4}$ of 8.

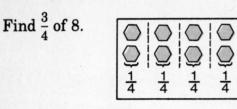

The denominator, 4, tells you to divide 8 into 4 groups of the same size.

First, find $\frac{1}{4}$ of 8.

$$\begin{array}{r} 2 \\ 4\overline{)8} \\ -8 \\ \hline 0 \end{array}$$

$\frac{1}{4}$ of 8 = 2

Then, multiply to find $\frac{3}{4}$ of 8.

Since $\frac{1}{4}$ of 8 is 2, multiply 3 by 2.

$$\begin{array}{r} 2 \\ \times 3 \\ \hline 6 \end{array}$$

$\frac{3}{4}$ of 8 = 6

EXERCISES *Complete.*

1.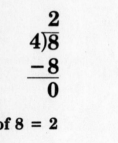

$\frac{1}{2}$ of 8 = ☐

2. ⬜ ○ ○ ● ○ ○ ⬜

$\frac{1}{5}$ of 5 = ☐

3. △△△△ △△△△ ▲▲▲▲

$\frac{1}{3}$ of 12 = ☐

4. $\frac{1}{6}$ of 12 = ☐

5. $\frac{1}{4}$ of 20 = ☐

6. $\frac{1}{8}$ of 24 = ☐

7. $\frac{1}{7}$ of 21 = ☐

8. $\frac{1}{2}$ of 20 = ☐

9. $\frac{1}{9}$ of 27 = ☐

10. ◇◇◇◇◇ ◇◇◇◇◇

$\frac{2}{5}$ of 10 = ☐

11. ○○○ ○○○ ○○○ ○○○

$\frac{3}{4}$ of 12 = ☐

12. ○○○○○○○○ ○○○○○○○○

$\frac{7}{8}$ of 16 = ☐

13. $\frac{2}{3}$ of 18 = ☐

14. $\frac{4}{7}$ of 14 = ☐

15. $\frac{5}{6}$ of 18 = ☐

16. $\frac{4}{5}$ of 20 = ☐

17. $\frac{5}{8}$ of 24 = ☐

18. $\frac{7}{9}$ of 27 = ☐

Problem Solving

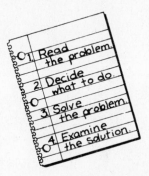

EXERCISES *Solve.*

1. Sarah has $\frac{3}{4}$ of a set of baseball cards. Hal has $\frac{1}{4}$ of a set. How much more does Sarah have?

2. Julie has $\frac{3}{8}$ of a yard of ribbon. She needs $\frac{5}{8}$ of a yard. How much more ribbon does she need?

3. After Fernandez gave $\frac{2}{5}$ of a pack of gum away, he has $\frac{1}{5}$ of a pack left. How much gum did he have in the beginning?

4. Dorian had some eggs. After he borrows $\frac{1}{4}$ of a dozen, he has $\frac{3}{4}$ of a dozen. How many eggs did he have in the beginning?

5. Hope ran $\frac{7}{8}$ of a mile. Barbara ran $\frac{2}{8}$ of a mile less than Hope. How far did Barbara run?

6. Marvin used $\frac{5}{8}$ of a cup of sugar for the punch. He has $\frac{7}{8}$ of a cup left. How much sugar did he have in the beginning?

7. Norah uses $\frac{2}{3}$ of a cup of white flour and $\frac{2}{3}$ of a cup of wheat flour in the bread. How much flour does she use in all?

8. Gerhardt read for $\frac{1}{4}$ of an hour. Scott read for $\frac{1}{4}$ of an hour longer than Gerhardt. How long did Scott read?

Name _____

Problem Solving

Horace drinks $\frac{2}{3}$ of a canteen of water.

Brad drinks $\frac{5}{6}$ of a canteen of water.

Who drinks more water?

Use the plan below to solve the problem.

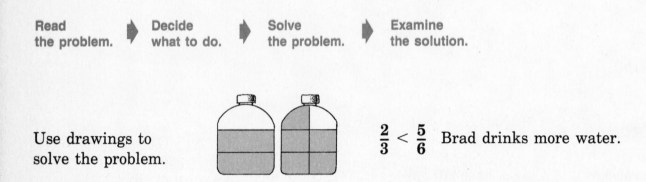

Read the problem. ▶ **Decide** what to do. ▶ **Solve** the problem. ▶ **Examine** the solution.

Use drawings to solve the problem.

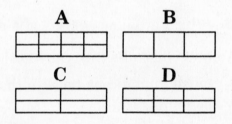

$\frac{2}{3} < \frac{5}{6}$ Brad drinks more water.

EXERCISES *Write the letter of two drawings that would help solve this problem.*

1. _____ Mother used $\frac{3}{8}$ pound of _____ butter making a cake and $\frac{1}{4}$ pound of butter making a pie. Which took the most butter?

A **B**
C **D**

Match each drawing with a problem. Then solve.

2. _____ Peggy wrote $\frac{3}{8}$ of the story.

Jamie wrote $\frac{1}{2}$ of the story.

Who wrote the most? _____

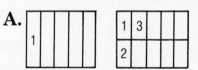

A.

3. _____ Jerry ate $\frac{1}{5}$ of a cake. Jill ate $\frac{3}{10}$ of a cake. Who ate less cake? _____

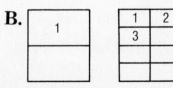

B.

134

Copyright © 1988 by Merrill Publishing Co., Columbus, Ohio 43216

Chapter 11 Test

Add. Write the sum in simplest form.

1. $\frac{2}{8} + \frac{4}{8}$

2. $\frac{3}{10} + \frac{2}{10}$

3. $\frac{7}{14} + \frac{2}{14}$

4. $\frac{8}{12} + \frac{5}{12}$

5. $\begin{array}{r} \frac{1}{3} \\ + \frac{3}{9} \\ \hline \end{array}$

6. $\begin{array}{r} \frac{3}{8} \\ + \frac{2}{4} \\ \hline \end{array}$

7. $\begin{array}{r} \frac{2}{12} \\ + \frac{2}{3} \\ \hline \end{array}$

8. $\begin{array}{r} \frac{2}{5} \\ + \frac{6}{10} \\ \hline \end{array}$

Subtract. Write the difference in simplest form.

9. $\frac{7}{8} - \frac{3}{8}$

10. $\frac{5}{9} - \frac{2}{9}$

11. $\frac{12}{12} - \frac{8}{12}$

12. $\frac{5}{18} - \frac{4}{18}$

13. $\begin{array}{r} \frac{5}{6} \\ - \frac{1}{3} \\ \hline \end{array}$

14. $\begin{array}{r} \frac{3}{4} \\ - \frac{1}{8} \\ \hline \end{array}$

15. $\begin{array}{r} \frac{9}{12} \\ - \frac{2}{3} \\ \hline \end{array}$

16. $\begin{array}{r} \frac{2}{5} \\ - \frac{1}{3} \\ \hline \end{array}$

Complete.

17. $\frac{1}{3}$ of $21 = \square$

18. $\frac{2}{3}$ of $30 = \square$

19. $\frac{1}{8}$ of $24 = \square$

20. $\frac{4}{5}$ of $25 = \square$

21. $\frac{1}{7}$ of $35 = \square$

22. $\frac{3}{7}$ of $28 = \square$

Solve.

23. Carlos has 18 coins. One third of them are nickels. How many nickels does Carlos have?

24. A bag of potting soil was $\frac{9}{10}$ full. Then Dee used $\frac{5}{10}$ of the bag. How much potting soil was left?

Maintenance

Standardized Format

Directions Work each problem on your own paper. Choose the letter of the correct answer. If the correct answer is not given, choose the letter for *none of the above*. Make no marks on this test.

1. Compute.

$(319 - 43) + 167$

a 367

b 453

c 502

d *none of the above*

2. Which digit is in the thousands place?

76,431

e 4

f 6

g 7

h *none of the above*

3. Which number is greater than 49,038?

a 48,997

b 49,009

c 49,083

d *none of the above*

4. Add.   4,374
               5,296
           +1,859

e 10,417

f 11,529

g 12,008

h *none of the above*

5. Subtract.

$42.50 - $7.99

a $32.49

b $33.69

c $34.51

d *none of the above*

6. Find the number of minutes between the two times.

1:45 and 2:20

e 25

f 30

g 35

h *none of the above*

7. What is the missing factor?

$\square \times 8 = 56$

a 6

b 7

c 8

d *none of the above*

8. Multiply.

   $367
 ×   5

e $1,745

f $1,835

g $1,845

h *none of the above*

9. Multiply.

   8,429
 ×   7

a 59,003

b 59,093

c 59,193

d *none of the above*

10. Multiply.

   4,276
 ×   28

e 118,648

f 119,728

g 120,568

h *none of the above*

11. Choose the best estimate.

36 × 94

a 2,700

b 3,600

c 4,000

d *none of the above*

12. Divide.

4)39

e 8 R3

f 9 R1

g 9 R3

h *none of the above*

13. Divide.

$6\overline{)210}$

a 30

b 35

c 40

d *none of the above*

14. What is the average of these numbers? 33, 27, 21, 19

e 23

f 24

g 25

h *none of the above*

15. What is this figure?

a line segment MN

b line MN

c ray MN

d *none of the above*

16. What fraction of the square is shaded?

e $\frac{3}{5}$

f $\frac{3}{8}$

g $\frac{5}{8}$

h *none of the above*

17. Which fraction is greater than $\frac{3}{4}$?

a $\frac{6}{8}$

b $\frac{7}{8}$

c $\frac{3}{8}$

d *none of the above*

18. Add. $\frac{3}{10} + \frac{4}{10}$

e $\frac{1}{10}$

f $\frac{7}{10}$

g $\frac{7}{20}$

h *none of the above*

19. What is $\frac{3}{4}$ of 20?

a 14

b 16

c 18

d *none of the above*

20. Which of the following shows intersecting lines?

e

g

f

h *none of the above*

21. Diane has 58 pictures to put in an album. She can put 4 pictures on a page. How many pages does she need?

a 13

b 14

c 15

d *none of the above*

22. There are 18 airplanes. Each airplane has 144 seats. How many seats are there?

e 1,296

f 2,194

g 2,592

h *none of the above*

Choose the more reasonable measurement.

1. paper clip

   3 g   3 kg

2. teacup

   200 L   200 mL

3. height of a doorway

   2 km   2 m

4. carton of sour cream

   2 c   2 gal

5. dog

   24 oz   24 lb

6. length of a shoe

   8 in.   8 yd

Complete.

7. 2 m = ☐ cm

8. ☐ kg = 3,000 g

9. 14 mL = ☐ L

10. 24 in. = ☐ ft

11. 7 tons = ☐ lb

12. ☐ qt = 3 gal

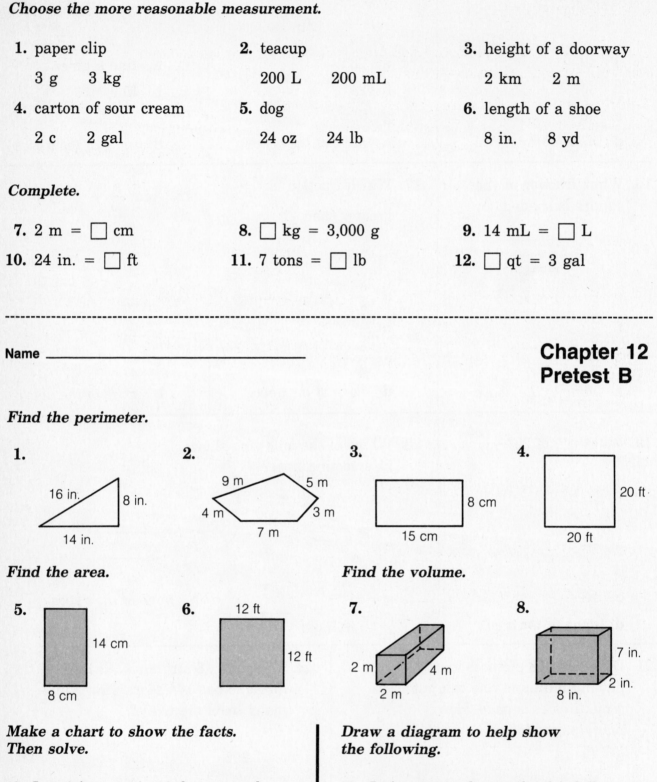

Find the perimeter.

1.
16 in. 8 in.
14 in.

2.
9 m 5 m
4 m 3 m
7 m

3.
8 cm
15 cm

4.
20 ft
20 ft

Find the area.

5.
14 cm
8 cm

6.
12 ft
12 ft

Find the volume.

7.
2 m 4 m
2 m

8.
7 in.
2 in.
8 in.

*Make a chart to show the facts.
Then solve.*

9. Laurie's room is 10 feet on each side. The family room is 10 feet by 15 feet. Which room has the larger perimeter?

Draw a diagram to help show the following.

10. Joe's aunt makes quilts for doll beds out of squares of material 4 inches on each side. What will the area be of a quilt that is made from 6 squares?

Centimeters, Meters, and Kilometers

The centimeter (cm), meter (m), and kilometer (km) are the most commonly used metric units of measurement.

A **centimeter** is used to measure small objects or distances. **1 cm**	A **meter** is 100 centimeters. It is used to measure larger objects or greater distances.	A **kilometer** is 1,000 meters. It is used to measure the greatest distances.

EXERCISES *Measure the length to the nearest centimeter.*

1. ▬▬▬▬▬▬▬▬▬▬▬   2. ▬▬▬▬▬▬

Name the unit that is best to measure each of the following.
Write CENTIMETER, METER, or KILOMETER.

3. length of a river

4. length of a toothbrush

5. width of a dollar bill

6. width of your bed

7. distance from where you live to school

Choose the most reasonable measurement.

8. length of a baseball bat	1 cm	1 m	1 km
9. height of a mountain	5 cm	5 m	5 km
10. thickness of a book	2 cm	2 m	2 km

Complete.

3 m = _____ cm 3 × 100 = 300 3 m = 300 cm	You need to change a larger unit to a smaller unit. So, *multiply.*

11. 8 m = _____ cm

12. 5 km = _____ m

13. 3 km = _____ m   14. 4 m = _____ cm   15. 9 km = _____ m

Capacity and Mass

The **liter** (L) and the **milliliter** (mL) are the metric units used to measure liquid.

> **1,000 milliliters = 1 liter**
> **1,000 mL = 1L**

The **gram** (g) and the **kilogram** (kg) are the metric units of mass.

> **1,000 grams = 1 kilogram**
> **1,000 g = 1 kg**

EXERCISES *Choose the unit that is better to measure each of the following. Write LITER or MILLILITER.*

1. a fish tank

2. a glass of juice

3. a drop of water

4. water in a swimming pool

Choose the unit that is better to measure each of the following. Write GRAM or KILOGRAM.

5. a car

6. an apple

7. an earthworm

8. yourself

Choose the more reasonable measurement.

9.

900 g   9 kg

10.

3 L   3 mL

11.

2 g   2 kg

12.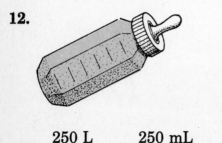

250 L   250 mL

13.

250 g   25 kg

14.

35 L   355 mL

Name _____

Inches, Feet, Yards, and Miles

Inches, feet, yards, and **miles** are the units used to
measure length in the customary system of measurement.
Study the chart below.

12 inches (in.) = 1 foot (ft)	1 mile (mi) = 5,280 feet (ft)
3 feet (ft) = 1 yard (yd)	1 mile (mi) = 1,760 yards (yd)
36 inches (in.) = 1 yard (yd)	

EXERCISES *Measure the length to the nearest inch.*

1.

2.

Measure the length to the nearest half-inch.

3.

4.

Match.

5.	length of a goldfish	**a.**	6 inches
6.	width of a door	**b.**	1 mile
7.	height of a basketball player	**c.**	1 inch
8.	length of 30 city blocks	**d.**	2 yards
9.	length of an envelope	**e.**	1 yard
10.	length of a couch	**f.**	3 miles
11.	length of a 15 minute walk	**g.**	6 feet

Complete.

2 yd = _____ ft 1 yd = 3 ft 3 × 2 = 6 2 yd = 6 ft	**To change from a larger unit to a smaller unit, *multiply.***

12. 3 yd = _____ ft   **13.** 4 ft = _____ in.

14. 2 yd = _____ in.   **15.** 2 mi = _____ ft.

Capacity and Weight

Cups, pints, quarts, and **gallons** are used to measure liquids in the customary system.

> **2 cups (c) = 1 pint (pt)**
> **2 pints (pt) = 1 quart (qt)**
> **4 quarts (qt) = 1 gallon (gal)**

Ounces, pounds, and **tons** are used to measure weight in the customary system.

> **16 ounces (oz) = 1 pound (lb)**
> **2,000 pounds (lb) = 1 ton**

EXERCISES   Choose the unit that is better to measure each of the following. Write CUPS or GALLONS.

1. a glass of juice

2. water for a garden

3. water for one plant

4. a thermos bottle

5. water to wash a car

6. milk for hot chocolate

Complete each sentence. Use oz, lb, or ton.

7. A baby weighs about 8 _____.

8. A bicycle weighs about 30 _____.

9. A slice of cheese weighs about 1 _____.

10. A gray whale weighs about 40 _____.

11. An airplane weighs about 10 _____.

12. A tube of toothpaste weighs about 9 _____.

Complete.

> 2 pts = _____ c
>
> 2 × 2 = 4
> 2 pt = 4 c

You need to change a larger unit to a smaller unit. So, *multiply*.

13. 4 pt = _____ c

14. 7 qt = _____ pt

15. 3 gal = _____ qt

16. 3 lb = _____ oz

17. 2 tons = _____ lb

142

Name _____

Maintenance

Write the number named by each 3.

1. 5,328
2. 43,109
3. 62,137
4. 938,241

Add, subtract, multiply, or divide.

5. $31,824
  + 7,069

6. 6)889

7. 57,842
  − 11,936

8. $0.63
  × 7

Estimate.

9. 314 × 4

10. 6,218 + 5,609

11. 572 × 41

Complete.

12. $\frac{2}{4} = \frac{\square}{8}$

13. $\frac{6}{8} = \frac{3}{\square}$

14. $\frac{2}{5} = \frac{4}{\square}$

15. $\frac{6}{9} = \frac{\square}{3}$

Add or subtract.

16. $\frac{1}{4} + \frac{1}{4}$

17. $\frac{8}{9} - \frac{3}{9}$

18. $\frac{1}{4} + \frac{5}{12}$

19. $\frac{3}{4} - \frac{3}{8}$

Complete.

20. $\frac{1}{5}$ of 15 = $\square$

21. $\frac{2}{3}$ of 18 = $\square$

22. $\frac{3}{8}$ of 24 = $\square$

Measure to the nearest centimeter.

23. _____

24. _____

25. _____

Solve.

26. Fernando's puppy weighs 2 pounds. How many ounces does the puppy weigh?

27. Mrs. Grey buys 3 yards of cloth to make curtains. How many feet of cloth does she buy?

Perimeter and Area

The distance around a polygon is the **perimeter.**

To find the perimeter, add the
lengths of the sides.

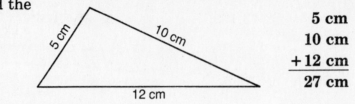

| 5 cm |
| 10 cm |
| +12 cm |
| 27 cm |

The perimeter of the triangle is 27 cm.

The **area** of a region is the number of square units needed
to cover the region.

Count the number of square units
needed to cover the region.

30 square units

To find the area of a square or rectangle,
multiply the length times the width.

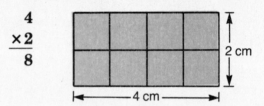

$$\begin{array}{r} 4 \\ \times 2 \\ \hline 8 \end{array}$$

The area is 8 square centimeters.

EXERCISES *Find the perimeter of each figure.*

1.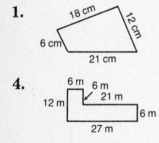

2.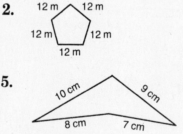

3.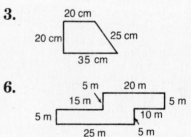

4.

5.

6.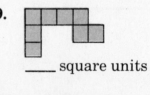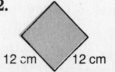

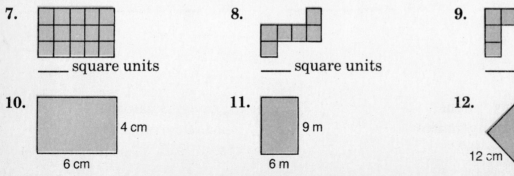

EXERCISES *Find the area of each figure.*

7.

_____ square units

8.

_____ square units

9.

_____ square units

10.

4 cm

6 cm

11.

9 m

6 m

12.

12 cm 12 cm

144

Patterns in Computation: Area of Triangles and Parallelograms

If you know how to find the area of rectangles, you can find the area of triangles and parallelograms. Study the pattern below.

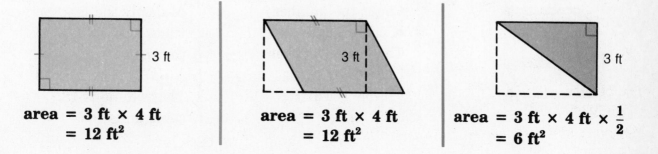

area = 3 ft × 4 ft
     = 12 ft²

area = 3 ft × 4 ft
     = 12 ft²

area = 3 ft × 4 ft × $\frac{1}{2}$
     = 6 ft²

> **To find the area of a parallelogram, multiply the base times the height.**
> **To find the area of a right triangle, multiply the base times the height and then multiply the product by $\frac{1}{2}$.**

Find the area of each figure.

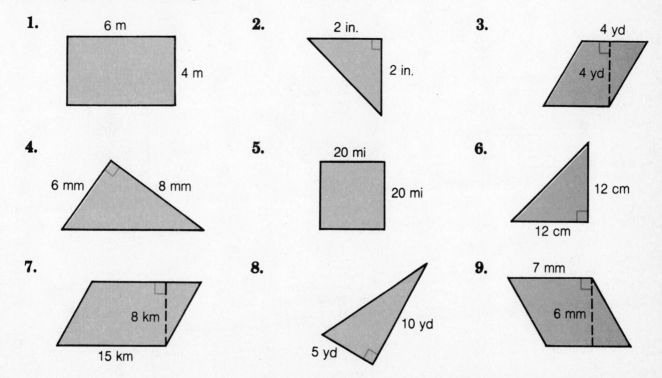

1. 6 m, 4 m

2. 2 in., 2 in.

3. 4 yd, 4 yd

4. 6 mm, 8 mm

5. 20 mi, 20 mi

6. 12 cm, 12 cm

7. 8 km, 15 km

8. 10 yd, 5 yd

9. 7 mm, 6 mm

Volume

Volume is the amount of space within a figure.
Measure volume in cubic units.

There are 2 ways to find the volume of the **rectangular prism** below.

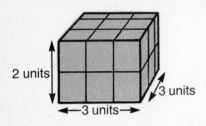

2 units
3 units
3 units

Count the number of cubic units. There are 18 cubes in all, so the volume is 18 cubic units.

Multiply the length times the width times the height.
3 × 3 × 2 = 18
The volume is 18 cubic units.

EXERCISES **Find the volume for each rectangular prism.**

1.

_____ cubic units

2.

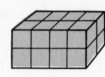

_____ cubic units

3.

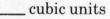

_____ cubic units

4.

2 units
6 units   1 unit

5.

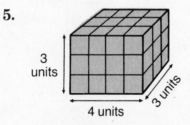

3 units
4 units   3 units

6.

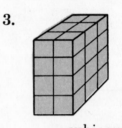

5 units
2 units   2 units

7.

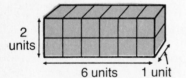

2 cm
5 cm
3 cm

8.

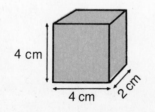

4 cm
4 cm   2 cm

9.

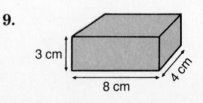

3 cm
8 cm   4 cm

Perimeter, Area, and Volume

- To find the perimeter, add the lengths of the sides.
- To find area, multiply the length times the width.
- To find volume, multiply the length times the width times the height.

EXERCISES *Find the perimeter and area of each figure.*

1.

12 ft
6 ft   6 ft
12 ft

2.

16 ft
14 ft   14 ft
16 ft

3.

200 m
120 m   120 m
200 m

4.

10 in.
10 in.   10 in.
10 in.

5.

5 yd
15 yd

6.

6 ft
30 ft   30 ft
6 ft

EXERCISES *Find the volume for each rectangular prism.*

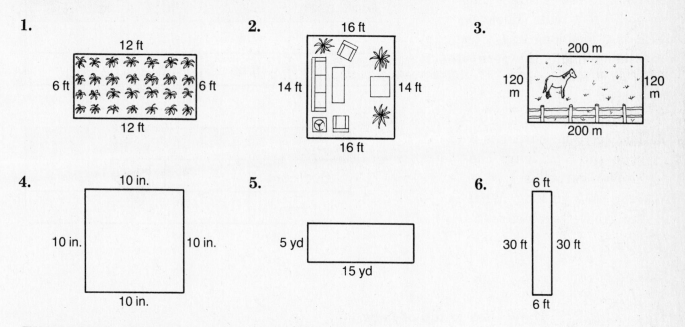

7.

1 ft
4 ft
1 ft

8.

4 in.
12 in.
4 in.

9.

15 in.
18 in.   10 in.

10.

3 ft
4 ft   3 ft

11.

12 yd
6 yd   6 yd

12.

12 in.
8 in.   24 in.

147

Problem Solving

Use the plan below to solve problems.

Read the problem. ▶ **Decide** what to do. ▶ **Solve** the problem. ▶ **Examine** the solution.

Complete each chart with the facts.

1. Bookcase A is 7 feet long and 3 feet wide. Bookcase B is 5 feet long and 4 feet wide. What is the perimeter of each bookcase?

Bookcase	Length	Width	Perimeter
A	7 ft	3 ft	
B	5 ft	4 ft	

2. The bedroom carpet is 5 yd wide and 6 yd long. The kitchen carpet is 4 yd wide by 5 yd long. What is the area of each carpet?

Carpet	Length	Width	Area
Bedroom			
Kitchen			

Make a chart to show each group of facts.

3. The new strawberry patch is 5 yd wide and 7 yd long. The old strawberry patch is 4 yd wide and 8 yd long. Show the length, width, area, and perimeter of each patch. Which perimeter is greater?

4. The school playground is 80 ft long and 60 ft wide. The park playground is 80 ft wide and 100 ft long. Show the length, width, area, and perimeter of each playground.

Problem Solving

EXERCISES *Draw a diagram to help solve each of the following.*

1. Marsha has a photo. It is 12 inches by 16 inches. She put a frame that was 2 inches wide around the photo. What are the length and width of the framed photo?

2. Toby is planting 8 tomato plants in each row. How many rows does he need if he has 104 plants?

3. The town playground has 5 sides. Each side is 40 feet long. How much fence will be needed to go around the playground?

4. Cleo is building shelves for his magic books. Fifteen books will fit on each shelf. How many books will fit on 7 shelves?

5. A toy is packed in a box whose base is 5 inches by 6 inches. How many of these boxes will fit in a shipping carton that is 15 inches by 24 inches?

6. Tim has a rectangular garden that is 20 feet by 25 feet. He plants $\frac{1}{5}$ of it in potatoes. How many square feet of the garden is planted in potatoes?

Chapter 12 Test

*Measure the length of each line segment
to the nearest centimeter.*

1. ___

2. _____

3. _____

Choose the more reasonable measurement.

4. length of a ladder

    2 m   2 km

5. juice in a glass

    300 mL   30 L

6. mass of a camera

    900 g   900 kg

7. length of a fishing pole

    5 ft   5 yd

8. water in a bucket

    2 pt   2 gal

9. weight of a sandwich

    3 oz   3 lb

Solve.

10. Find the perimeter.

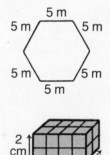

11. Find the area.

12. Find the volume.

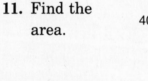

13. Find the perimeter.

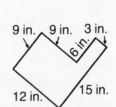

Draw a diagram to help solve the following.

14. Don had 2 square pieces of material.
The squares measured 5 inches on each
side. He sewed the squares together
on one side. Find the perimeter of
the new piece of material.

Write a decimal for each of the following.

1.   2.   3.   4.

5. $9\frac{7}{10}$ 6. $12\frac{37}{100}$ 7. nine tenths   8. $4\frac{7}{100}$

Order from least to greatest.

9. 1.18, 1.08, 1.81   10. 14.94, 14.49, 14.5   11. 25.08, 25.9, 25.11

Add or subtract.

1. $\begin{array}{r} 15.6 \\ + 32.75 \\ \hline \end{array}$ 2. $\begin{array}{r} 63.94 \\ - 28.48 \\ \hline \end{array}$ 3. $\begin{array}{r} 7.65 \\ + 7 \\ \hline \end{array}$ 4. $\begin{array}{r} 72.03 \\ - 15.8 \\ \hline \end{array}$ 5. $\begin{array}{r} 36.28 \\ + 14.92 \\ \hline \end{array}$

6. 68.2 − 32.27   7. 58.7 + 26.47   8. 9.8 − 7.94

Estimate.

9. $\begin{array}{r} 2.3 \\ + 0.9 \\ \hline \end{array}$ 10. $\begin{array}{r} 15.37 \\ - 2.9 \\ \hline \end{array}$ 11. $\begin{array}{r} 36.28 \\ + 14.92 \\ \hline \end{array}$ 12. $\begin{array}{r} 92.54 \\ - 19.27 \\ \hline \end{array}$

Write the number of possible outcomes.

13. tossing a penny

14. choosing a month of the year

Solve.

15. A box contains 15 marbles. Four of them are red. What is the probability of choosing a marble that is not red?

16. Angela wants to buy a new book bag that costs $3.65. She has $1.79 in her bank. How much more money does she need?

Decimals and Fractions

The shaded part of the square shows the fraction $\frac{7}{10}$.

It also shows a **decimal**.

Write 0.7   **Say** *seven tenths.*

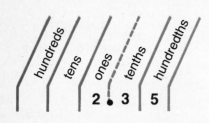

Write 1.4   **Say** *one and four tenths.* | **Write 0.33**   **Say** *thirty-three hundredths.*

A place value chart can help you read and write decimals.

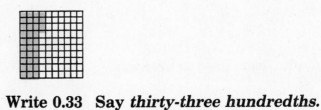

The digit 2 is in the ones position.
The digit 3 is in the tenths position.
The digit 5 is in the hundredths position.

Write 2.35   **Say** *two and thirty-five hundredths.*

EXERCISES   *Write a fraction and a decimal for the shaded part.*

1.   **2.**   **3.**   **4.**

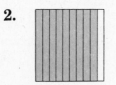

Write a decimal for the shaded part.

5.   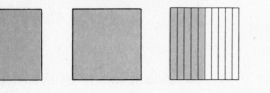   **6.**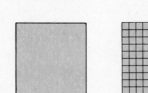

Write as a decimal.

7. $\frac{6}{10}$ **8.** $12\frac{1}{10}$ **9.** $\frac{21}{100}$ **10.** $\frac{76}{100}$

11. $\frac{3}{100}$ **12.** $24\frac{32}{100}$ **13.** $68\frac{68}{100}$ **14.** $88\frac{2}{100}$

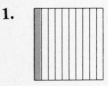
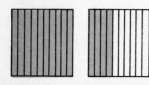
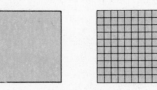
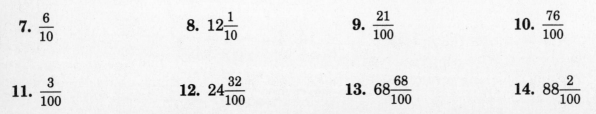

Patterns in Place Value: Reading and Writing Decimals

Study the pattern below. Each group of numbers can be written using only two different digits. Notice where the digits are placed in the place-value chart.

Using only 3s and 0s:

	hundreds	tens	ones	tenths	hundredths

3 hundredths   three hundredths

3 tenths   three tenths

3 ones   three

3 tens   thirty

3 hundreds   three hundred

hundreds	tens	ones	tenths	hundredths
		0	0	3
		0	3	
		3		
	3	0		
3	0	0		

Remember that 3 is the same as 3.00.

Using only 8s and 0s:

eight

eight and eight tenths

eight and eighty-eight hundredths

eighty and eight tenths

hundreds	tens	ones	tenths	hundredths
		8		
		8	8	
		8	8	8
	8	0	8	

Use the pattern above to name the following numbers.

1. _____
2. _____
3. _____
4. _____
5. _____
6. _____
7. _____
8. _____
9. _____
10. _____

hundreds	tens	ones	tenths	hundredths
		4		
		0	4	
	4	0		
6	0	0		
		0	0	6
		6	6	
	7	7		
	7	0	7	
		7	0	7
7	0	7	7	

Write the following numbers in the place-value chart.

11. twenty
12. fifty and five tenths
13. ninety-nine and nine hundredths
14. three hundred thirty and three tenths
15. two hundred twenty-two and two hundredths

Comparing and Ordering Decimals

Compare decimals by using place-value positions.

Compare 2.63 and 2.67.

ones	tenths	hundredths
2 .	6	3
2 .	6	7

Compare the ones.

The ones are the same.

Compare the tenths.

The tenths are the same.

Compare the hundredths.

3 hundredths < 7 hundredths

2.63 < 2.67

Remember, you can place a zero to the right of the
decimal point without changing the value of the decimal.

EXERCISES *Fill each* ◯ *with <, >, or = to make a true sentence.*

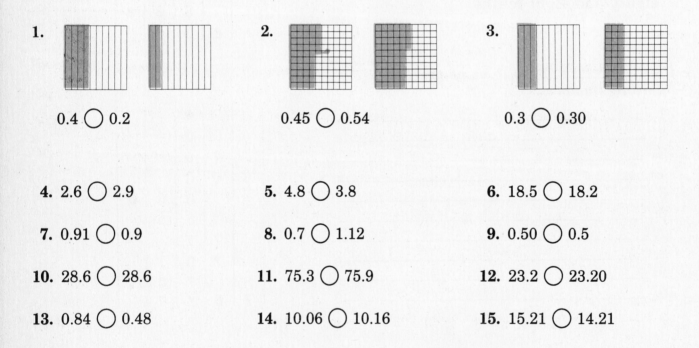

1. 0.4 ◯ 0.2

2. 0.45 ◯ 0.54

3. 0.3 ◯ 0.30

4. 2.6 ◯ 2.9

5. 4.8 ◯ 3.8

6. 18.5 ◯ 18.2

7. 0.91 ◯ 0.9

8. 0.7 ◯ 1.12

9. 0.50 ◯ 0.5

10. 28.6 ◯ 28.6

11. 75.3 ◯ 75.9

12. 23.2 ◯ 23.20

13. 0.84 ◯ 0.48

14. 10.06 ◯ 10.16

15. 15.21 ◯ 14.21

Order from least to greatest.

16. 0.7, 0.1, 0.3

17. 0.44, 0.39, 0.48

18. 18.31, 18.25, 18.27

19. 6.9, 6.87, 6.91

Maintenance

Add, subtract, multiply, or divide.

1. 27,841
  − 16,923

2. 500
  × 7

3. $653.18
  + 241.26

4. 8)2,544

Find the average.

5. 24, 15, 27

6. 48, 73, 55, 44

7. 112, 129, 164, 131

Write a fraction for the shaded part.

8. 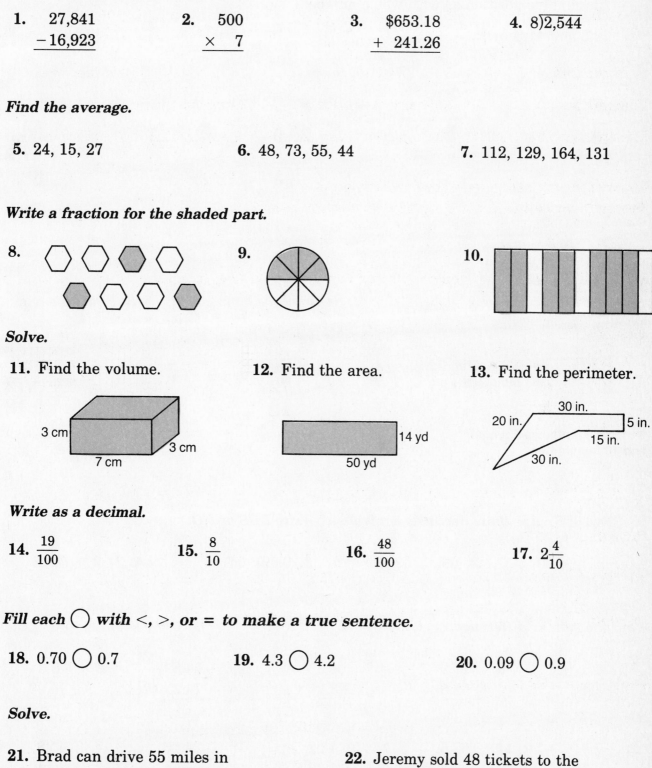 **9.** **10.**

Solve.

11. Find the volume.

3 cm
7 cm
3 cm

12. Find the area.

14 yd
50 yd

13. Find the perimeter.

20 in.
30 in.
5 in.
15 in.
30 in.

Write as a decimal.

14. $\frac{19}{100}$

15. $\frac{8}{10}$

16. $\frac{48}{100}$

17. $2\frac{4}{10}$

Fill each ◯ with <, >, or = to make a true sentence.

18. 0.70 ◯ 0.7

19. 4.3 ◯ 4.2

20. 0.09 ◯ 0.9

Solve.

21. Brad can drive 55 miles in one hour. How far can he drive in 8 hours?

22. Jeremy sold 48 tickets to the school play. Sandy sold 29 tickets. How many more tickets did Jeremy sell?

Name _____

Adding and Subtracting Decimals

To add or subtract decimals, add or subtract in
each place-value position as with whole numbers.

Add 26.5 and 41.8.

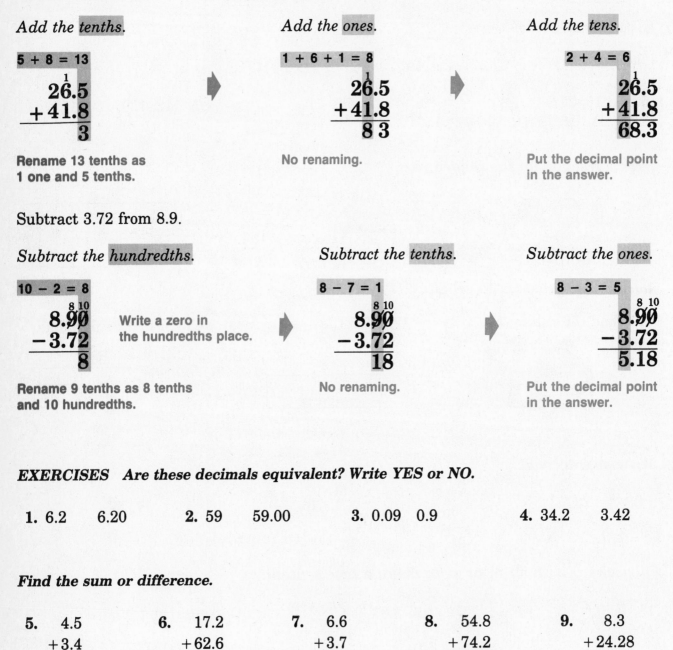

Add the tenths.

$5 + 8 = 13$

$$\begin{array}{r} 2\overset{1}{6}.5 \\ +41.8 \\ \hline .3 \end{array}$$

**Rename 13 tenths as
1 one and 5 tenths.**

Add the ones.

$1 + 6 + 1 = 8$

$$\begin{array}{r} 2\overset{1}{6}.5 \\ +41.8 \\ \hline 8.3 \end{array}$$

No renaming.

Add the tens.

$2 + 4 = 6$

$$\begin{array}{r} 2\overset{1}{6}.5 \\ +41.8 \\ \hline 68.3 \end{array}$$

Put the decimal point
in the answer.

Subtract 3.72 from 8.9.

Subtract the hundredths.

$10 - 2 = 8$

$$\begin{array}{r} 8.\overset{8\ 10}{9\not{0}} \\ -3.72 \\ \hline .8 \end{array}$$

**Rename 9 tenths as 8 tenths
and 10 hundredths.**

Write a zero in
the hundredths place.

Subtract the tenths.

$8 - 7 = 1$

$$\begin{array}{r} 8.\overset{8\ 10}{9\not{0}} \\ -3.72 \\ \hline .18 \end{array}$$

No renaming.

Subtract the ones.

$8 - 3 = 5$

$$\begin{array}{r} 8.\overset{8\ 10}{9\not{0}} \\ -3.72 \\ \hline 5.18 \end{array}$$

Put the decimal point
in the answer.

EXERCISES *Are these decimals equivalent? Write YES or NO.*

1. 6.2   6.20   2. 59   59.00   3. 0.09   0.9   4. 34.2   3.42

Find the sum or difference.

5. $\begin{array}{r} 4.5 \\ +3.4 \\ \hline \end{array}$ 6. $\begin{array}{r} 17.2 \\ +62.6 \\ \hline \end{array}$ 7. $\begin{array}{r} 6.6 \\ +3.7 \\ \hline \end{array}$ 8. $\begin{array}{r} 54.8 \\ +74.2 \\ \hline \end{array}$ 9. $\begin{array}{r} 8.3 \\ +24.28 \\ \hline \end{array}$

10. $\begin{array}{r} 7.8 \\ -2.5 \\ \hline \end{array}$ 11. $\begin{array}{r} 67.9 \\ -33.5 \\ \hline \end{array}$ 12. $\begin{array}{r} 4.82 \\ -1.36 \\ \hline \end{array}$ 13. $\begin{array}{r} 24.16 \\ -\ 5.34 \\ \hline \end{array}$ 14. $\begin{array}{r} 46.8 \\ -22.46 \\ \hline \end{array}$

15. $5.3 + 6.72$ 16. $18.3 - 4.41$ 17. $14 + 9.83$

Rounding and Estimation

Round 5.85 to the nearest whole number.

On the number line, 5.85 is closer to 6 than 5.

To the nearest whole number, 5.85 rounds to 6.

To estimate sums or differences, first round each number to the nearest whole number. Then add or subtract.

Estimate 10.9 + 8.2.

$$
\begin{array}{rcr}
10.9 & \to & 11 \\
+\ 8.2 & \to & +\ 8 \\
\hline
 & & 19
\end{array}
$$

10.9 rounds to 11.
8.2 rounds to 8
The sum is about 19.

EXERCISES *Round to the nearest whole number. Use the number line.*

1. 7.2   **2.** 8.8   **3.** 10.1   **4.** 6.9   **5.** 9.8

6. 10.6   **7.** 7.8   **8.** 6.4   **9.** 10.7   **10.** 6.5

Choose the correct answer for rounding to the nearest whole number.

11. 4.6   **a.** 4   **b.** 5   **12.** 23.19   **a.** 23   **b.** 24

13. 53.5   **a.** 53   **b.** 54   **14.** 16.91   **a.** 16   **b.** 17

Round to the nearest whole number. Then estimate.

15.
$$
\begin{array}{rcr}
6.9 & \to & 7 \\
+5.3 & \to & +5 \\
\hline
\end{array}
$$

16.
$$
\begin{array}{r}
24.2 \\
-\ 9.7 \\
\hline
\end{array}
$$

17.
$$
\begin{array}{r}
26.5 \\
+\ 3.2 \\
\hline
\end{array}
$$

18.
$$
\begin{array}{r}
10.4 \\
-\ 3.6 \\
\hline
\end{array}
$$

19.
$$
\begin{array}{r}
52.8 \\
+36.7 \\
\hline
\end{array}
$$

20.
$$
\begin{array}{r}
49.5 \\
-24.8 \\
\hline
\end{array}
$$

21.
$$
\begin{array}{r}
21.89 \\
+16.03 \\
\hline
\end{array}
$$

22.
$$
\begin{array}{r}
76.42 \\
-31.58 \\
\hline
\end{array}
$$

Problem Solving

Use the plan below to solve a problem.

Read the **problem.** ▶ **Decide** what to do. ▶ **Solve** the problem. ▶ **Examine** the solution.

Solve. Check each answer.

1. Sandy has $4.50. She wants to buy shoes for $12.65. How much more money does she need?

2. Joni buys an ice cream cone with one scoop for 50¢ and one with three scoops for 80¢. What is the total cost?

3. George buys shorts for $3.00, socks for $1.50, and pencils for $1.39. How much does he spend?

4. Sue has $4.00. She buys slippers for $2.75. How much change does she get?

5. Tony has $1.50. He buys a ball for 69¢. How much money does he have left?

6. Bertha has $6.75. She wants to buy a purse for $9.25. How much more money does she need?

7. Lori buys a medium pizza with topping. How much change does she receive from $5.00?

Pizza	Cost
Small	$1.90
Medium	$3.25
Large	$6.00
Topping	50¢

Outcomes and Probability

The bag at the right contains 5 white blocks and 4
other blocks. One block is chosen at random.
At random means that each choice is equally
likely. What is the chance, or **probability,**
that a white block is chosen?

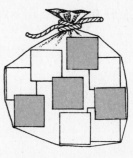

There are 9 possible outcomes, or choices. Five of the
outcomes are white. So, the probablity is 5 out of 9, or $\frac{5}{9}$.

EXERCISES *Write the number of possible outcomes.*

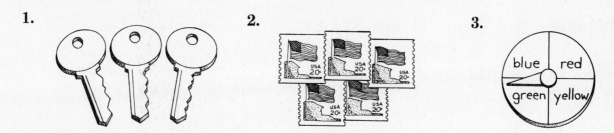

1.

2.

3.

blue | red

green | yellow

***Choose a coin from those shown. Write
the probability of choosing each of the following.***

4. a nickel

5. a dime

6. a penny

7. NOT a penny

8. NOT a nickel

9. NOT a dime

10. a quarter

11. any coin

12. a coin worth more than 5¢

Solve.

13. A die is rolled. What is the probability
of rolling a number greater than 4?

Chapter 13 Test

Write a decimal for each of the following.

1. $\frac{43}{100}$

2. $18\frac{5}{10}$

3. $37\frac{51}{100}$

4. $98\frac{9}{10}$

5. two and eight hundredths

6. twenty-two and six tenths

Write each missing decimal.

7. 3.4, _____, 3.6

8. 62.16, _____, 62.18

9. 14.89, _____, 14.91

Order from least to greatest.

10. 43.6, 43.2, 43.5

11. 8.07, 8.71, 8.27

12. 74.8, 74.68, 74.72

Add or subtract.

13. 9.2
   +3.9

14. 6.8
   +2.5

15. 28.7
   +13.2

16. 49.6
   −34.7

17. 66.8
   +47.4

18. 6.86
   −2.79

19. 5.4
   +19.83

20. 56.7
   −14.24

21. 84.26
   +17.8

22. 93.19
   −52.3

Estimate.

23. 8.6
   +5.4

24. 11.3
   − 7.2

25. 44.02
   +12.17

26. 87.9
   −18.32

Solve.

27. The high temperature on Wednesday was 63.8 degrees. The low temperature was 44.5 degrees. Find the difference between the two temperatures.

28. There are 3 green apples and 5 red apples in the refrigerator. One apple is chosen at random. What is the probability of choosing a green apple?

Divide.

1. 5)874

2. 7)3,826

3. 9)$69.12

4. 8)6,529

5. 16)32

6. 14)84

7. 36)84

8. 50)98

Solve.

9. There are 252 mums to be planted in 42 pots. How many mums should be planted in each pot?

10. Twenty-nine scouts want to sell 261 boxes of pencils. How many boxes must each scout sell?

Divide.

1. 40)920

2. 50)546

3. 67)890

4. 97)992

5. 17)637

6. 26)998

7. 34)870

8. 48)646

Solve.

9. Dawn needs to buy some tomatoes. Grocery A has them for 8¢ per oz. At Grocery B, they cost $1.44 per pound. Where is the better buy?

10. Mrs. Thomas bought 4 dozen roses for $60.00. Find the cost of each rose.

Name _____

Dividing 3- and 4-Digit Numbers

Divide 5,664 by 4.

Divide the thousands.

```
   1
4)5,664
 -4      4 × 1 thousand
  1      = 4 thousands
```

Divide the hundreds.

```
   1,4
4)5,664
 -4↓
  16
 -16     4 × 4 hundreds
   0     = 16 hundreds
```

Divide the tens and ones.

```
   1,416
4)5,664
 -4↓
  16
 -16
   06
  - 4    4 × 1 ten
   24    = 4 tens
  -24    4 × 6 = 24
    0
```

EXERCISES Divide.

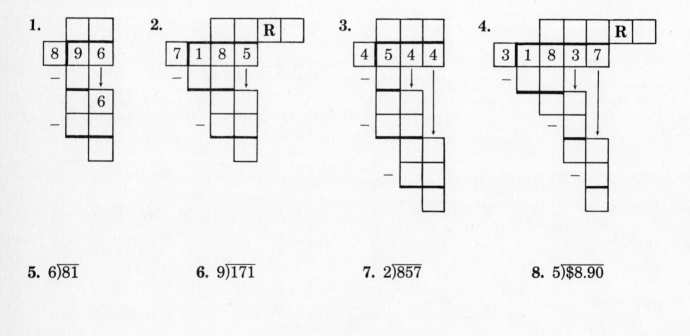

1. 8)96

2. 7)185 R

3. 4)544

4. 3)1837 R

5. 6)81

6. 9)171

7. 2)857

8. 5)$8.90

9. 8)920

10. 4)778

11. 3)1,587

12. 9)$75.78

Dividing by Tens

Divide 240 by 40.

$$\begin{array}{r} 6 \\ 40\overline{)240} \\ -240 \\ \hline 0 \end{array}$$

40 × ⬚6⬚ = 240
Write a 6 in
the ones place.

Divide 280 by 30.

$$\begin{array}{r} 9 \text{ R10} \\ 30\overline{)280} \\ -270 \\ \hline 10 \end{array}$$

30 × ⬚9⬚ = 270
Write the remainder
with an R.

Don't forget that when you divide and get a remainder,
the remainder must be *less* than the divisor.

EXERCISES *Divide.*

1. $20\overline{)40}$ **2.** $30\overline{)120}$ **3.** $40\overline{)160}$ **4.** $50\overline{)200}$

5. $60\overline{)360}$ **6.** $70\overline{)420}$ **7.** $80\overline{)480}$ **8.** $90\overline{)540}$

Divide. Write the remainder next to the quotient.

9. $\overset{7}{40\overline{)288}}$ **10.** $\overset{7}{30\overline{)224}}$ **11.** $\overset{4}{50\overline{)207}}$ **12.** $\overset{4}{80\overline{)336}}$

13. $60\overline{)442}$ **14.** $90\overline{)398}$ **15.** $70\overline{)500}$ **16.** $20\overline{)83}$

Solve.

17. A shelf can hold 40 books. How many shelves are needed
to hold 320 books?

Patterns in Computation: Dividing by Tens

If you know basic division facts, you can divide whole
numbers by tens. Study the pattern below.

$3\overline{)6}^{\,2}$ | $3\text{ tens}\overline{)6\text{ tens}}^{\,2} \longrightarrow 30\overline{)60}^{\,2}$ | $3\text{ tens}\overline{)60\text{ tens}}^{\,20} \longrightarrow 30\overline{)600}^{\,20}$

$3\overline{)7}^{\,2\text{ R1}}$ | $3\text{ tens}\overline{)7\text{ tens}}^{\,2\text{ R10}}$ | $30\overline{)70}^{\,2\text{ R10}}$ | $30\overline{)700}^{\,23\text{ R10}}$

Use the pattern above to divide.

1. $4\overline{)8}$ 2. $4\overline{)80}$ 3. $40\overline{)80}$ 4. $40\overline{)800}$

5. $9\overline{)9}$ 6. $9\overline{)90}$ 7. $90\overline{)90}$ 8. $90\overline{)900}$

9. $5\overline{)35}$ 10. $5\overline{)350}$ 11. $50\overline{)350}$ 12. $50\overline{)3,500}$

Divide. Write any remainder next to the quotient.

13. $20\overline{)84}$ 14. $90\overline{)98}$ 15. $60\overline{)180}$ 16. $40\overline{)320}$

17. $30\overline{)237}$ 18. $90\overline{)470}$ 19. $50\overline{)164}$ 20. $60\overline{)105}$

21. $50\overline{)117}$ 22. $30\overline{)252}$ 23. $20\overline{)66}$ 24. $60\overline{)512}$

Dividing by 2-Digit Numbers

Divide 187 by 21.

First, *guess* the quotient. Round the divisor to the nearest 10.

$21\overline{)187}$ Try 9 as a quotient.

$20 \times \boxed{9} = 180$

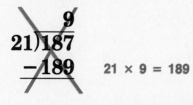

$21\overline{)187}$
-189 $21 \times 9 = 189$

You cannot subtract. Change the quotient from 9 to 8.

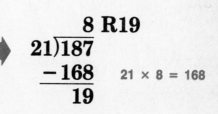

$8 \text{ R}19$
$21\overline{)187}$
-168 $21 \times 8 = 168$
19

This quotient is correct.

EXERCISES Divide.

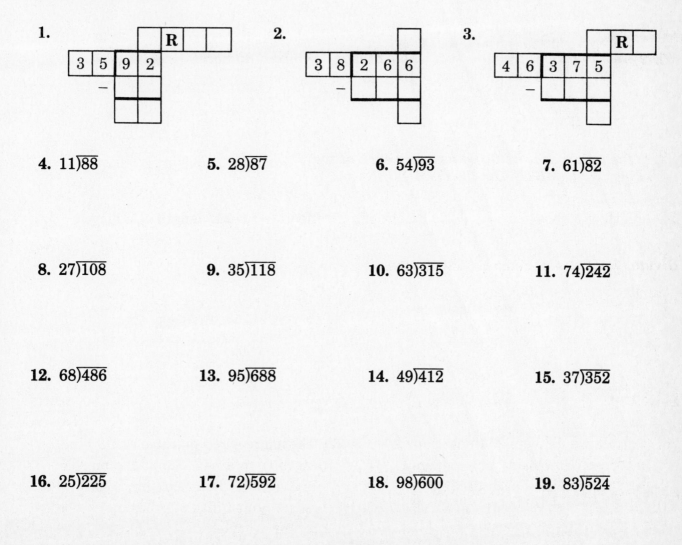

1.

| 3 | 5 | 9 | 2 | | R | | |

2.

| 3 | 8 | 2 | 6 | 6 |

3.

| 4 | 6 | 3 | 7 | 5 | | R | |

4. $11\overline{)88}$

5. $28\overline{)87}$

6. $54\overline{)93}$

7. $61\overline{)82}$

8. $27\overline{)108}$

9. $35\overline{)118}$

10. $63\overline{)315}$

11. $74\overline{)242}$

12. $68\overline{)486}$

13. $95\overline{)688}$

14. $49\overline{)412}$

15. $37\overline{)352}$

16. $25\overline{)225}$

17. $72\overline{)592}$

18. $98\overline{)600}$

19. $83\overline{)524}$

Maintenance

Add, subtract, multiply, or divide.

1. 3,264
   +6,195

2. 16,208
   − 8,109

3. 56,821
   +12,179

4. $37.28
   − 10.67

5. 432
   876
   +362

6. 43
   ×15

7. 4)258

8. 3,517
   × 8

9. 12)104

10. $6.38
    × 14

Replace each ◯ with <, >, or = to make a true sentence.

11. $\frac{4}{6}$ ◯ $\frac{5}{6}$

12. $\frac{3}{4}$ ◯ $\frac{5}{8}$

13. $\frac{1}{2}$ ◯ $\frac{1}{3}$

14. $\frac{1}{2}$ ◯ $\frac{3}{6}$

Write each improper fraction as a whole number or mixed numeral.

15. $\frac{5}{4}$

16. $\frac{16}{4}$

17. $\frac{17}{6}$

18. $\frac{28}{9}$

Name the unit that is better to measure each of the following. Write METER or CENTIMETER.

19. length of a shoe

20. height of a giraffe

21. length of a bicycle

Add or subtract.

22. 34.8
    +25.3

23. 58.7
    −17.35

24. $\frac{2}{5} + \frac{1}{10}$

25. $\frac{14}{16} - \frac{3}{4}$

Solve.

26. Sally Rowe delivers 234 newspapers in 9 days. How many newspapers does Sally deliver each day?

27. There are 4 red marbles and 3 blue marbles in a bag. Suppose a marble is chosen without looking. What is the probability of choosing a blue marble?

2-Digit Quotients

Sometimes when you divide, the quotient has more than one digit.
Divide in each place-value position from left to right.

Divide 366 by 30.

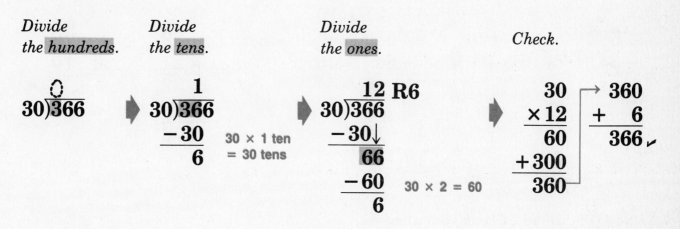

Divide the hundreds.   *Divide the tens.*   *Divide the ones.*   Check.

EXERCISES   *Divide. Check your answers.*

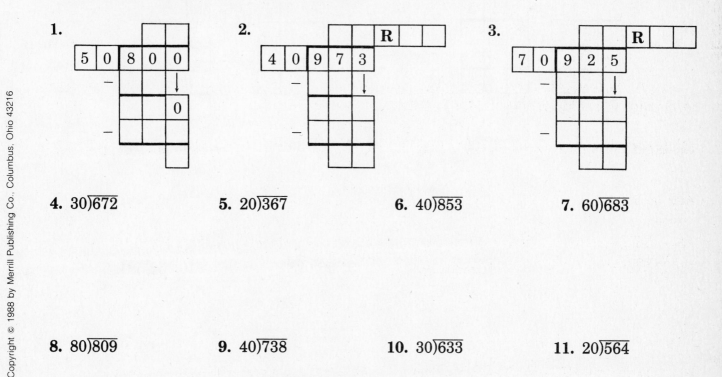

4. 30)672   **5.** 20)367   **6.** 40)853   **7.** 60)683

8. 80)809   **9.** 40)738   **10.** 30)633   **11.** 20)564

More 2-Digit Quotients

Divide 682 by 32.

Divide the tens.   *Divide the ones.*   *Check.*

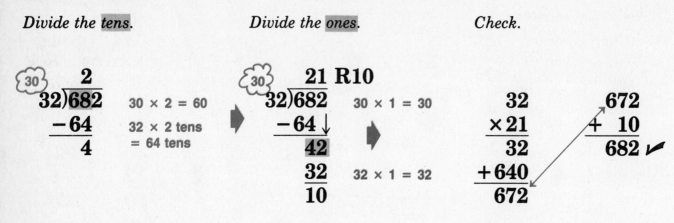

EXERCISES   Divide. Check your answers.

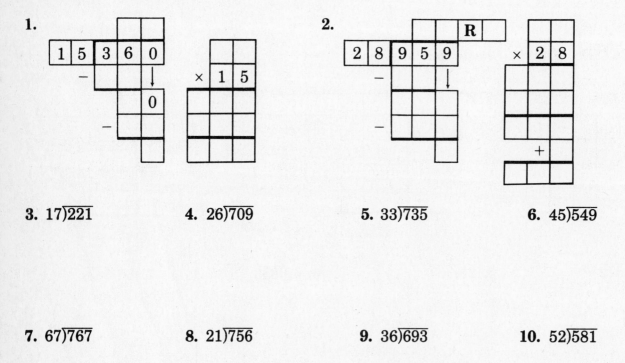

3. 17)221   **4.** 26)709   **5.** 33)735   **6.** 45)549

7. 67)767   **8.** 21)756   **9.** 36)693   **10.** 52)581

Solve.

11. The hardware store orders nails in boxes of 50 nails each.
The store orders 600 nails. How many boxes do they receive?

Problem Solving

EXERCISES *Solve.*

1. Jill's aunt bought a pair of table lamps for $96. How much did each lamp cost?

2. Carl bought 3 gallons of punch for the party. Each quart serves 6 people. How many people will the 3 gallons serve?

3. Each roll contains 16 yards of ribbon. David needs 2 feet of ribbon to make a bow. How many bows can he make from one roll?

4. Andrea bought four 8-ounce packages of cream cheese. How many pounds of cream cheese did she buy?

5. Brian is 180 cm tall. The snow drifts near his home are 3 meters high. How many centimeters higher than Brian are the drifts?

6. Long-stemmed roses cost $30.00 per dozen at the florist. How much does 1 rose cost?

7. Tina cuts yarn into 18-inch pieces to make the hair for a rag doll. How many pieces can she get from a ball of yarn 24 feet long?

8. It is about 100 meters from Karen's house to the mailbox. How many times must she run back and forth from her house to the mailbox to run a distance of 1 kilometer?

Chapter 14 Test

Divide.

1. $7\overline{)80}$ **2.** $8\overline{)125}$ **3.** $3\overline{)1,275}$ **4.** $2\overline{)5,223}$

5. $9\overline{)\$78.75}$ **6.** $4\overline{)9,604}$ **7.** $20\overline{)140}$ **8.** $60\overline{)420}$

9. $50\overline{)436}$ **10.** $80\overline{)424}$ **11.** $24\overline{)98}$ **12.** $43\overline{)356}$

13. $84\overline{)588}$ **14.** $28\overline{)267}$ **15.** $30\overline{)480}$ **16.** $50\overline{)557}$

17. $20\overline{)709}$ **18.** $24\overline{)756}$ **19.** $43\overline{)992}$ **20.** $61\overline{)879}$

Copyright © 1988 by Merrill Publishing Co., Columbus, Ohio 43216

Solve.

21. Lee can buy an 8-ounce bottle of shampoo for $1.92 or a 12-ounce bottle for $2.64. Which is the better buy?

22. Randy spent $2.09 on a notebook and 6 pencils. The pencils cost 15¢ each. How much did the notebook cost?

Name _____

Maintenance

Standardized Format

Directions Work each problem on your own paper. Choose the letter
of the correct answer. If the correct answer is not given, choose
the letter for *none of the above*. Make no marks on this test.

1. Add.

86,752 + 45,679

a 132,431

b 133,441

c 143,341

d *none of the above*

2. What is the number?

6,000 + 40 + 3

e 643

f 6,043

g 6,403

h *none of the above*

3. Subtract.

$72.83
− 49.85

a $21.98

b $22.98

c $23.98

d *none of the above*

4. Multiply.

700 × 7

e 49

f 409

g 490

h *none of the above*

5. Choose the best
estimate.   781
                  × 6

a 4,200

b 420

c 4,800

d *none of the above*

6. Multiply.

309 × 25

e 7,585

f 7,725

g 7,985

h *none of the above*

7. Divide.

4)795

a 189 R2

b 196 R1

c 198 R3

d *none of the above*

8. How many lines of
symmetry are there?

e 0

f 2

g 4

h *none of the above*

9. What is $\frac{8}{18}$ in
simplest form?

a $\frac{1}{2}$

b $\frac{2}{5}$

c $\frac{4}{9}$

d *none of the above*

10. Which fraction
is greater than 1?

e $\frac{3}{8}$

f $\frac{11}{9}$

g $\frac{1}{6}$

h *none of the above*

11. Subtract.

$\frac{3}{4} - \frac{1}{2}$

a $\frac{2}{2}$

b $\frac{2}{7}$

c $\frac{1}{4}$

d *none of the above*

12. What is the
perimeter?

20 m / 30 m

e 60 m

f 100 m

g 600 m

h *none of the above*

13. How many meters are in 1 kilometer?

a 1,000

b 100

c 10

d *none of the above*

14. Find the area.

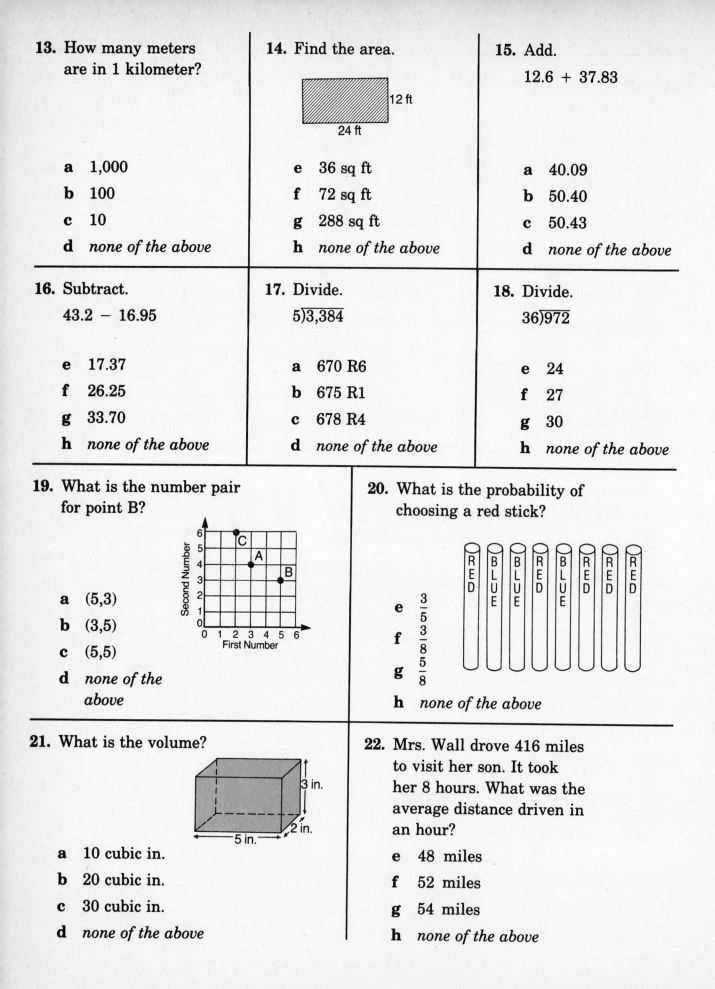

12 ft

24 ft

e 36 sq ft

f 72 sq ft

g 288 sq ft

h *none of the above*

15. Add.

12.6 + 37.83

a 40.09

b 50.40

c 50.43

d *none of the above*

16. Subtract.

43.2 − 16.95

e 17.37

f 26.25

g 33.70

h *none of the above*

17. Divide.

5)3,384

a 670 R6

b 675 R1

c 678 R4

d *none of the above*

18. Divide.

36)972

e 24

f 27

g 30

h *none of the above*

19. What is the number pair for point B?

a (5,3)

b (3,5)

c (5,5)

d *none of the above*

20. What is the probability of choosing a red stick?

e $\frac{3}{5}$

f $\frac{3}{8}$

g $\frac{5}{8}$

h *none of the above*

21. What is the volume?

3 in.

2 in.

5 in.

a 10 cubic in.

b 20 cubic in.

c 30 cubic in.

d *none of the above*

22. Mrs. Wall drove 416 miles to visit her son. It took her 8 hours. What was the average distance driven in an hour?

e 48 miles

f 52 miles

g 54 miles

h *none of the above*

Add or subtract.

1. $5 + 6$ 2. $8 + 0$ 3. $2 + 9$ 4. $7 + 3$

5. $9 - 4$ 6. $11 - 3$ 7. $14 - 5$ 8. $7 - 0$

Name the property shown by each of the following.

9. $7 + 5 = 12$
   $5 + 7 = 12$

10. $9 + 0 = 9$

11. $8 + 6 = 14$
    $6 + 8 = 14$

Find the missing addend.

12. $2 + \square = 7$ 13. $\square + 6 = 15$ 14. $\square + 5 = 13$

Write the fact family for each group of numbers.

15. $8, 6, 14$ 16. $11, 5, 6$ 17. $9, 12, 3$

Add or subtract.

18. $\begin{array}{r} 12 \\ + \ 7 \\ \hline \end{array}$ 19. $\begin{array}{r} 48 \\ + 51 \\ \hline \end{array}$ 20. $\begin{array}{r} 56 \\ - \ 4 \\ \hline \end{array}$ 21. $\begin{array}{r} 73 \\ - 61 \\ \hline \end{array}$

22. $\begin{array}{r} 369 \\ + 620 \\ \hline \end{array}$ 23. $\begin{array}{r} 8{,}704 \\ + 1{,}195 \\ \hline \end{array}$ 24. $\begin{array}{r} 595 \\ - 372 \\ \hline \end{array}$ 25. $\begin{array}{r} 7{,}644 \\ - 5{,}321 \\ \hline \end{array}$

Write in standard form.

26. six thousand, eight hundred fifty

27. four hundred seventy thousand, one hundred twenty-five

Complete.

28. $1{,}700 = \square$ hundreds   29. $4{,}800 = \square$ tens

Round each number to the nearest thousand.

30. $7{,}742$ 31. $9{,}289$ 32. $52{,}876$ 33. $4{,}139$

Write in words.

34. 4,198,367   **35.** 21,047,138   **36.** 193,830,002

Add.

37.   54
        + 33

38.   182
        + 763

39.   349
        + 275

40.   607
        + 196

41.   2,315
        + 2,869

42.   5,834
        + 1,177

43.   145,248
        +   7,975

44.   56,390
           48,625
        +   2,319

Subtract.

45.   87
        − 35

46.   609
        − 84

47.   931
        − 469

48.   800
        − 176

49.   4,053
        − 1,826

50.   8,142
        − 3,563

51.   75,066
        − 29,827

52.   291,428
        − 135,579

Estimate.

53.   622
        + 181

54.   2,193
        + 4,738

55.   417
        − 168

56.   8,532
        − 2,099

Write each time. Use numerals and A.M. *or* P.M.

57.   **58.**   **59.**   **60.**

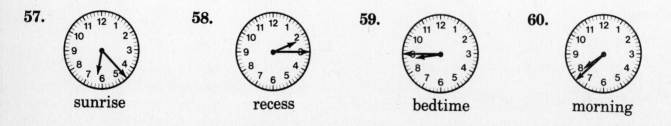

sunrise   recess   bedtime   morning

What time is it?

61. 25 minutes after 7:10 A.M.

62. 20 minutes before 1:00 P.M.

Write the total amount of money. Use a dollar sign and a decimal point.

63. 2 quarters
3 nickels
4 pennies

64. 4 dollars
1 half dollar
2 dimes

65. 7 dollars
3 quarters
2 pennies

66. 6 dollars
1 half dollar
5 nickels

Add or subtract.

67. $4.75
 + 0.86

68. $9.70
 − 3.93

69. $45.62
 + 15.79

70. $12.00
 − 7.67

Write the coins and bills needed for change.
Use as few as possible.

	Price	Amount Given		Price	Amount Given
71.	27¢	50¢	**72.**	$1.91	$5.00

Multiply.

73.   8
 × 4

74.   7
 × 7

75.   4
 × 6

76.   3
 × 9

Divide.

77. 9)‾72‾

78. 5)‾45‾

79. 3)‾18‾

80. 6)‾42‾

Complete each list of multiples.

81. Multiples of 4: 4, _____, 12, 16, 20, _____, 28, _____, _____

82. Multiples of 7: 7, 14, _____, 28, _____, 42, _____, _____, 63

Write two related multiplication facts for each of the following.

83. 48 ÷ 8 = 6   **84.** 56 ÷ 7 = 8   **85.** 21 ÷ 3 = 7

Multiply.

86.   10
        × 6

87.   500
        × 7

88.   39
        × 2

89.   47
        × 4

90. 7 × 121   **91.** 5 × 136   **92.** 104 × 9

93.   4,700
          × 6

94.   6,754
          × 4

95. $0.96
          × 4

96. $48.72
          × 6

97. 6 × 4 × 5   **98.** 3 × 8 × 7   **99.** 9 × 2 × 4

Estimate.

100.   51
         × 4

101.   461
         × 7

102.   324
         × 6

103.   6,395
           × 3

Multiply.

104. 85 × 10   **105.** 500 × 70   **106.** 300 × 47

107.   48
         × 29

108.   753
         × 28

109.   1,264
           × 19

110. $9.06
           × 54

Estimate.

112.   51
         × 47

113.   914
         × 68

114.   380
         × 84

Divide.

115. 7)‾6‾3‾   **116.** 5)‾3‾3‾   **117.** 3)‾9‾9‾   **118.** 4)‾9‾4‾

119. 9)‾2‾0‾7‾   **120.** 6)‾9‾0‾6‾   **121.** 4)‾9‾5‾1‾   **122.** 7)‾9‾9‾8‾

Find the average.

123. 9, 5, 12, 10, 14   **124.** 18, 26, 31, 24, 21

Name each figure.

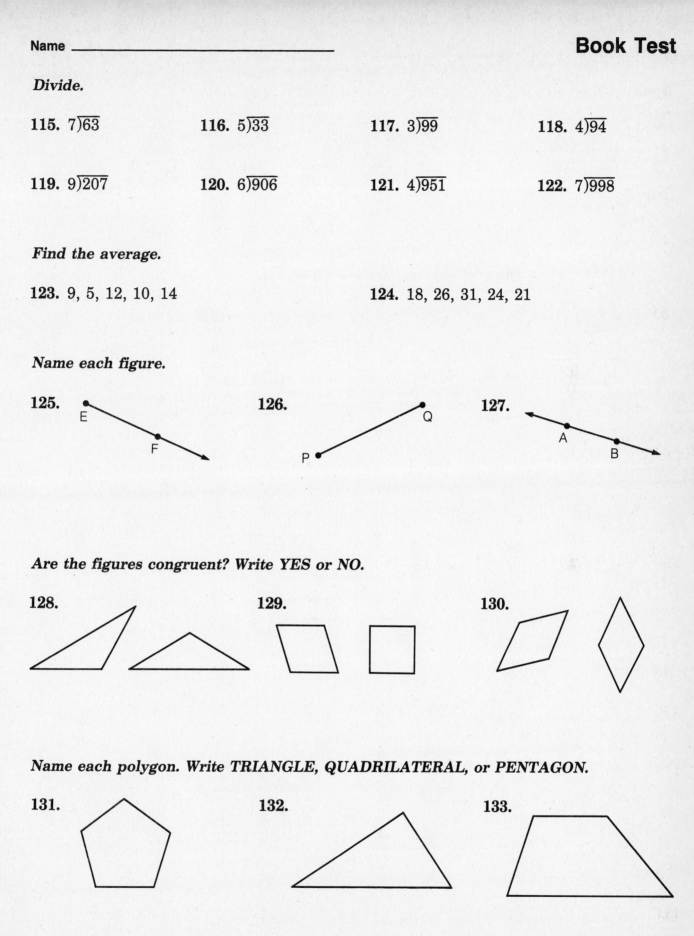

125.   **126.**   **127.**

Are the figures congruent? Write YES or NO.

128.   **129.**   **130.**

Name each polygon. Write TRIANGLE, QUADRILATERAL, or PENTAGON.

131.   **132.**   **133.**

Name each shape.

134.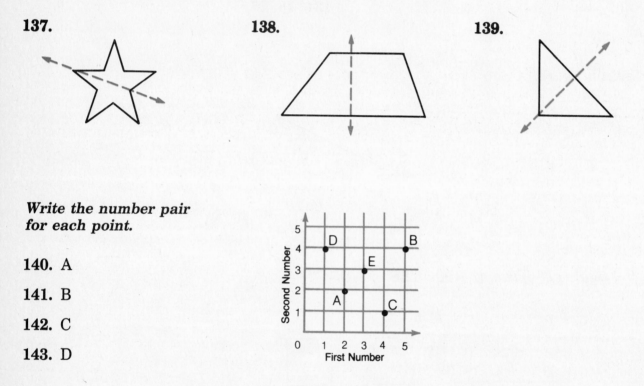

135.

136.

Is the dashed line a line of symmetry? Write YES or NO.

137.

138.

139.

Write the number pair for each point.

140. A

141. B

142. C

143. D

Write a fraction for the shaded part.

144.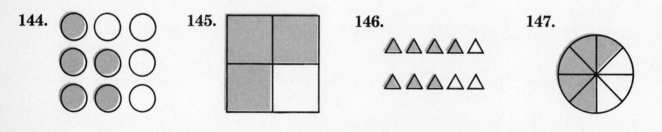

145.

146.

147.

Replace each ☐ with a number so the fractions are equivalent.

148. $\frac{1}{3} = \frac{\square}{6}$

149. $\frac{4}{5} = \frac{12}{\square}$

150. $\frac{6}{15} = \frac{2}{\square}$

151. $\frac{10}{20} = \frac{\square}{2}$

Replace each $\bigcirc$ with <, >, or = to make a true sentence.

152. $\frac{4}{5} \bigcirc \frac{8}{10}$ **153.** $\frac{5}{8} \bigcirc \frac{5}{6}$ **154.** $\frac{8}{9} \bigcirc \frac{8}{11}$

Write each improper fraction as a whole number or a mixed numeral.
Write the fraction part in simplest form.

155. $\frac{20}{4}$ **156.** $\frac{26}{3}$ **157.** $\frac{37}{6}$ **158.** $\frac{30}{8}$

Add or subtract. Write each sum or difference in simplest form.

159. $\frac{2}{7} + \frac{2}{7}$ **160.** $\frac{5}{12} + \frac{5}{12}$ **161.** $\frac{4}{5} - \frac{1}{5}$ **162.** $\frac{5}{6} - \frac{1}{6}$

163. $\begin{array}{r} \frac{1}{2} \\ + \frac{3}{8} \\ \hline \end{array}$ **164.** $\begin{array}{r} \frac{1}{4} \\ + \frac{1}{3} \\ \hline \end{array}$ **165.** $\begin{array}{r} \frac{1}{4} \\ - \frac{1}{8} \\ \hline \end{array}$ **166.** $\begin{array}{r} \frac{3}{4} \\ - \frac{1}{3} \\ \hline \end{array}$

Complete.

167. $\frac{1}{2}$ of 14 = $\square$ **168.** $\frac{5}{6}$ of 36 = $\square$ **169.** $\frac{5}{8}$ of 40 = $\square$

Measure to the nearest centimeter.

170. $\longmapsto\!\longmapsto$ **171.** $\longmapsto\!\!\!\!\!\!\!\!\longmapsto$

Choose the more reasonable measurement.

172. weight of a package of butter
     1 lb   1 ton

173. thermos jug of juice
     1 cup   1 gal

Solve. Use the figures.

174. Find the area.

175. Find the perimeter.

176. Find the volume.

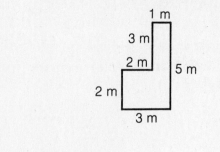

12 km

15 km

1 m
3 m
2 m
2 m
5 m
3 m

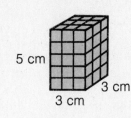

5 cm
3 cm
3 cm

Write a decimal for each of the following.

177. $\frac{37}{100}$

178. $4\frac{7}{10}$

179. twenty-nine and eight tenths

Order from least to greatest.

180. 1.74, 1.47, 4.17

181. 39.4, 39.1, 39

182. 56.04, 56.5, 56.44

Add or subtract.

183.   5.84
+ 2.59

184.   4.6
+ 4.57

185.   27.18
+ 37.95

186.   3.92
+ 1.1

187.   7.13
− 1.76

188.   8.04
− 5.76

189.   53.1
− 27.85

190.   72.6
− 2.11

Round to the nearest whole number. Then estimate.

191.   21.6
+ 2.3

192.   75.62
− 19.29

193.   18.6
+ 9.64

194.   14.2
− 6.01

Divide.

195. 3)4,852

196. 5)5,945

197. 8)$96.16

198. 6)9,872

199. 24)72

200. 90)810

201. 32)205

202. 62)708

Copyright © 1988 by Merrill Publishing Co., Columbus, Ohio 43216

Index

of whole numbers, 53–55,
  59–60, 68–71, 73–75,
  80–81, 84
by zero, 55

Number pairs, 110
Number lines
  used for fractions, 121
  used in multiplication, 53
  used in rounding, 19, 157
Numerators, 113

Odd numbers, 31, 60
One, 15–17, 21
  division by, 61
  multiplication by, 55
Ordering
  decimals, 154
  fractions, 120
  whole numbers, 18
Ounces, 142
Outcomes, 159

Parallelograms, 107
Patterns in computation
  adding fractions, 130
  area of triangles and
    parallelograms, 145
  checking sums and
    differences, 7
  clock arithmetic, 44
  counting money, 49
  dividing by tens, 164
  dividing whole numbers, 92
  divisibility, 62
  equivalent fractions, 117
  even and odd numbers, 31
  multiplying whole numbers,
    75
  relating addition and
    multiplication, 82
Patterns in geometry
  tessellations, 105
Patterns in place value
  reading and writing
    decimals, 153
Pentagon, 107
Perimeter, 144, 147
Period, 21
Pints, 142
Place value
  charts, 15, 152–154
  decimals, 152–153
  whole numbers, 15–17
Plane, 103
Points, 110
Polygon, 103, 107

Pounds, 142
Pretests, 1, 14, 25, 41, 52, 67,
  79, 89, 102, 112, 125, 138,
  151, 161
Probability, 159
Problem solving
  addition and subtraction of
    fractions, 133
  choosing the operation, 11,
    64
  dividing to find equivalent
    fractions, 122
  draw a diagram, 149
  estimating, 30
  guess and check, 100
  hidden steps, 169
  making and using a chart,
    148
  meaning of remainders, 99
  missing facts, 12, 50, 77
  reading charts and graphs,
    22
  too many facts, 23
  two-step problems, 37, 65
  using a calendar, 45
  using drawings, 134
  using money, 158
  using multiplication, 76, 85
  working backwards, 123
Product, 54
Properties
  of addition, 2
  of multiplication, 55, 70
Pyramids, 108

Quadrilaterals, 107
Quarts, 142
Quotients, 57, 90
  3-digit, 98
  2-digit, 91, 94, 167–168

Rays, 104
Rectangles, 107
Rectangular prisms, 108
Remainders, 90, 94, 97–99,
  163–165, 167–168
  meaning of, 99
Rounding
  decimals, 157
  whole numbers, 19

Simplest form, 119
Solid figures, 108
Sphere, 108
Squares, 107
**Standard form of whole
  numbers,** 15–16

Subtraction
  checking, 7
  of decimals, 156
  estimating, 36
  facts, 5
  of fractions, 127, 131
  of money, 48
  related to addition, 6
  renaming in, 33–35
  of whole numbers, 5, 7, 10,
    26, 33–36
  with zeros, 34
Sum, 2
Symmetry, 109

Tens
  division by, 163–164
  multiplication by, 81
Tenths, 152
Tessellations, 105
Thousands, 16–17, 21
Time, 42–43
Tons, 142
Triangles, 107

Volume, 146–147

Weeks, 45
Weight, 142
Whole numbers
  adding, 2–4, 7, 9, 26–29
  comparing, 5
  dividing, 56–57, 61, 90–94,
    97–98, 162–165, 167–168
  estimating differences of, 36
  estimating products of, 74,
    84
  estimating sums of, 29
  even, 31, 60
  expanded form, 15–16
  multiplying, 53–55, 59–60,
    68–71, 73–75, 80–81, 84
  odd, 31, 60
  ordering, 18
  place value, 15–17
  rounding, 19
  standard form, 15–16
  subtracting, 5, 7, 10, 26,
    33–36
  in words, 15–16

Yards, 141

Zeros
  in addition, 2
  in division, 61
  in multiplication, 55
  in subtraction, 34

Answers

CHAPTER 1

Page 2 **1.** 8 **2.** 12 **3.** 10 **4.** 9 **5.** 3 **6.** 15 **7.** 6 **8.** 10 **9.** 11 **10.** 9 **11.** 8 **12.** 18 **13.** 10 **14.** 5 **15.** 13 **16.** 15 **17.** 7 **18.** 7 **19.** 6 **20.** 4 **21.** 0 **22.** 6 kittens **23.** 12 children

Page 3 **1.** 12 **2.** 12 **3.** 9 **4.** 13 **5.** 19 **6.** 16 **7.** 18 **8.** 13 **9.** 14 **10.** 12 **11.** 18 **12.** 11 **13.** 14 **14.** 16 **15.** 16 animals **16.** 13 gloves **17.** 15 homes **18.** 17 children

Page 4 **1.** 8 **2.** 8 **3.** 6 **4.** 9 **5.** 7 **6.** 5 **7.** 8 **8.** 0 **9.** 5 **10.** 4 **11.** 8 **12.** 4 **13.** 4 **14.** 9 **15.** 9 **16.** 4 **17.** 3 **18.** 5 **19.** 1 **20.** 5 **21.** 6 **22.** 5 **23.** 8 **24.** 6 **25.** 9 **26.** 7 **27.** 5 robins **28.** 9 balloons

Page 5 **1.** 2 **2.** 7 **3.** 5 **4.** 9 **5.** 4 **6.** 8 **7.** 6 **8.** 8 **9.** 9 **10.** 7 **11.** 4 **12.** 8 **13.** 8 **14.** 7 **15.** 9 **16.** 0 **17.** 3 **18.** 8 **19.** 4 are black **20.** 7 more

Page 6 **1.** $9 - 6 = 3$ **2.** $5 + 1 = 6$ **3.** $5 + 7 = 12$ **4.** $12 - 4 = 8$ **5.** $9 + 8 = 17$ **6.** $13 - 8 = 5$ **7.** $14 - 7 = 7$ **8.** $10 - 6 = 4$ **9.** $6 - 4 = 2$ **10.** $7 + 8 = 15$ **11.** $6 + 6 = 12$ **12.** $16 - 8 = 8$ **13.** $7 + 8 = 15; 8 + 7 = 15;$ $15 - 8 = 7; 15 - 7 = 8$ **14.** $5 + 4 = 9;$ $4 + 5 = 9; 9 - 4 = 5; 9 - 5 = 4$ **15.** $4 + 8 = 12; 8 + 4 = 12; 12 - 8 = 4;$ $12 - 4 = 8$ **16.** $7 + 6 = 13; 6 + 7 = 13;$ $13 - 6 = 7; 13 - 7 = 6$ **17.** 4 pies **18.** 12 pictures

Page 7 Patterns in Computation **1.** 9 **2.** 99 **3.** 999 **4.** 2,222 **5.** 7,777 **6.** 75 **7.** 889 **8.** 53 **9.** 111 **10.** 272 **11.** 383 **12.** 996 **13.** 2,787 **14.** 522 **15.** 5,124 **16.** 8,798 **17.** 8,759 **18.** 2,182 **19.** 2,810 **20.** 1,151

Page 8 Maintenance **1.** 10 **2.** 13 **3.** 6 **4.** 13 **5.** 16 **6.** 4 **7.** 16 **8.** 12 **9.** 11 **10.** 14 **11.** 18 **12.** 8 **13.** 7 **14.** 6 **15.** 9 **16.** 2 **17.** 1 **18.** 8 **19.** 3 **20.** 9 **21.** 5 **22.** 9 **23.** 0 **24.** 4 **25.** 9 **26.** 3 **27.** 7 **28.** 6 **29.** 14 houses **30.** 5 donuts **31.** 8 runs **32.** 6¢

Page 9 **1.** 46 **2.** 77 **3.** 89 **4.** 246 **5.** 377 **6.** 438 **7.** 548 **8.** 2,389 **9.** 4,998 **10.** 3,589 **11.** 68; $22 + 46 = 68$ **12.** 956; $152 + 804 = 956$ **13.** 5,776; $1,455 + 4,321 = 5,776$ **14.** 95 points **15.** 374 miles

Page 10 **1.** 34 **2.** 22 **3.** 23 **4.** 11 **5.** 222 **6.** 421 **7.** 532 **8.** 333 **9.** 2,203 **10.** 2,524 **11.** 21; $24 + 21 = 45$ **12.** 21; $63 + 21 = 84$ **13.** 311; $57 + 311 = 368$ **14.** 410; $409 + 410 = 819$ **15.** 2,312; $3,114 + 2,312 = 5,426$ **16.** 510; $8,243 + 510 = 8,753$ **17.** 12 books **18.** 13¢

Page 11 **1.** add **2.** subtract **3.** 9 cups **4.** 17 cookies **5.** 16 apples **6.** 15¢

Page 12 **1.** 6 **2.** 121 **3.** 99 **4.** 287 **5.** 86 **6.** 163 **7.** 14 **8.** 121

CHAPTER 2

Page 15 **1.** 80 **2.** 700 **3.** 5 **4.** 63 **5.** 290 **6.** 841 **7.** 904 **8.** 19 **9.** 72 **10.** 813 **11.** 542 **12.** seventeen **13.** forty-four **14.** eighty-seven **15.** one hundred ninety-eight **16.** five hundred seventy-nine **17.** nine hundred nineteen **18.** $30 + 3$ **19.** $10 + 2$ **20.** $80 + 8$ **21.** $400 + 60 + 1$ **22.** $700 + 20 + 9$ **23.** $900 + 90 + 9$ **24.** $200 + 9$ **25.** $500 + 10 + 8$ **26.** $700 + 30$

Page 16 **1.** 500 **2.** 5,000 **3.** 500,000 **4.** 50,000 **5.** 2,506 **6.** 15,089 **7.** 8,749 **8.** 305,068 **9.** 933,107 **10.** seven thousand, six hundred nine **11.** seventeen thousand, five hundred forty **12.** ninety four thousand, sixty-two **13.** three hundred twenty-one thousand, two **14.** nine hundred eighty-three thousand, four hundred four **15.** $5,000 + 300 + 10 + 4$ **16.** $20,000 + 8,000 + 100 + 40$ **17.** $50,000 + 9,000 + 20 + 1$ **18.** $70,000 + 9,000 + 900 + 80 + 1$ **19.** $300,000 + 80,000 + 4,000 + 200 + 8$ **20.** $900,000 + 90,000 + 9,000 + 900 + 9$

Page 17 **1.** 2 **2.** 5 **3.** 9 **4.** 23 **5.** 56 **6.** 2 **7.** 8 **8.** 34 **9.** 683 **10.** 47 **11.** 288 **12.** 91 **13.** 590, 600, 610 **14.** 3,500, 3,600 **15.** 6,770; 6,780; 6,800; 6,810 **16.** 300 minutes **17.** 100¢ or $1.00

Page 18 **1.** $28 < 29$ **2.** $463 > 462$ **3.** $747 = 747$ **4.** $3,664 > 3,649$ **5.** $8,233 < 8,238$ **6.** $<$ **7.** $>$ **8.** $<$ **9.** $=$ **10.** $>$ **11.** $<$ **12.** $>$ **13.** $>$

14. 52 15. 44 16. 558 17. 612 18. 994
19. 2,812 20. 4,080 21. 8,301
22. 467, 576, 671 23. 1,426; 2,610; 4,338

Page 19 1. 900 2. 800 3. 900 4. 800
5. 900 6. 900 7. 800 8. 800 9. 900
10. 800 11. 3,000 12. 7,000 13. 19,000
14. 79,000 15. 2,030 16. 4,700 17. 960
18. 8,260 19. 18,800 20. 27,000 21. 51,000
22. 48,800 23. 79,340 24. 91,000
25. 32,860 26. 19,200 27. 29,000
28. 42,400 29. 99,900

Page 20 Maintenance 1. 10 2. 9 3. 13
4. 11 5. 12 6. 79 7. 89 8. 889 9. 11
10. 13 11. 5 12. 8 13. 8 14. 7 15. 7
16. 15 17. 46 18. 51 19. 32 20. 35
21. 60 22. 600 23. 6 24. 6,000 25. 60,000
26. 629 27. 8,102 28. 53,013 29. 400,011
30. > 31. > 32. = 33. > 34. 340
35. 700 36. 8,000 37. 5,300 38. 9,120
39. 13,000 40. 25,000 41. 63,140
42. 83,000 43. 77,800

Page 21 1. 37,214 2. 248,309 3. 8,832,117
4. 98,026,707 5. 630,126,789 6. 200
7. 20,000 8. 2,000,000 9. 20,000,000
10. 200,000 11. 20,000 12. 2,000
13. 2,000,000 14. 3,047,200 15. 53,208,023
16. 33,510,017 17. five million, forty thousand,
six hundred 18. sixty-three million, seventy
thousand, four 19. < 20. =

Page 22 1. 12 2. 6 3. 18 4. 8
5. ice cream, jello 6. cookies, fruit
7. ice cream, 14; cake, 8; pie, 10;
cookies, 6; jello, 12; fruit, 6

Page 23 1. 1,082 melons 2. 516 balloons
3. $10.73 4. 239 empty seats 5. 413 tickets
6. 27 children

CHAPTER 3

Page 26 1. 12 2. 7 3. 5 4. 15 5. 8 6. 16
7. 11 8. 9 9. 12 10. 6 11. 13 12. 6
13. 19 14. 53 15. 39 16. 33 17. 42 18. 3
19. 97 20. 68 21. 25 22. 69 23. 87 papers
24. 13 more donuts

Page 27 1. 75 2. 85 3. 463 4. 647 5. 737
6. 2,058 7. 3,837 8. 765 9. 847 10. 832
11. 951 12. 6,552 13. 4,261 14. 5,336
15. 3,853 16. 684 steps
17. 445 pennies and nickles

Page 28 1. 6,153 2. 7,182 3. 14,234
4. 40,347 5. 55,823 6. 139,403 7. 80,029

8. 214,140 9. 513,226 10. 22,263 11. 104
12. 154 13. 398 14. 778 15. 7,149 16. 154
17. 200 18. 484 19. 917 20. 6,418
21. 110 toothbrushes 22. 681,115 papers

Page 29 1. 40 + 30 = 70 2. 60 + 30 = 90
3. 50 + 40 = 90 4. 70 + 70 = 140
5. 70 + 50 = 120 6. 300 + 600 = 900
7. 300 + 700 = 1,000 8. 500 + 800 = 1,300
9. 600 + 300 = 900 10. 800 + 300 = 1,100
11. 2,000 + 5,000 = 7,000
12. 4,000 + 7,000 = 11,000
13. 4,000 + 4,000 = 8,000
14. 6,000 + 6,000 = 12,000
15. 70 + 60 = 130, 130 miles
16. 200 + 400 = 600, 600 miles of lines

Page 30 1. c 2. a 3. b

Page 31 Patterns in Computation 1. even
2. odd 3. even 4. even 5. even 6. odd
7. odd 8. odd 9. even 10. even 11. odd
12. odd 13. odd, 17 14. even, 14
15. odd, 15 16. odd, 29 17. even, 38
18. even, 166 19. odd, 189 20. odd, 831
21. even, 1,172 22. even, 1,194

Page 32 Maintenance 1. 60 2. 6 3. 6,000
4. 600 5. > 6. = 7. > 8. < 9. 40
10. 2,000 11. 400 12. 9,000 13. 697
14. 232 15. 613 16. 647 17. 374
18. 12,264 19. 979 20. 1,356
21. 600 + 300 = 900 22. 500 + 200 = 700
23. 500 + 400 = 900 24. 800 + 600 = 1,400
25. 2,000 + 7,000 = 9,000
26. 8,000 + 4,000 = 12,000 27. 28¢
28. estimate 700 + 600 = 1,300 visitors

Page 33 1. 27 2. 28 3. 308 4. 362 5. 236
6. 732 7. 142 8. 176 9. 365 10. 75
11. 454 12. 256 13. 1,376 14. 1,754
15. 775 16. 228 miles 17. 350 miles

Page 34 1. 59, 10 2. 10 3. 39 4. 10 5. 10
6. 39 7. 14 8. 173 9. 156 10. 154
11. 2,557 12. 537 13. 1,427 14. 1,516
15. 2,586 16. 688 17. 577 records 18. $26

Page 35 1. 2,882 2. 1,868 3. 3,335
4. 1,379 5. 907 6. 26,488 7. 16,787
8. 27,354 9. 7,539 10. 44,415 11. 147,793
12. 165,293 13. 57,257 14. 97,778
15. 476,038 16. 188,597 17. 47,768 copies
18. 5,068 people

Page 36 1. 60 − 20 = 40 2. 40 − 30 = 10
3. 80 − 40 = 40 4. 80 − 50 = 30
5. 80 − 50 = 30 6. 500 − 400 = 100
7. 400 − 200 = 200 8. 800 − 400 = 400

9. $600 - 600 = 0$ 10. $500 - 200 = 300$
11. $5,000 - 3,000 = 2,000$
12. $5,000 - 2,000 = 3,000$
13. $6,000 - 3,000 = 3,000$
14. $9,000 - 6,000 = 3,000$
15. $\$400 - \$300 = \$100$
16. $6,000 - 4,000 = 2,000$ more miles

Page 37 1. 41 sheets 2. 6 packages
3. 45 cookies 4. 7 more desks 5. 53 trays
6. 53 light bulbs

CHAPTER 4

Page 42 1. 8:19 2. 6:52 3. 4:45 4. 12:30
5. 9:30; past 9 6. 5:15; past 5
7. 10:45; quarter 11 8. 2:45; quarter till 3
9. 8:30; half past 8 10. 5:15; quarter past 5
11. 9:20; 20 minutes after 9 12. A.M. 13. P.M.
14. P.M. 15. A.M.

Page 43 1. 6:25 P.M. 2. 5:45 A.M.
3. 4:30 A.M. 4. 12:15 A.M. 5. 3:00 P.M.
6. 6:15 A.M. 7. 11:30 A.M. 8. 11:50 P.M.
9. 5 hours 10. 20 minutes 11. 50 minutes
12. 3 hours 13. 6 hours 14. 35 minutes

Page 44 Patterns in Computation 1. 1:00
2. 5:00 3. 7:00 4. 10:00 5. 12:00 6. 4
7. 2 8. 10 9. 3 10. 7 11. 8 12. 6 13. 12
14. 1 15. 8 16. 6 17. 3 18. 9:30 P.M.
19. 4:00 P.M.

Page 45 1. January 8 2. January 17
3. February 17 4. January 20 5. February 3
6. February 8 7. February 22 8. January 23
9. 5 paychecks; January 3, January 17,
January 13, February 14, February 28
10. January 24, February 28 11. February 6
12. January 22

Page 46 Maintenance 1. 1,808 2. 7,032
3. 585 4. 7,038 5. 1,820 6. 61,128 7. 225
8. 2,128 9. 14 10. 5 11. 7 12. 8, 10, 15, 17
13. 95, 97, 100, 101, 102 14. 79, 97, 709, 907
15. 3, 13, 30, 31, 33 16. $900 + 700 = 1,600$
17. $900 + 500 = 1,400$ 18. $400 - 200 = 200$
19. $150 - 40 = 110$ 20. $80 + 90 + 90 = 260$
21. $40 + 70 + 50 = 160$
22. $7,000 + 4,000 + 3,000 = 14,000$
23. $10,000 - 8,000 = 2,000$ 24. 7:30 25. 6:15

Page 47 1. $2.87 2. $1.78 3. $2.46 4. $1.95
5. $1.20 6. $3.00 7. 37¢, $0.37 8. 25¢, $0.25
9. 40¢, $0.40 10. 100¢, $1.00 11. 2¢; $0.02
12. 60¢, $0.60 13. fifty cents
14. sixty-three cents
15. four dollars and eighty-seven cents

Page 48 1. $6.51 2. $3.74 3. $2.79
4. $4.28 5. $8.80 6. $1.57 7. $1.52
8. $7.41 9. $6.23 10. $5.33 11. 4 pennies,
1 quarter, 1 half-dollar; change: 79¢
12. 2 pennies, 1 nickel, 1 dime, 1 half-dollar;
change: 67¢ 13. 2 dimes, 1 quarter, 3 dollars;
change: $3.45 14. 4 pennies, 2 dimes, 3 dollars;
change: $3.24

Page 49 Patterns in Computation 1. $1.27
2. $0.80 3. $2.02 4. 1 quarter 5. $0.75
6. 1 half-dollar, 1 quarter 7. $0.45
8. 1 quarter, 2 dimes 9. $1.28 10. $0.15

Page 50 1. b. amount of money given
2. b. amount of money received 3. b. time she
arrived 4. a. time put in the oven; b. amount of
time to bake 5. a. minutes jogged in morning;
b. minutes jogged in afternoon 6. b. additional
time it took Karen 7. a. amount of money Suzy
had 8. b. amount of money left

CHAPTER 5

Page 53 1. 9 2. 8 3. 16 4. 20 5. 18
6. 14 7. 12 8. 8 9. 10 10. 9 11. 8 12. 12

Page 54 1. 6 2. 21 3. 10 4. 8 5. 9 6. 12
7. 20 8. 27 9. 16 10. 28 11. 24 12. 12
13. 35 14. 18 15. 32 16. 36 17. f 18. g
19. e 20. a 21. c 22. b 23. d 24. 40 hours

Page 55 1. 10 2. 24 3. 4 4. 0 5. 18 6. 0
7. 32, 32 8. 45, 45 9. 30, 30 10. 24, 24
11. 7, 7 12. 0, 0 13. 1 14. 0 15. 2 16. 4
17. 3 18. 4 19. 5 20. 7 21. 6 22. 8
23. 2 24. 1 25. 5 26. 2

Page 56 1. 7 2. 5 3. 4 4. 6 5. 7 6. 8
7. 9 8. 8 9. 6 10. 5, 5 11. 4, 4 12. 9, 9
13. 6, 6 14. 7, 7 15. 5, 5 16. 2, 2 17. 4, 4
18. 4, 4

Page 57 1. 5 2. 7 3. 7 4. 8 5. 9 6. 4
7. 2 8. 6 9. 4 10. 1 11. 7 12. 9 13. 3
14. 7 15. 5 16. 8 17. 6 18. 8 19. 6
20. 8 21. 2 22. 9 23. 9 children
24. 6 balloons

Page 58 Maintenance 1. 3 2. 3 3. 4 4. 8
5. 0 6. 5 7. 7 8. 7 9. 1,634 10. 131
11. 3,884 12. 3,408 13. 18,359 14. 125,421
15. 3,316 16. 11,369 17. 1,401 18. 234
19. 80,000 20. 8,000 21. 8 22. 800
23. $34.52 24. $15.11 25. $3.61 26. $4.17
27. 32 28. 30 29. 27 30. 5 31. 4 32. 8
33. August 31 34. 25¢

Page 59 **1.** 42 **2.** 54 **3.** 56 **4.** 36 **5.** 30 **6.** 16 **7.** 18 **8.** 35 **9.** 24 **10.** 7 **11.** 18 **12.** 32 **13.** 21 **14.** 6 **15.** 63 **16.** 28 **17.** 24 **18.** 14 **19.** 45 **20.** 27 **21.** 40 **22.** 48 hours **23.** 42 days

Page 60 **1.** 35 **2.** 12, 24 **3.** 6, 12, 18 **4.** 6, 12, 18, 24 **5.** odd **6.** even **7.** even **8.** odd **9.** even **10.** odd **11.** even **12.** even **13.** even **14.** odd **15.** odd **16.** odd

Page 61 **1.** 3 **2.** 2 **3.** 5 **4.** 7 **5.** 9 **6.** 0 **7.** 3 **8.** 6 **9.** 0 **10.** 7 **11.** 8 **12.** 4 **13.** 7 **14.** 1 **15.** 6 **16.** 2 **17.** 0 **18.** 4 **19.** 5 **20.** 0 **21.** 9 **22.** 1 **23.** 6 **24.** 5 **25.** 5 blocks **26.** 4 rows

Page 62 Patterns in Computation **1.** 3 **2.** 2, 3 **3.** 3 **4.** 5 **5.** 5 **6.** 2, 3 **7.** 2, 3, 5 **8.** 2, 5 **9.** 3 **10.** 2 **11.** 5 **12.** 2, 3 **13.** 2, 3, 5 **14.** 2 **15.** 3, 5 **16.** 2, 3 **17.** yes **18.** no **19.** A whole number is divisible by 10 if its ones digit is 0.

Page 63 **1.** $5 \times 7 = 35$; $7 \times 5 = 35$; $35 \div 7 = 5$; $35 \div 5 = 7$ **2.** $4 \times 8 = 32$; $8 \times 4 = 32$; $32 \div 8 = 4$; $32 \div 4 = 8$ **3.** $3 \times 9 = 27$; $9 \times 3 = 27$; $27 \div 9 = 3$; $27 \div 3 = 9$ **4.** $6 \times 5 = 30$; $5 \times 6 = 30$; $30 \div 5 = 6$; $30 \div 6 = 5$ **5.** $2 \times 1 = 2$; $1 \times 2 = 2$; $2 \div 1 = 2$; $2 \div 2 = 1$ **6.** $3 \times 7 = 21$; $7 \times 3 = 21$; $21 \div 7 = 3$; $21 \div 3 = 7$ **7.** $4 \times 4 = 16$; $16 \div 4 = 4$ **8.** $5 \times 1 = 5$; $1 \times 5 = 5$; $5 \div 1 = 5$; $5 \div 5 = 1$ **9.** $9 \times 6 = 54$; $6 \times 9 = 54$; $54 \div 6 = 9$; $54 \div 9 = 6$ **10.** $3 \times 4 = 12$; $4 \times 3 = 12$; $12 \div 4 = 3$; $12 \div 3 = 4$ **11.** $5 \times 4 = 20$; $4 \times 5 = 20$; $20 \div 4 = 5$; $20 \div 5 = 4$ **12.** $7 \times 9 = 63$; $9 \times 7 = 63$; $63 \div 9 = 7$; $63 \div 7 = 9$ **13.** $6 \times 7 = 42$; $7 \times 6 = 42$; $42 \div 7 = 6$; $42 \div 6 = 7$ **14.** $5 \times 5 = 25$; $25 \div 5 = 5$ **15.** $1 \times 4 = 4$; $4 \times 1 = 4$; $4 \div 1 = 4$; $4 \div 4 = 1$ **16.** $5 \times 9 = 45$; $9 \times 5 = 45$; $45 \div 9 = 5$; $45 \div 5 = 9$

Page 64 **1.** SUBTRACT; $14.00 **2.** MULTIPLY, SUBTRACT; $1.00 **3.** DIVIDE; 5 rides **4.** DIVIDE; 9 floors **5.** DIVIDE; 7 planters; 1 plant remains **6.** SUBTRACT, DIVIDE; 4 show areas

Page 65 **1.** 287 miles **2.** $6.00 **3.** $24.00 **4.** $1.00 **5.** 45 cases **6.** 63 tablets

CHAPTER 6

Page 68 **1.** 5 **2.** 50 **3.** 500 **4.** 5,000 **5.** 21 **6.** 210 **7.** 2,100 **8.** 21,000 **9.** 32 **10.** 320 **11.** 3,200 **12.** 32,000 **13.** 30 **14.** 300

15. 3,000 **16.** 30,000 **17.** 40 **18.** 400 **19.** 4,000 **20.** 4,200 **21.** 560 **22.** 1,200 **23.** 36,000 **24.** 24,000 **25.** 66 **26.** 55 **27.** 80 **28.** 62 **29.** 69 **30.** 70 **31.** 28 **32.** 86 **33.** 66 **34.** 60 **35.** 48 **36.** 30

Page 69 **1.** 90 **2.** 68 **3.** 85 **4.** 54 **5.** 70 **6.** 258 **7.** 318 **8.** 252 **9.** 264 **10.** 365 **11.** 96 **12.** 70 **13.** 87 **14.** 90 **15.** 57 **16.** 60 **17.** 94 **18.** 504 **19.** 384 **20.** 304 **21.** 304 **22.** 440 **23.** $752 **24.** $495 **25.** $602 **26.** 432 **27.** $376 **28.** 185 **29.** $343 **30.** 260

Page 70 **1.** 0 **2.** 6 **3.** 9 **4.** 10 **5.** 35 **6.** 28 **7.** 32 **8.** 56 **9.** 54 **10.** 75 **11.** 64 **12.** 90 **13.** 80 **14.** 64 **15.** 32 **16.** 72 **17.** 140 **18.** 200 **19.** 0 **20.** 360 **21.** 16 **22.** 60 **23.** 0

Page 71 **1.** 472 **2.** 696 **3.** 924 **4.** 789 **5.** 956 **6.** 959 **7.** 963 **8.** 980 **9.** 326 **10.** 815 **11.** 832 **12.** 792 **13.** 822 **14.** 770 **15.** 864 **16.** 438 fliers **17.** 476 miles

Page 72 Maintenance **1.** 6,204 **2.** 14,212 **3.** 95,756 **4.** 17,678 **5.** 32,653 **6.** 14,602 **7.** 88,043 **8.** 462,791 **9.** > **10.** < **11.** < **12.** 2:05 **13.** 7:50 **14.** 4:45 **15.** 69 **16.** 45 **17.** 2,800 **18.** 920 **19.** 6 **20.** 5 **21.** 6 **22.** 8 **23.** $1.21 **24.** 4 times

Page 73 **1.** 1,630 **2.** 1,701 **3.** 1,602 **4.** 3,618 **5.** 1,718 **6.** 3,040 **7.** 4,944 **8.** 5,826 **9.** 925 **10.** 2,391 **11.** 14,498 **12.** 26,190 **13.** 24,260 **14.** 27,097 **15.** 32,088 **16.** $3,680 **17.** $5,728

Page 74 **1.** $9.42 **2.** $42.00 **3.** $32.48 **4.** $182.76 **5.** $284.15 **6.** $32.41; $35 **7.** $206.55; $180 **8.** $227.44; $240 **9.** 1,384; 1,200 **10.** 3,498; 3,600 **11.** 23,183; 25,000 **12.** 21,084; 21,000 **13.** 12,476; 12,000 **14.** 32,124; 30,000 **15.** $63.92; $80 **16.** 67,384; 64,000

Page 75 Patterns in Computation **1.** = **2.** 7,000 **3.** 888 **4.** 22 **5.** 6 **6.** 66 **7.** 666 **8.** 6,666 **9.** 66,666 **10.** 45 **11.** 495 **12.** 4,995 **13.** 49,995 **14.** 499,995

Page 76 **1.** 25 students **2.** 21 cars **3.** 32 pictures **4.** 27 pieces of paper **5.** 5 students **6.** 15 students **7.** 20 students

Page 77 **1.** The points for Elm Park School's team are missing. **2.** 147 empty seats **3.** 234 coupons **4.** The number of horses is missing. **5.** $1,551 **6.** 9,998 people

CHAPTER 7

Page 80 **1.** 30 **2.** 70 **3.** 140 **4.** 760 **5.** 600
6. 2,470 **7.** 460; 552 **8.** 830; 1,328
9. 162; 540; 702 **10.** 448; 640; 1,088 **11.** 1,008
12. 648 **13.** 858 **14.** 1,425 **15.** 513
16. 1,242 **17.** 1,092 **18.** 912 **19.** 490
20. 782

Page 81 **1.** 390 **2.** 2,380 **3.** 1,800 **4.** 2,250
5. 5,840 **6.** 26,400 **7.** 435; 6,525
8. 252; 1,400; 1,652 **9.** 168; 1,680; 1,848
10. 322; 4,140; 4,462 **11.** 672 **12.** 5,712
13. 2,418 **14.** 3,534 **15.** 6,225 **16.** 1,484
17. 6,270 **18.** 3,159 **19.** 1,998 **20.** 2,430

Page 82 Patterns in Computation
1. 210; 21; 231 **2.** 980; 980; 980; 98; 3,038
3. 390; 39; 39; 468 **4.** 460; 460; 460; 46; 46;
1,472 **5.** 640; 64; 64; 64; 832 **6.** 5,700; 570; 57;
6,327 **7.** 1,242 **8.** 3,066 **9.** 2,015 **10.** 4,606

Page 83 Maintenance **1.** 46, 48, 50, 84, 88
2. 1,333, 3,133, 3,313, 3,331 **3.** 46, 49, 50, 79,
82 **4.** 247, 402, 740, 742 **5.** 12,415
6. 105,780 **7.** 36,669 **8.** $5.13 **9.** 11:30 P.M.
10. 11:30 A.M. **11.** 10:00 P.M. **12.** 7:00 A.M.
13. 63 **14.** 6 **15.** 5 **16.** 42 **17.** 4,900
18. $498 **19.** 2,872 **20.** 30,635 **21.** 370
22. yes **23.** 12 tickets

Page 84 **1.** 1,372; 10,290; 11,662 **2.** $204.12
3. 24,096 **4.** 10,350 **5.** $509.62 **6.** 49,533
7. 15,392 **8.** $275.50 **9.** 62,528 **10.** 118,188
11. $2,564.45 **12.** 197,220 **13.** 120,495
14. $2,356.48 **15.** 70 × 30 = 2,100
16. 100 × 90 = 9,000 **17.** 100 × 50 = 5,000
18. 300 × 100 = 30,000

Page 85 **1.** $149.50 **2.** $122.10
3. 4,000 pencils **4.** $24.30 **5.** $113.96
6. 800 crayons **7.** 10,000 sheets **8.** $57.44

CHAPTER 8

Page 90 **1.** 2 **2.** 3 **3.** 5 R6 **4.** 8 R5 **5.** 0
6. 4 R1 **7.** 4 R3 **8.** 8 **9.** 1 **10.** 7 R7 **11.** 3
12. 4 **13.** 5 R5 **14.** 1 **15.** 8 **16.** 2 R7
17. 6 R3 **18.** 0 **19.** 4 **20.** 9 R3 **21.** 4 weeks,
3 days left **22.** 7 pairs, 1 extra shoe

Page 91 **1.** 21 **2.** 12 **3.** 10 **4.** 23 **5.** 22
6. 34 **7.** 11 **8.** 33 **9.** 24 **10.** 11 **11.** 10
12. 32 **13.** 11 **14.** 42 **15.** 20
16. 12 squares **17.** 10 tags

Page 92 Patterns in Computation **1.** 2
2. 2 tens **3.** 20 **4.** 2 hundreds **5.** 200 **6.** 3
7. 3 hundreds **8.** 300 **9.** 330 **10.** 3,000

11. 1 **12.** 10 **13.** 100 **14.** 1,000 **15.** 1,010
16. 3 **17.** 33 **18.** 3,000 **19.** 3,300 **20.** 3,303
21. 2 **22.** 202 **23.** 222 **24.** 2,000 **25.** 2,002

Page 93 **1.** 8, 6, 2, 2, 4, 0 **2.** 7, 5, 3, 3, 5, 0
3. 6, 4, 1, 1, 2, 0 **4.** 8, 4, 3, 3, 2, 0 **5.** 12
6. 38 **7.** 13 **8.** 13 **9.** 26 **10.** 24 **11.** 14
12. 15 **13.** 15 **14.** 14

Page 94 **1.** 1, 4, 3, 5, 1, 4, 2, 2, 0, 7, 0, 3, 3, 7, 3
2. 2, 5, 1, 4, 2, 5, 1, 1, 1, 0, 5, 0, 1, 1, 5, 1
3. 1, 3, 2, 5, 1, 3, 1, 7, 1, 5, 6, 5, 2, 2, 6, 7
4. 21 R3 **5.** 16 R4 **6.** 19 R1 **7.** 14 R4
8. 18 R3 **9.** 27 R1 **10.** 49 R1 **11.** 15 R2
12. 11 R4 **13.** 12 R4 **14.** 15 R2 **15.** 10 R5

Page 95 **1.** 7 **2.** 24; 8 **3.** 32; 8 **4.** 30; 6
5. 76; 19 **6.** 84; 21 **7.** 80; 16 **8.** 96; 24
9. 78; 26 **10.** 70; 14 **11.** 64; 16 **12.** 15 cans
13. $14

Page 96 Maintenance **1.** 23,746 **2.** $134.52
3. 96,739 **4.** 4,574 **5.** 35 **6.** 41 **7.** 38
8. 30 **9.** 56 **10.** 36 **11.** 6 **12.** 7 **13.** 574
14. 16 **15.** $270 **16.** 18 **17.** 288 **18.** 2,187
19. 3,780 **20.** 14 R1 **21.** 16 R3 **22.** 11 R2
23. 26 **24.** 9 weeks **25.** week 2 **26.** 18

Page 97 **1.** 8, 2, 4, 3, 3, 2, 0
2. 7, 5, 4, 2, 4, 4, 2, 5 **3.** 1, 1, 6, 1, 1, 2, 1
4. 84 **5.** 37 R2 **6.** 75 R3 **7.** 73 **8.** 81
9. 48 R2 **10.** 78 **11.** 63 R5 **12.** 59
13. 66 R6 **14.** 43 teams **15.** 96 papers

Page 98 **1.** 7, 4, 4, 2, 0 **2.** 2, 0, 6, 0
3. 0, 9, 1, 0, 3, 3, 6, 1 **4.** 127 R1 **5.** 186
6. 105 R4 **7.** 284 R2 **8.** 121 **9.** 163 papers
10. 13 students

Page 99 **1.** 26¢ **2.** 32¢ **3.** 25¢ **4.** 89¢
5. 49¢ **6.** 31¢ **7.** $1.03 **8.** $2.18

Page 100 **1.** 2 patterns, 2 yarns **2.** 3, 8
3. 2, 3, 9; 4, 5, 6, 7, 8 **4.** 1, 5, 3; 6, 2, 4 **5.** 45
6. 9—22¢ stamps; 1—8¢ stamp

CHAPTER 9

Page 103 **1.** yes **2.** no **3.** yes **4.** no **5.** no
6. yes **7.** yes **8.** yes **9.** no **10.** no **11.** no
12. yes

Page 104 **1.** line JK or line KJ **2.** angle Y
3. line segment RS or SR **4.** ray PQ **5.** angle B
6. line VW or WV **7.** parallel **8.** intersecting
9. parallel **10.** intersecting **11.** intersecting

Page 105 Patterns in Geometry **1.-8.** See
students' work. **9.** no **10.** yes **11.** yes
12. no

Page 106 Maintenance 1. $40 + 8$
2. $600 + 70 + 1$ **3.** $1,000 + 400 + 9$
4. $10,000 + 8,000 + 200 + 30 + 5$ **5.** 7,821
6. 1,015 **7.** 79,515 **8.** 28,246 **9.** 7,128
10. 32 **11.** 9 **12.** 56 **13.** 7 **14.** 168
15. 16 R2 **16.** 2,496 **17.** 26 **18.** 84
19. 216 R1 **20.** 636 **21.** 67 **22.** line segments
OP, PN, NO **23.** line segments EF, FG, GH, HE
24. 90 papers **25.** $30

Page 107 1. yes **2.** no **3.** no **4.** pentagon
5. quadrilateral **6.** triangle **7.** pentagon
8. A,G **9.** A, B, C, E, G, H
10. A, B, C, E, F, G, H

Page 108 1. pyramid **2.** cylinder **3.** cube
4. sphere **5.** rectangular prism **6.** cone
7. cylinder **8.** rectangular prism **9.** pyramid

Page 109 1. yes **2.** yes **3.** no **4.** yes **5.** 1
6. 2 **7.** 0 **8.** 2 **9.** 1 **10.** 0 **11.** 1 **12.** 1

Page 110 1. G **2.** B **3.** I **4.** N **5.** P **6.** R
7. D **8.** S **9.** Q **10.** K **11.** E **12.** J
13. (4,4) **14.** (11,8) **15.** (2,2) **16.** (6,12)
17. (7,1) **18.** (6,5)

CHAPTER 10

Page 113 1. $\frac{3}{4}$ **2.** $\frac{4}{7}$ **3.** $\frac{2}{6}$ **4.** $\frac{3}{9}$ **5.** $\frac{7}{8}$ **6.** $\frac{5}{10}$
7. $\frac{1}{8}$ **8.** $\frac{3}{5}$ **9.** $\frac{1}{4}$ **10.** $\frac{3}{7}$ **11.** $\frac{1}{6}$ **12.** $\frac{1}{2}$ **13.** $\frac{6}{6}$
14. $\frac{2}{4}$

Page 114 1. 3 **2.** 6 **3.** 8 **4.** 6 **5.** 6 **6.** 20
7. $\frac{5}{15}$; $\frac{1}{3}$ **8.** $\frac{3}{4}$; $\frac{12}{16}$ **9.** $\frac{2}{3}$; $\frac{6}{9}$ **10.** $\frac{3}{6}$; $\frac{1}{2}$ **11.** $\frac{2}{6}$; $\frac{1}{3}$

Page 115 1. 6 **2.** 12 **3.** 8 **4.** 2; $\frac{4}{10}$ **5.** 3; $\frac{15}{27}$
6. $\frac{3}{3}$; 18 **7.** 3 **8.** 12 **9.** 8 **10.** 15 **11.** 8
12. 18 **13.** 16 **14.** 27 **15.** 10 **16.** 12
17. 20 **18.** 24 **19.** 3; 10; 7 **20.** 12; 4; 20
21. $\frac{6}{9}$ **22.** $\frac{9}{12}$

Page 116 1. 4 **2.** 1 **3.** 2; 4 **4.** 2; $\frac{2}{5}$ **5.** 3; $\frac{2}{3}$
6. 2; $\frac{4}{8}$ **7.** 5; 1 **8.** 6; $\frac{1}{5}$ **9.** 3; $\frac{2}{5}$ **10.** 4 **11.** 6
12. 2 **13.** 5 **14.** 4 **15.** 3 **16.** 1 **17.** 5
18. 5 **19.** 7 **20.** 2 **21.** 4

Page 117 Patterns in Computation

1. $\frac{2}{4}$ **2.** $\frac{3}{6}$ **3.** $\frac{4}{8}$ **4.** $\frac{5}{10}$ **5.** $\frac{6}{12}$ **6.** $\frac{9}{12}$ **7.** $\frac{12}{16}$ **8.** $\frac{15}{20}$
9. $\frac{20}{22}$ **10.** $\frac{30}{33}$ **11.** $\frac{40}{44}$ **12.** $\frac{50}{55}$ **13.** $\frac{14}{16}$, $\frac{21}{24}$, $\frac{28}{32}$, $\frac{35}{40}$, $\frac{70}{80}$,
$\frac{700}{800}$ **14.** $\frac{18}{20}$, $\frac{27}{30}$, $\frac{36}{40}$, $\frac{45}{50}$, $\frac{90}{100}$, $\frac{900}{1,000}$ **15.** $\frac{22}{24}$, $\frac{33}{36}$, $\frac{44}{48}$,
$\frac{55}{60}$, $\frac{110}{120}$, $\frac{1,100}{1,200}$

Page 118 Maintenance 1. $<$ **2.** $>$ **3.** $=$
4. $5 \times 6 = 30$; $6 \times 5 = 30$; $30 \div 5 = 6$;
$30 \div 6 = 5$ **5.** $1 \times 9 = 9$; $9 \times 1 = 9$; $9 \div 1 = 9$;
$9 \div 9 = 1$ **6.** $4 \times 9 = 36$; $9 \times 4 = 36$;
$36 \div 9 = 4$; $36 \div 4 = 9$ **7.** 3,616 **8.** 14
9. 1,536 **10.** 128 R2 **11.** 18,000 **12.** 10 R5
13. $200 + 700 = 900$ **14.** $6,000 - 5000 = 1,000$
15. $700 \times 5 = 3,500$ **16.** $400 \times 20 = 8,000$
17. line segment CD or DC **18.** angle Y
19. ray MN **20.** $\frac{3}{8}$ **21.** $\frac{4}{9}$ **22.** $\frac{10}{12}$ **23.** $\frac{4}{4}$; 8
24. 2, 5 **25.** $\frac{8}{8}$; 2 **26.** No. She only has 94¢

Page 119 1. no **2.** no **3.** yes **4.** no **5.** no
6. yes **7.** no **8.** no **9.** $\frac{3}{5}$ **10.** $\frac{2}{9}$ **11.** $\frac{1}{4}$ **12.** $\frac{2}{3}$
13. $\frac{3}{7}$ **14.** $\frac{1}{6}$ **15.** $\frac{1}{5}$ **16.** $\frac{5}{9}$ **17.** $\frac{3}{8}$ **18.** $\frac{4}{7}$ **19.** $\frac{4}{5}$
20. $\frac{2}{3}$ **21.** $\frac{1}{5}$ **22.** $\frac{2}{7}$ **23.** $\frac{1}{8}$ **24.** $\frac{1}{10}$ **25.** $\frac{3}{4}$ are
blue **26.** $\frac{1}{2}$ are girls

Page 120 1. $>$ **2.** $<$ **3.** $>$ **4.** $<$
5. $>$ **6.** $=$ **7.** $>$ **8.** $=$ **9.** $<$
10. $>$ **11.** $<$ **12.** $<$ **13.** $<$ **14.** $>$
15. $<$ **16.** $>$ **17.** $<$ **18.** $>$
19. $\frac{3}{11}$, $\frac{6}{11}$, $\frac{8}{11}$, $\frac{10}{11}$ **20.** $\frac{1}{6}$, $\frac{5}{12}$, $\frac{7}{12}$, $\frac{5}{6}$

Page 121 1. $>$ **2.** $<$ **3.** $>$ **4.** $=$
5. A **6.** B **7.** D **8.** G **9.** H **10.** E
11. $2\frac{3}{5}$ **12.** $3\frac{1}{2}$ **13.** $1\frac{2}{3}$ **14.** $2\frac{3}{4}$ **15.** $1\frac{1}{2}$ **16.** 3
17. $4\frac{2}{5}$ **18.** $9\frac{1}{3}$

Page 122 1. $\frac{1}{2}$ **2.** yes, $\frac{1}{2} = \frac{5}{10}$ **3.** yes, $\frac{2}{4} = \frac{1}{2}$
4. no, $\frac{3}{8} \neq \frac{3}{4}$ **5.** yes, $\frac{3}{6} = \frac{1}{2}$ **6.** 8 photos **7.** yes,
6 albums **8.** 1 stamp

Page 123 1. 6 shells **2.** 12 apples
3. 35 stickers **4.** 50¢ **5.** 39¢ **6.** 13 meatballs

CHAPTER 11

Page 126 1. 3 **2.** 5 **3.** 5 **4.** $\frac{1}{2}$ **5.** 10; 6 **6.** 2;
$\frac{1}{2}$ **7.** $\frac{2}{3}$ **8.** $\frac{7}{8}$ **9.** $1\frac{2}{7}$ **10.** 1 **11.** $\frac{3}{4}$ **12.** $1\frac{1}{3}$
13. $\frac{5}{6}$ **14.** $1\frac{1}{10}$ **15.** $\frac{7}{9}$ **16.** 1 **17.** $1\frac{1}{4}$ **18.** 1
19. $\frac{1}{2}$ **20.** $1\frac{3}{8}$

Page 127 1. 1 **2.** 1 **3.** 1 **4.** $\frac{3}{4}$ **5.** $\frac{2}{3}$ **6.** 2; 2
7. $\frac{3}{8}$ **8.** $\frac{2}{5}$ **9.** $\frac{2}{5}$ **10.** $\frac{3}{7}$ **11.** $\frac{2}{3}$ **12.** $\frac{1}{2}$ **13.** $\frac{4}{11}$
14. $\frac{5}{6}$ **15.** $\frac{3}{4}$ **16.** $\frac{7}{18}$ **17.** $\frac{1}{2}$ **18.** $\frac{2}{3}$ **19.** $\frac{4}{15}$ **20.** $\frac{1}{2}$

Page 128 Maintenance 1. $146.13 **2.** 3,908
3. 47,296 **4.** 9 R4 **5.** $171.15 **6.** 1,157
7. 150 **8.** $3,000 + 5,000 = 8,000$
9. $1,000 - 400 = 600$ **10.** $300 \times 9 = 2,700$

11. $60 \times 50 = 3,000$ 12. $\frac{3}{4}$ 13. $\frac{5}{6}$ 14. $\frac{2}{3}$ 15. $\frac{3}{8}$, $\frac{4}{8}, \frac{6}{8}, \frac{7}{8}$ 16. $\frac{2}{5}, \frac{6}{10}, \frac{9}{10}$ 17. $4\frac{1}{2}$ 18. 3 19. $3\frac{1}{7}$ 20. 2 21. $\frac{5}{8}$ 22. $\frac{5}{9}$ 23. $\frac{2}{3}$ 24. $\frac{5}{12}$ 25. $\frac{1}{2}$ mile

Page 129 1. 5; 6; $\frac{11}{15}$ 2. 2; $\frac{3}{4}$ 3. 4; 5; $\frac{9}{10}$ 4. 3; 14; $\frac{17}{21}$ 5. $\frac{3}{5}$ 6. $\frac{7}{9}$ 7. $\frac{9}{16}$ 8. $\frac{11}{12}$ 9. $1\frac{7}{15}$ 10. $\frac{3}{4}$ 11. $\frac{5}{6}$ 12. 1 13. $\frac{6}{7}$ 14. $\frac{5}{6}$ 15. $\frac{2}{3}$ 16. $\frac{15}{16}$

Page 130 Patterns in Computation
1. $\frac{5}{6}$ 2. $\frac{8}{15}$ 3. $\frac{9}{20}$ 4. $\frac{13}{14}$ 5. $\frac{7}{10}$ 6. $\frac{9}{14}$ 7. $\frac{11}{15}$ 8. $\frac{11}{30}$ 9. $\frac{13}{20}$ 10. $\frac{11}{28}$

Page 131 1. 12; 10; $\frac{2}{15}$ 2. 9; 2; $\frac{7}{12}$ 3. 8; 1; $\frac{7}{10}$ 4. 3; 2; $\frac{1}{6}$ 5. $\frac{2}{3}$ 6. $\frac{1}{8}$ 7. $\frac{1}{2}$ 8. $\frac{2}{5}$ 9. $\frac{3}{10}$ 10. $\frac{1}{6}$ 11. $\frac{3}{10}$ 12. $\frac{5}{12}$ 13. $\frac{5}{8}$ 14. $\frac{1}{16}$ 15. $\frac{1}{3}$ 16. $\frac{5}{16}$

Page 132 1. 4 2. 1 3. 4 4. 2 5. 5 6. 3 7. 3 8. 10 9. 3 10. 4 11. 9 12. 14 13. 12 14. 8 15. 15 16. 16 17. 15 18. 21

Page 133 1. $\frac{1}{2}$ of a set 2. $\frac{1}{4}$ yd 3. $\frac{3}{5}$ of a pack 4. $\frac{1}{2}$ doz 5. $\frac{5}{8}$ of a mile 6. $1\frac{1}{2}$ of a cup 7. $1\frac{1}{3}$ of a cup 8. $\frac{1}{2}$ hr

Page 134 1. A; C 2. B; Jamie 3. A; Jerry

CHAPTER 12

Page 139 1. 6 cm 2. 4 cm 3. kilometer 4. centimeter 5. centimeter 6. centimeter or meter 7. meter or kilometer 8. 1 m 9. 5 km 10. 2 cm 11. 800 12. 5,000 13. 3,000 14. 400 15. 9,000

Page 140 1. liter 2. milliliter 3. milliliter 4. liter 5. kilogram 6. gram 7. gram 8. kilogram 9. 900 g 10. 3 L 11. 2 kg 12. 250 mL 13. 250 g 14. 355 mL

Page 141 1. 3 inches 2. 2 inches 3. $2\frac{1}{2}$ inches 4. $3\frac{1}{2}$ inches 5. c 6. e 7. g or d 8. f 9. a 10. d or g 11. b 12. 9 13. 48 14. 72 15. 10,560

Page 142 1. cups 2. gallons 3. cups 4. cups 5. gallons 6. cups 7. lb 8. lb 9. oz 10. ton 11. ton 12. oz 13. 8 14. 14 15. 12 16. 48 17. 4,000

Page 143 1. 300 2. 3,000 3. 30 4. 30,000 5. $38,893 6. 148 R1 7. 45,906 8. $4.41 9. $300 \times 4 = 1,200$ 10. $6,000 + 6,000 = 12,000$

11. $600 \times 40 = 24,000$ 12. 4 13. 4 14. 10 15. 2 16. $\frac{1}{2}$ 17. $\frac{5}{9}$ 18. $\frac{2}{3}$ 19. $\frac{3}{8}$ 20. 3 21. 12 22. 9 23. 4 cm 24. 3 cm 25. 5 cm 26. 32 oz 27. 9 feet

Page 144 1. 57 cm 2. 60 m 3. 100 cm 4. 78 m 5. 34 cm 6. 90 m 7. 15 8. 6 9. 8 10. 24 sq cm 11. 54 sq m 12. 144 sq cm

Page 145 Patterns in Computation
1. 24 sq m 2. 2 sq in. 3. 16 sq yd 4. 24 sq mm 5. 400 sq mi 6. 72 sq cm 7. 120 sq km 8. 25 sq yd 9. 42 sq mm

Page 146 1. 9 2. 16 3. 24 4. 12 cubic units 5. 36 cubic units 6. 20 cubic units 7. 30 cubic cm 8. 32 cubic cm 9. 96 cubic cm

Page 147 1. 36 ft; 72 sq ft 2. 60 ft; 224 sq ft 3. 640 m; 24,000 sq m 4. 40 in., 100 sq in. 5. 40 yd; 75 sq yd 6. 72 ft; 180 sq ft 7. 4 cubic ft 8. 192 cubic in. 9. 2,700 cubic in. 10. 36 cubic ft 11. 432 cubic yd 12. 2,304 cubic in.

Page 148 1. 20 ft; 18 ft 2. 6 yd; 5 yd; 30 square yards; 5 yd; 4 yd; 20 square yards 3. neither; Strawberry Patch; Length; Width; Area; Perimeter; New; 7 yd; 5 yd; 35 square yards; 24 yards; Old; 8 yd; 4 yd; 32 square yards; 24 yards 4. Playground; Length; Width; Area; Perimeter; School; 80 ft; 60 ft; 4,800 square feet; 280 ft; Park; 100 ft; 80 ft; 8,000 square feet; 360 ft

Page 149 1. 14 in. by 18 in. 2. 13 rows 3. 200 ft 4. 105 books 5. 12 boxes 6. 100 sq ft

CHAPTER 13

Page 152 1. $\frac{1}{10}$; 0.1 2. $\frac{9}{10}$; 0.9 3. $\frac{19}{100}$; 0.19 4. $\frac{64}{100}$; 0.64 5. 2.5 6. 2 7. 0.6 8. 12.1 9. 0.21 10. 0.76 11. 0.03 12. 24.32 13. 68.68 14. 88.02

Page 153 Patterns in Place Value
1. four 2. four tenths 3. forty 4. six hundred 5. six hundredths 6. six and six tenths 7. seventy-seven 8. seventy and seven tenths 9. seven and seven hundredths 10. seven hundred seven and seven tenths 11. 2; 0 12. 5; 0; 5 13. 9; 9; 0; 9 14. 3; 3; 0; 3 15. 2; 2; 2; 0; 2

Page 154 1. > 2. < 3. = 4. < 5. > 6. > 7. > 8. < 9. = 10. =

11. < **12.** = **13.** > **14.** < **15.** >
16. 0.1, 0.3, 0.7 **17.** 0.39, 0.44, 0.48 **18.** 18.25, 18.27, 18.31 **19.** 6.87, 6.9, 6.91

Page 155 Maintenance 1. 10,918 **2.** 3,500
3. $894.44 **4.** 318 **5.** 22 **6.** 55 **7.** 134 **8.** $\frac{3}{8}$
9. $\frac{4}{8}$ or $\frac{1}{2}$ **10.** $\frac{7}{10}$ **11.** 63 cubic cm **12.** 700 sq yd
13. 100 in. **14.** 0.19 **15.** 0.8 **16.** 0.48
17. 2.4 **18.** = **19.** > **20.** < **21.** 440
miles **22.** 19 tickets

Page 156 1. yes **2.** yes **3.** no **4.** no **5.** 7.9
6. 79.8 **7.** 10.3 **8.** 129.0 **9.** 32.58 **10.** 5.3
11. 34.4 **12.** 3.46 **13.** 18.82 **14.** 24.34
15. 12.02 **16.** 13.89 **17.** 23.83

Page 157 1. 7 **2.** 9 **3.** 10 **4.** 7 **5.** 10
6. 11 **7.** 8 **8.** 6 **9.** 11 **10.** 7 **11.** b **12.** a
13. b **14.** b **15.** 12 **16.** 24 − 10 = 14
17. 27 + 3 = 30 **18.** 10 − 4 = 6
19. 53 + 37 = 90 **20.** 50 − 25 = 25
21. 22 + 16 = 38 **22.** 76 − 32 = 44

Page 158 1. $8.15 **2.** $1.30 **3.** $5.89
4. $1.25 **5.** 81¢ **6.** $2.50 **7.** $1.25

Page 159 1. 3 **2.** 5 **3.** 4 **4.** $\frac{3}{9}$ **5.** $\frac{4}{9}$ **6.** $\frac{2}{9}$
7. $\frac{7}{9}$ **8.** $\frac{6}{9}$ **9.** $\frac{5}{9}$ **10.** 0 **11.** 1 **12.** $\frac{4}{9}$ **13.** $\frac{2}{6}$

CHAPTER 14

Page 162 1. 1; 2; 8; 1; 1; 6; 0 **2.** 2; 6; 3; 1; 4; 4; 5; 4; 2; 3 **3.** 1; 3; 6; 4; 1; 4; 1; 2; 2; 4; 2; 4; 0
4. 6; 1; 2; 1; 1; 8; 0; 3; 3; 0; 7; 6; 1 **5.** 13 R3
6. 19 **7.** 428 R1 **8.** $1.78 **9.** 115
10. 194 R2 **11.** 529 **12.** $8.42

Page 163 1. 2 **2.** 4 **3.** 4 **4.** 4 **5.** 6 **6.** 6
7. 6 **8.** 6 **9.** R8 **10.** R14 **11.** R7 **12.** R16

13. 7 R22 **14.** 4 R38 **15.** 7 R10 **16.** 4 R3
17. 8 shelves

Page 164 Patterns in Computation
1. 2 **2.** 20 **3.** 2 **4.** 20 **5.** 1 **6.** 10 **7.** 1
8. 10 **9.** 7 **10.** 70 **11.** 7 **12.** 70 **13.** 4 R4
14. 1 R8 **15.** 3 **16.** 8 **17.** 7 R27 **18.** 5 R20
19. 3 R14 **20.** 1 R45 **21.** 2 R17 **22.** 8 R12
23. 3 R6 **24.** 8 R32

Page 165 1. 2; 2; 2; 7; 0; 2; 2 **2.** 7; 2; 6; 6; 0
3. 8; 7; 3; 6; 8; 7 **4.** 8 **5.** 3 R3 **6.** 1 R39
7. 1 R21 **8.** 4 **9.** 3 R13 **10.** 5 **11.** 3 R20
12. 7 R10 **13.** 7 R23 **14.** 8 R20 **15.** 9 R19
16. 9 **17.** 8 R16 **18.** 6 R12 **19.** 6 R26

Page 166 Maintenance 1. 9,459 **2.** 8,099
3. 69,000 **4.** $26.61 **5.** 1,670 **6.** 645
7. 64 R2 **8.** 28,136 **9.** 8 R8 **10.** $89.32
11. < **12.** > **13.** > **14.** = **15.** $1\frac{1}{4}$
16. 4 **17.** $2\frac{5}{6}$ **18.** $3\frac{1}{9}$ **19.** centimeter
20. meter **21.** meter or centimeter **22.** 60.1
23. 41.35 **24.** $\frac{5}{10}$ or $\frac{1}{2}$ **25.** $\frac{2}{16}$ or $\frac{1}{8}$ **26.** 26
papers **27.** $\frac{3}{7}$

Page 167 1. 1; 6; 5; 0; 3; 0; 3; 0; 0; 0
2. 2; 4; 1; 3; 8; 0; 1; 7; 3; 1; 6; 0; 1; 3
3. 1; 3; 1; 5; 7; 0; 2; 2; 5; 2; 1; 0; 1; 5 **4.** 22 R12
5. 18 R7 **6.** 21 R13 **7.** 11 R23 **8.** 10 R9
9. 18 R18 **10.** 21 R3 **11.** 28 R4

Page 168 1. 2; 4; 3; 0; 6; 0; 6; 0; 0; 2; 4; 1; 2; 0; 2; 4; 0; 3; 6; 0 **2.** 3; 4; 7; 8; 4; 1; 1; 9; 1; 1; 2; 7; 3; 4; 2; 7; 2; 6; 8; 0; 9; 5; 2; 7; 9; 5; 9 **3.** 13
4. 27 R7 **5.** 22 R9 **6.** 12 R9 **7.** 11 R30 **8.** 36
9. 19 R9 **10.** 11 R9 **11.** 12 boxes

Page 169 1. $48 **2.** 72 people **3.** 24 bows
4. 2 pounds **5.** 120 cm **6.** $2.50 **7.** 16 pieces
8. 10 times